Lone Stars and Legends

The Story of Texas Music

Paula Felps

Republic of Texas Press
Plano, Texas

on Data

music / Paula Felps.

p. cm.

Includes discography (p.), bibliographical references (p.) and index.

ISBN 1-55622-798-1 (pbk.)

1. Popular music—Texas—History and criticism. I. Title.

ML3477.7.T4 F45 2001

781.64'09764—dc21 2001019030

Republic of Texas Press is an imprint of Wordware Publishing, Inc.

Printed in the United States of America

ISBN 1-55622-798-1

10 9 8 7 6 5 4 3 2 1

0102

All inquiries for volume purchases of this book should be addressed to Wordware Publishing, Inc., at 2320 Los Rios Boulevard, Plano, Texas 75074. Telephone inquiries may be made by calling:

(972) 423-0090

Contents

Dedication

For John Bitunjac, who taught me to
shut up, sit down, and write.

Acknowledgments

The Internet provided a valuable means of gathering information and cross-checking facts, and websites that provided some of the information contained in these pages include: All Music Guide, Bluesnet, Blue Flame Café, Red Hot Jazz, Roughstock's History of Country Music, Handbook of Texas Music Online, Texas Monthly's Texas Music Source, CNN.com, Famous Texans, iMusic, iCast, Blues and Two J's, Country Music Hall of Fame, and Southern Music of the 20th Century.

Obviously it takes brainpower well beyond my own to track down all this information, so from the "It Takes a Village" department, here's my heartfelt thanks:

For reading, discussing, and pointing out new resources, thanks to Mike Bogle, Paula Bosse, Steve Burklund, and Jeff Morrison. Those who deserve special mention for providing me with background information, photos, and big bits of trivia well worth tracking down include Pat Boone; Denardo Coleman; Rufus Coleman; David Dennard and Dragon Street Records; Herb Ellis; Carl Finch; Jim Flansburg and the Denton Record-Chronicle; Johnny Gimble; Neil Harpe; Ron Harwood; Bubba Hernandez; Paul Hilcoff; Trini Lopez; the University of North Texas Music Library; John Meekings, Casey Monahan, and the Texas Music Office; Kelley Reese and the University of North Texas public information office; Billy Sills; Tommie Ritter Smith; Chris Strachwitz and Arhoolie Records; Julius Tupa and the Texas Polka News; the The Texas Country Music Hall of Fame; Texas Folklife Resources; and the Scott Joplin Foundation.

Thanks to Ginnie Bivona at Republic of Texas Press for giving me the chance (and the extra time) to pull it all together, and to Dr. Cindy Hart, who kept my hands working long after they wanted to quit. For those of you who had to hear about this through much of the year 2000, thanks for the support and all apologies for the whining. Finally, special thanks to Louise Weston for an endless supply of patience and perspective, and to Charlie Martin for the chance to make this happen.

Introduction

Piecing together something as all-encompassing as the history of Texas music isn't exactly a small task, but the great thing about a project like this is that you never realize how daunting it is until you're already committed. By then, it's too late and there's nothing to do but finish it.

The passion and interest for this book actually goes back about a decade, when, after creating a weekly entertainment magazine in Denton, I began to look at what made that little burg so rife with musical talent. Not sure if it was something in the air, something in the water, or simply a happy geographical coincidence, I studied more about the city's influence on music through its world-renowned jazz studies program at the University of North Texas. That program had attracted enough talent to produce more than a handful of pop and avant-garde bands through the years, a tradition that dates back to Pat Boone and Roy Orbison in the fifties, took a sharp turn with experimental groups in the seventies such as the jazz fusion act Schwantz Lefantz, and continues today, evidenced by such diverse Denton-grown offerings as polka proselytizers Brave Combo and alt country boys Slobberbone.

What became clear in studying those early days of jazz, pop, and rock in Denton is that it's nearly impossible to quarantine and study just one element of music; the genres are all so deeply connected that at times it's hard to tell where one ends and the other begins. What may initially seem like clear-cut boundaries begin to blur under closer examination. So when Republic of Texas Press expressed interest in that very topic, it seemed like the ideal time to take a closer look at how this magnificent beast called Texas music came to life.

Some of this information came from files I've kept for several years, adding to, for reasons that weren't clear to me at the time, with every interview. Much of the early information came from a diverse number of printed resources that oftentimes contradicted one another, which of course made this research much more entertaining. For a complete list of published resources—and some great in-depth reading on some of music's earliest days—check out the bibliography at the end of the book. Liner notes provided another invaluable source of information that's too often left out of the history books. Some of the most noteworthy resources are listed in the bibliography, but if you choose to follow through on the "Recommended Listening" at the end of each chapter, be sure you read the liner notes—you never know what you might find.

This book is not designed as a definitive history, but rather as a starting point. Hopefully, it will provide readers with a bit more information than they might have had, introduce a new artist, or connect the musical dots between the sounds you enjoy but never knew how they got here. Many of these artists deserve an entire book of their own, and hopefully the following chapters will encourage listeners to learn a bit more about the music and where it came from.

Chapter One

Where it All Began

Like most things to come out of the state of Texas, its music is legendary and larger than life. The state that prides itself on proving bigger is better has a rich soundtrack to back up its bragging rights, a soundtrack that is as complex and diverse as the people who penned it.

Understanding or appreciating Texas music is not nearly as difficult as defining it. Depending on who you ask, Texas music may mean the deep southern blues of Blind Lemon Jefferson or the western swing of Bob Wills and the Texas Playboys. Some think of the enduring country songs of the legendary Willie Nelson, while others conjure up images of conjunto legends like Santiago Jiménez and Narciso Martínez. And for some, Texas music means the rock 'n' roll foundation laid by Buddy Holly, or the guitar-god licks of Stevie Ray Vaughan, or the unforgettable velvet growls of Janis Joplin. As personal and universal as religion, Texas music means something different to each individual.

Quite possibly, the only link that the sounds created in Texas have to one another are their geographical boundaries. (One certainly can't listen to Bob Wills and the Butthole Surfers and imagine that they have anything in common, other than the bands' birthplaces.) However, to say that Texas music is nothing more than music made in the Lone Star State somehow downplays its power, for that single shared characteristic alone gives the music a proud pedigree, regardless of its genre. Each note owes a debt to a long line of pioneers who poured their sweat and spirit into the music, continuously adding a new texture to the diverse tapestry that wraps itself around the ears of every listener today.

That makes creating a "definitive" history of Texas music something that borders on the impossible. Attempting to compress the complete contributions of the state's musical masters between two covers is a Herculean task that is destined to fail, which explains why so many books on Texas music focus on a particular genre. In the pages that follow, the focus is on the individuals who lived for their music, despite whatever odds and obstacles they encountered. In a time when the landscape is overpopulated with albums and acts, it's difficult to imagine the struggles that once were required simply to be able to create music. It is, however, possible to see how each musical pioneer created a foundation that was built upon by the next genre and/or generation, constructing a solid framework that allows us to enjoy the diverse and thriving scene that exists in Texas today.

Many of those who live outside of the Lone Star State have often equated Texas music with Stetsons and cowboy boots, but that misperception is changing. True, Texas has generated more than its fair share of cowboy-friendly songs, but it has also spawned an enviable bounty of renegade rockers, of blues masters, and song crafters who provide constant proof that the state's music is nothing if not special. While New Orleans, Chicago, and New York get most of the credit for the birth of jazz music, Texas certainly served as a busy midwife, delivering and nurturing talent that later would staff some of jazz music's finest bands.

History's music books are packed with Texas tunes. There are songs about Texas, for Texas, and about missing Texas; songs about leaving Texas, getting back to Texas, or living long enough to die in Texas. Not many states can make that claim—when's the last time someone heard a song romanticizing life on the plains of Kansas? The same enthusiastic pride that generates such friendly warnings as "Don't Mess With Texas" is evident in the musical heritage that grew up on the plains and remains, at least to a certain extent, rooted in that determined spirit.

Texas music has long reflected the fusion of the state's inhabitants, defying and ignoring the boundaries of genres from the very beginning, and effortlessly intertwining disparate influences to create a fluid presence. Had it not been for its broad ancestry, it is likely that Texas music never would have discovered such a powerful voice. However, the state's cultural melting pot (fortunately) provided it with a more relaxed, creative climate than most of its northern counterparts from the very beginning. It is that complex stew of humanity that also provided the state with more roots to delve into and draw upon as it nurtured its multilayered musical heritage.

Central Texas's German and Czech influences, the Spanish folk music imported across the Mexican border by soldiers and settlers at the early missions, the Creole songs smuggled across the border from Louisiana, and the gospel tradition delivered through the spirituals of slaves all flowed together into the state's young, developing veins to begin bringing to life the sound of Texas music.

While other states or regions may choose to stake their claim in a particular sound, Texas wins the prize for music that flourishes in the most diverse manner possible. Grunge brought the not-short-enough-lived "Seattle sound," making that the unofficial home of alternative rock. Chicago is generally considered to be the home of the modern-day blues; New Orleans claims ownership as the birthplace of jazz; and Nashville proudly bears the mantle as the capital of country music—a title that, in the early fifties, many believed would belong to

Dallas. While the Lone Star State likely will never bear the flag for a single musical movement, each and every one of those genres thrives in Texas, and all genres must acknowledge more than just a trace of a southern accent.

It may not differ from other music in any way other than its birthplace, but that is enough to set Texas music apart. Music history's halls of fame are lined with Texas troubadours who helped give a voice to the state's spirited melodic heritage. Along the way there have also been countless, faceless contributors who believed in the music as fervently as any Baptist preacher in a pulpit on Sunday morning. Each contribution, whether historically noted or not, has altered the sound—sometimes almost imperceptibly—and allowed it to evolve and grow. The unsung heroes are as much a part of Texas's music history as its celebrated legends; and whether or not their names are recalled, their spirit remains alive through the music they created.

Texas Royalty

King of Ragtime – Scott Joplin

King of the Twelve-string Guitar –
Huddie "Leadbelly" Ledbetter

The King of the Country Blues – Blind Lemon Jefferson

King of the Hillbilly Piano Players –
Aubrey "Moon" Mullican

Trumpet King of the West – Hot Lips Page

King of Western Swing – Bob Wills

Queen of Western Swing – Laura Lee Owens McBride

King of the Jukebox – Lefty Frizzell

The history lesson of Texas music begins long before the state actually existed, and its early days went something like this:

The unsettled pre-Texas frontier of the 1500s saw the area populated by tribes of Indians, who brought the first music to the plains. Before European settlers decided to set up camp, the area's only inhabitants were a number of Indian tribes occupying the area between the Rio Grande and the Red River. Their first taste of European music came from Mexico, where a school of music had been built in 1525.

Spanish explorers crossed the border from Mexico in a futile search for gold in the early 1500s, bringing with them missionaries who set out to mine for souls. At missions in El Paso and San Antonio, the explorers' Spanish folk music and guitars proved to be a drawing card for the natives, who probably weren't the first (and certainly weren't the last) folks ever to be lured into a house of worship by the music.

The Spanish influence remained the dominant musical force for years to come and still is entrenched in the music and traditions of Texas culture. In the late 1700s, however, a new flavor of ethnic music had begun working its way across the Louisiana border. The new French accent brought a colorful, raucous brand of Creole dance music later known as zydeco. It provided a brilliant kick to the budding culture and quickly was added to the ever-expanding musical mix.

Meanwhile, German immigrants were discovering the Hill Country and, by the mid-1840s, the early German music scene was flourishing. Even in areas where the population wasn't predominantly German, the music was proving infectious, sneaking into the Spanish sound and infusing it with a high-energy sophistication that characterized the early sounds imported by German immigrants. Tejano musicians began incorporating some of the European flavors into their repertoire, adding polkas, waltzes, and schottisches to the mix.

German Texans began hiring Tejano players for their celebrations, and the South Texas Spanish culture began embracing the sound of the German accordion. By the end of the century, the collision of Texas and German music had given way to a sound that was no longer distinctively European or Mexican, but could only be called Tex Mex.

The German music tradition was kept alive and thriving through male singing societies in Galveston, Houston, and New Braunfels, among other cities, which became centers of activity thanks to an impressive range of instrumentation and instruction. The Germans even were responsible for creating the first symphony orchestras ever to play in Texas, which began appearing in the 1870s.

With the introduction of European music and instruments, the live concert scene began taking off, although they weren't exactly the kind of Saturday nights that are enjoyed in Texas today. Thanks to the Anglo-American presence in the state, influences of English, Scottish, and Irish music had infiltrated the mix, and the 1840s saw Texas become part of a circuit for visiting bands—all of the concert variety, of course. In the larger communities, military bands became a popular form of musical entertainment, and by the time the century ended, most towns had a band they could call their own.

At the same time—but at a much different level—another musical influence was being created, one that laid the foundation for the very soul of Texas music.

As early as 1825 settlers began bringing slaves to Texas, and between 1840 and 1860 the presence of slaves had become common in the state. In the fields where they worked, the slaves relied upon music to help them pass the days and keep their work moving at a steady pace. In the field songs, the slaves expressed their hurts and their hope, and much of the music reflected the combination of their African traditions and the Christian evangelism of their Southern owners. Those spirituals, which are sometimes now referred to as "the sorrow songs," were rife with biblical references for redemption and the inevitable human longing for freedom.

The music became a cornerstone for gospel music, as well as laying a solid foundation for the blues, which promptly splintered to give birth to jazz but ultimately spawned that tradition known as rock 'n' roll.

It was in the Spanish missions that early Texans found the first formalized music presentations, and the church-related theme would not leave the music for many years.

By the 1800s, Southern preachers went back to basics, deciding the music of the day needed to get back into the holy land. Faced with an abundance of parishioners and a shortage of music, they improvised, borrowing popular folk tunes of the time and changing the words to have religious themes. Already on its way to becoming the buckle of the Bible belt, Texas found its deep religious roots fit well into secular music—once it was given a lyrical makeover. Pop tunes and penitence proved to be a powerful combination, doing its part to punch up the religious services and creating a lasting treasure chest of hymns.

A livelier version of the religious folk-inspired music soon emerged as traveling preachers hit the circuit, delivering a more sophisticated version of the simple sacred music to rural areas. Needing to capture a congregation rather than preach to a captive one, the traveling preachers couldn't depend on the solemn hymns of worship, and instead adopted more invigorating songs to help parlay their message. The evangelistic enthusiasm with which the upbeat salvation songs were delivered helped boost the audience participation level, bringing gospel to the forefront as a bona fide trend and creating the foundation for Texas's deep, religious musical traditions.

Of course, folk music had its place on the range as well as in religious rites; cowboy songs and ballads have remained something of a Texas trait despite the fact that they were sung all over the country. The cowboy songs remain linked to the Lone Star State's image, eventually evolving into country music and western swing and, later, giving way to the honky-tonk tradition.

None of these different styles of music can be called distinctly Texan, but they certainly took on a unique Texas accent once they crossed state lines. Like many of its residents, both early and contemporary, the music may not have been born in Texas but it took on a new identity once it got there.

Songs About Texas

Texas has been immortalized in many ways, but perhaps nothing better captures the wide-reaching spirit of Texas better than the catalog of music devoted to it. Few (if any) states can claim as many musical numbers that pay homage to it as thoroughly as the Lone Star State. Here's a sampling of some of the many songs written about Texas—feel free to add your own to the list.

All My Exes Live in Texas
Beautiful, Beautiful Texas
Blind in Texas
Blue Yodel No. 1 (T for Texas)
Bluest Eyes in Texas
Deep in the Heart of Texas
Denton, Texas
Ghost of a Texas Ladies' Man
God Blessed Texas
I Can't See Texas From Here
If You're Gonna Play in Texas
I Like Texas
Luckenbach, Texas

At its heart, Texas music may be no different from its counterparts in the other states. But even to the novice Yankee listener, who may only acknowledge the occasional superstar musician to come out of the Lone Star State, there is something different, something uniquely dynamic about the Texas music scene. It has played an important part in the evolution of music and has been an influential player in everything from country and western music to jazz and blues to rock 'n' roll. Or, as the

Rockabilly Blues (Texas 1955)
San Antonio Rose
Streets of Laredo
Short Texas
Stars Over Texas
Texas
Texas Flood
Texas in My Rearview Mirror
Texas, Our Texas (state song)
Texas Ranger
Texas Size Heartache
Texas Tornado
Texas (When I Die)
Tcxas Women
That's Right (You're Not From Texas)
The Eyes of Texas
The Yellow Rose of Texas
There's a Girl in Texas
Town of El Paso
Waltz Across Texas
West Texas Holiday
What I Like About Texas

Texas Music Office slogan says, "You can't hear American music without hearing Texas."

What follows in these pages is a glimpse into how the dreams and talent of young musicians grew into legendary accomplishments and changed the direction of music. Depending on the genre, the stories end in the late fifties or early sixties, simply because those years were a pivotal turning point for the music. Radio, television, and mass marketing collided to change not only the way music was viewed, but how it was presented and where it was heard. What happened after that point is another matter entirely.

This is the story of just some of the lone stars who helped it get there.

Chapter Two

Ragtime and the Birth of the Blues

As the nineteenth century drew to a close, a cultural shift propelled a musical revolution. Music changed dramatically after the Civil War, with American artists and musicians turning their attention to themes of the United States rather than continuing to borrow heavily from the native lands of the country's founding fathers. While the rhythms still were borrowed from abroad, the rhymes became much more relevant to the topics of the day.

By the mid-1840s, no American composer had found more popularity than Stephen Foster, who chronicled the spirit of the era with homespun, familiar tales that catered perfectly to the Anglo-Americans. Foster's musical stories deeply romanticized the South—although he actually had never been to many of the areas he wrote about—and they struck a lasting, far-reaching chord in the hearts of a young, growing nation.

Meanwhile, the music of the African-Americans, like their white counterparts, reflected the experiences of the day. Unlike Foster's compositions, however, the songs of the black population were primarily born of pain and personal experience. They didn't have the need to "borrow" from the worlds that others lived in; their own worlds were painfully rife with creative inspiration. And while Foster's anthems romanticized the South, the music of those blacks living in the South depicted a much different landscape.

The mistreatment at the hands of slave owners, the loss and separation of family members, and the hope for a better life all were reflected in the songs that became popular among the black population in the mid-1800s. Field hollers and early spirituals, songs about the hard life in the cotton fields, sad laments about life in prison and in the railroad yards all comprised the African-American music of the era and laid the foundation for what would soon become the blues.

Spirituals were one of the most widely utilized ways for slaves to express their discontent, and they borrowed from both African lullabies and European hymns to provide a distinctive precursor to the blues. Despite the hardship expressed in the vocals, the songs also were filled with hope and the dream of freedom, either in this life or the next.

Jubilees and shouts, which used a call-and-response format, helped slaves pass the long hours of backbreaking labor. The shouts began as musical expressions of the singer's mood but later grew into extended phrases and verses, setting the tone for the early vocals of blues music.

Work songs were another means of musical expression and resonated through both the cotton fields and prison yards, where workers kept beat with their tools as they sang of the hard hand that life had dealt them. Solidly grounded in the African-American tradition of chanting, work songs focused on the idea of becoming so tired of the oppression in their lives that the slaves, workers, or prisoners would finally run away and find freedom, either in a spiritual or physical sense.

The groundwork laid by these early, often simplistic songs provided the backbone for the coming musical movement. After black Texans gained their freedom in 1865, they began building their own communities throughout the state. Although still saddled with a second-class status, they created forward-thinking schools, churches, and social organizations. They created their own newspapers and grocery stores; founded their own colleges and industries. All the while, they nurtured the creativity of music and other art forms that freed their spirits.

One of the first forms of black musical entertainment that caught the attention of the white population were coon songs, a genre that obviously was named after the racial slur of "coon." Coon songs involved whooping and hollering as loud and creatively as possible, and once the white population caught on to the pleasure of such unbridled expression, they began having coon shouting matches at social functions. The matches took the songs out of the cotton fields and prison yards, cleaned them up, and dusted them off to fit the more proper social settings of the white population. Although they undoubtedly lost some of their spirit and meaning through this sterilization process, the songs remained a popular form of entertainment for quite some time.

A second form of musical entertainment that contributed to the rise of ragtime also was based in plantation life, but this time came from the other side of the fence. The cakewalk became a popular social pastime among the well-to-do whites in the late 1890s. Like the coon shouting matches, it provided a friendly competition, only this particular activity brought a more socially refined dimension. The cakewalk was a dance that required couples in fancy clothing to promenade a short distance, with the best walkers of the event taking home a nice cake. The cakewalk eventually became so popular that it progressed all the way to vaudeville and even went on to Europe.

Both these versions of music contributed heavily to the foundation of ragtime music. African rhythms were incorporated into the music of both coon songs and cakewalks, and Anglo ears and feet were instantly taken with the powerful, lively rhythms. Whites became more interested in black folk music, cultivating a fascination that had begun as early as 1848, when the black-face minstrel craze took over.

Propelled by Stephen Foster's false Negro minstrels, the fad of whites mimicking blacks on stage became a huge industry after the Civil War. By the end of the century, however, African-American artists were able to override the cartoonish mimics of minstrels and replace it with an authentic and lasting form of American music.

Without a doubt, the availability of musical instruments through mail-order houses dramatically changed the complexion of music. Drums had long been the staple of the African-American community, although nervous plantation owners frequently confiscated such instruments when they realized their slaves used the drums to send messages to one another. As slavery disappeared and blacks were allowed to explore their musical possibilities, they began adding banjos, guitars, violins, and pianos to their reserves, creating "jig bands," the precursor to ragtime.

In the Lone Star State, the African-American community clung to its musical roots while at the same time incorporating some of the European sounds that had been imported to Texas. They presented more refined versions of black music, preparing the largely white population for a brand new sound.

Pinpointing the exact birth date of that sound is all but impossible, but it undoubtedly coincides with Scott Joplin's discovery of music.

Joplin was born into a musically gifted family, and although the commonly accepted birthday for the pianist is November 14, 1868, author Ed Berlin, one of the foremost experts on Joplin's life, says the correct date of his birth actually was sometime between June 1867 and January 1868. What is readily agreed upon, however, is that as a young child Joplin's family moved from his birthplace of Linden to Texarkana, the community that is most often cited as his hometown.

Joplin's parents were former slaves who became laborers after finding their freedom. His father, Giles (also spelled "Jiles" in some documents), showed a certain level of musical ability on the violin, and his mother, Florence, sang and played the banjo. Despite their financial limits, the parents encouraged all six of their children to stretch their musical muscles. The middle Joplin child mastered the guitar and cornet, but it was only after his mother found work as a maid for a wealthy attorney that he found his true musical calling.

On the piano in the home of W.G. Cook, Joplin began experimenting on the keys. He showed early signs of musical proficiency and so impressed Julius Weiss, a musical tutor, that Weiss offered him piano lessons for free. His mother took him to different places around town to practice his music until she finally saved enough money to buy him a second-hand piano to play at home.

By the time he was a teenager, Joplin had formed his first band, the Texas Medley Quartette, and was playing at everything from brothels and saloons to church gatherings. The band included two of his brothers and toured for about four years, creating a substantial musical reputation for the young pianist but ultimately contributing to his desire to join the growing ranks of musicians who were in great demand in the Midwest.

He settled in St. Louis sometime around 1890, where the type of music called jig piano was popular. Using a bouncing bass line and syncopated melodies, the sound later became called "ragged time," because of its seemingly erratic tempo.

In the red light districts of St. Louis, the budding ragtime sound thrived. Joplin honed his skills alongside other up-and-comers, then headed to Chicago by 1893, where the Columbian Exposition was taking place. He stayed there for an undetermined amount of time, playing with a band in areas near the expo, then moved to Sedalia, Missouri, using that as his home base while he toured with his eight-man band.

Joplin was one of the pioneers of ragtime brass, a sound that ultimately influenced the rise of jazz. He added horns to the piano-driven music, doubling the size of his popular Texas Medley Quartette and dramatically enriching the sound of the music. While in Chicago, he had discovered the confidence that his music had previously lacked, and he now began publishing his own compositions. His first published works weren't ragtime—the sentimental ballads "A Picture of Her Face" and "Please Say You Will" both were printed in 1895.

Back in Sedalia in 1897, Joplin enrolled in the George R. Smith College for Negroes, where he studied piano and music theory. He became the "entertainer" at the Maple Leaf Club, and it was during his tenure in that club that he wrote his best-known composition, "The Maple Leaf Rag." He took the composition to music publisher John Stark, who paid Joplin $50 for the song, which was published in 1899, and Joplin earned one cent royalty on every copy sold. It was the first piece of sheet music published by a Texan and became the first million-selling piece of sheet music ever.

At the time, with the recording industry yet to be created, sheet music was the only means of distributing music to the masses. Publishers found a lucrative niche in the music industry, and Joplin ranked among one of the fortunate few in his business arrangement with Stark. Before copyright laws took effect in 1909, most composers were paid only a flat fee for their music, with publishers receiving the profits from sales. Many great composers of the 1800s—including Stephen Foster—died penniless while their publishers became rich. Joplin's agreement with Stark was enough to provide him with a limited but continuous income for the rest of his life. By 1909 his "Maple Leaf Rag" had sold more than 500,000 copies, and it continued selling half a million copies a decade for the next twenty years.

Although Joplin is universally regarded as the King of Ragtime, the first published rag actually belonged to a white man, Ben Harney of Louisville, who has been credited with making ragtime popular in New York City. "You've Been a Good Old Wagon" was published in 1895, and two years later the first instrumental rag, "Mississippi Rag" by William Krell, was published. Even though it had started the movement, Negro ragtime didn't find its place in the publishing world until Tom Turpin's "Harlem Rag" in 1897.

Like many musicians before and after him, Joplin's life was restless, and he criss-crossed the country, publishing a number of well-known rags that included "The Entertainer," a song that enjoyed its greatest popularity more than fifty years after Joplin's death when it found its way into the 1973 movie *The Sting*. Joplin eventually composed dozens of sophisticated rags, but he also turned his attention to opera and ballet. Regardless of the medium, they all carried his ragtime influence, even when delivered with classical aplomb.

His first stage work was an ambitious folk ballet called *The Ragtime Dance*, and it incorporated singing narration with the type of dancing found in the clubs of that era. It was first performed in Sedalia in 1899, although the music wasn't published until 1902. By then Joplin was working on his first full-scale opera, *A Guest of Honor.* The opera chronicled Booker T. Washington's historic dinner at the White House with President Roosevelt in 1901.

A Guest of Honor opened in St. Louis in 1903 then embarked on an ill-fated five-state midwestern tour. The tour came to an abrupt and irreparable halt when someone in the thirty-person traveling troupe stole the box office receipts, and, unable to meet payroll, Joplin was forced to cancel the tour. When he was unable to pay for the troupe's stay at the theatrical boardinghouse in Pittsburgh, Kansas, Joplin's belongings were confiscated as payment. To this day the sheet music from the opera has never been recovered.

Although he continued composing great rags, Joplin himself never quite recovered from the incident, either. The next few years saw the breakup of his first marriage, followed by the sudden death of his second wife just ten weeks after their marriage. The financial fallout from the *Guest of Honor* fiasco led him to pick up insignificant jobs, playing music in unlikely places for very little money, although he still managed to publish several more new rags.

As the new century came into its own, recorded music began to surface, although flat record albums would not appear as a successful format for at least another ten years. Joplin recorded some piano rolls, which provided popular soundtracks for the "player pianos" sported in many wealthy parlors. His rolls boosted ragtime music's popularity, but as many other musicians would discover in years to come, popularity of one art form typically leads to its dilution. Other players began recording their own piano rags, many of them far less challenging than Joplin's complicated formal compositions, and even the watered-down, anemic spin-offs of the music became a part of the soundtrack for that generation.

The lucrative sheet music market had given birth to an industry of its own, one that saw the creation of Tin Pan Alley. Originally the nickname of a street in Manhattan where many music publishers set up shop, Tin Pan Alley became the moniker of the publishing industry that penned and pushed sheet music, regardless of where the individual publisher might be located.

For the first time—and certainly not the last—publishers hired songwriters and composers for the specific purpose of cranking out mass-produced, easy-on-the-ears songs for the general public. The rise of this industry gave Joplin a wealth of publishing options, but it also would ultimately cause him even greater frustration.

By 1907 Joplin had set his sights on creating yet another opera, also a large-scale production with heavy ragtime influences. This time around the opera was called *Treemonisha*, and he already had been working on the piece for several years. Now he turned his full attention to it, and he spent the next three years pouring his heart and soul into completing the opera. Once he finished the work, he was unable to get it published, despite the fact that his other works continued selling well.

Although he penned more than a dozen new works between 1907 and 1909, Joplin's health was beginning to deteriorate from a case of syphilis he had contracted in his younger, wilder days. He found himself unable to play many of the new works as his mental and physical state declined, and in the years that followed, music scholars would note just how inconsistent his creative process was in crafting those works. Some leaned heavily toward jazz, while others seemed little more than carbon copies of his earlier works.

As his health waned, Joplin's obsession with seeing *Treemonisha* published and performed intensified. He claimed to have turned the completed opera over to a young songwriter named Irving Berlin, who worked for one of the Tin Pan Alley publishers who printed many of Joplin's pieces. The opera was turned down for publication.

When Berlin's hit song "Alexander's Ragtime Band" was published early in 1911, Joplin told numerous friends that the song's verse borrowed heavily from one of the numbers in *Treemonisha* called "A Real Drag." Angry and frustrated, he reworked the song and then published the opera himself.

Joplin made several attempts to have the opera staged over the next few years, but none came to fruition. He managed to pull together a small production of it—sans costumes or orchestra—for a Harlem audience in 1915, but many close to him believed that the utter rejection of what he considered to be the greatest work of his lifetime contributed heavily to Joplin's rapid physical and emotional demise.

By the time Lottie Stokes, his wife of eleven years, had him committed to a Manhattan mental institution in 1916, Joplin, like ragtime, was already becoming part of history. Sadly, the piano rolls recorded during the final year of his life are erratic and inconsistent, reflecting his often tormented mental state and showing little resemblance to the genius who once had reigned supreme on the keyboard.

Joplin died on April 1, 1917, and although his passing seemed to mark the end of the ragtime era, his music continued to live on, albeit in more sophisticated and improvisational varieties. In 1976 his treasured *Treemonisha*, which finally had been staged in full in 1972, won Joplin a posthumous Pulitzer Prize.

Through Tin Pan Alley, ragtime reached a more mainstream population and became one of the first pop music trends. Fort Worth native Euday Bowman settled in Kansas City, where he immortalized the city's busy strip of pawn shops with "Twelfth Street Rag." That song later would be recorded by jazz great Louis Armstrong in 1927, the first of many outstanding jazz musicians to commit the number to vinyl.

Bowman composed a number of rags in the wake of that song's popularity, many of them named after other streets in Kansas City. Eventually, he based his rag compositions on the blues movement, including songs like "Kansas City Blues."

Pop rags and piano solos like "Ragging the Scale," released in 1915, and "Nola," published a year later, took the ragtime craze to a new level. Other influences were infiltrating the music, changing its sound into something more digestible to early mainstream pop audiences. George Gershwin found his first hit with the rag-flavored "Swanee," sung by Al Jolsen in 1919's Broadway run of *Sinbad*. By that time ragtime had even caught the ears of classical composers, with both Stravinsky and Debussy incorporating ragtime rhythms into some of their works. But the sound was changing, evolving into something that would quickly splinter into various forms of music, making it difficult to pigeonhole as ragtime but impossible to classify under any other genres of the era.

Scott Joplin's influence obviously reached far beyond the ragtime of the day and set the stage for the coming Jazz Age of the 1920s. Joplin's inimitable style echoed through the hands of many of jazz's early composers, who both paid tribute to the master and seemed to loot his treasure chest of musical tricks.

The prolific composer/pianist James P. Johnson took Joplin's jaunty ragtime style and boldly led it in a new direction entirely. His splicing of ragtime and early jazz played a key role in the birth of the jazz revolution, a revolution that was spread across the country via player piano rolls.

Even more notably, one of the first jazz composers, the legendary Ferdinand "Jelly Roll" Morton, credited Joplin with influencing his works. Morton even paid tribute to the ragtime king by performing his own jazz-infused renditions of "Maple Leaf Rag" and "Original Rags." Morton was the first in a long line of musicians to give such a nod to Joplin's handiwork, and the distinctive rag sound would be heard in the music of others for years to come.

That sound would also show up in the blues, but blues purists will argue that the blues have always been around, and ragtime was merely an offshoot of the early blues. As far as blues and ragtime are concerned—or blues and jazz, for that matter—it's definitely the same question as that of the chicken and the egg. Which came first is debatable and, for the most part, a moot point. What's clear is that each deeply affected the other, and all lent themselves to building a rock-solid foundation for the future of music.

Morton often is credited with "inventing" jazz shortly after the turn of the century, and his music was heavily influenced the by both ragtime and blues. Some of his first compositions contained the word "blues" in their titles, evidence that the blues already were alive and well.

Many scholars put the official birth of the blues sometime in the first decade of the 1900s, but other historians are quick to note that the blues song "Nobody There" was actually transcribed in 1890 by Gates Thomas, who began publishing song texts that had been collected from the black communities in South Texas. Where these points of contention find a common connection is in the agreement that, by the early 1900s, the blues were everywhere in Texas.

Growing out of the spirituals, work songs, and field hollers, the blues originally served the same purpose as those early songs—to provide a momentary musical escape from the harsh reality of everyday living. Although freedom among the blacks was now a given, most were still enslaved in many ways. The plantation economy still was thriving, and although they were no longer considered property, the blacks continued providing the hard labor to keep the plantations in business. Sharecropping and tenant farming took the place of slavery, and blacks gave up most of their crops to white landowners in exchange for the use of land, tools, and clothing. At the end of the day, most ended up still owing more to the landholders than they could produce.

It comes as no surprise, then, that the common theme of many early blues songs was mobility. Families moved frequently to escape their debt to white landowners, and like the work songs before them, the blues frequently embraced the idea of becoming so frustrated with the conditions around them that one runs away.

While ragtime's driving musical force was the piano, the guitar played an equally important role in the emergence of the blues. The guitar and harmonica replaced the instrumentation of banjo and fiddle, and the music became more percussive, usually offering a steady ground beat that had been lacking in previous incarnations of African-American music.

The itinerant lifestyle chronicled in the blues is the very thing that led to its widespread growth. Although the entertainment industry roared to life in the early 1900s, Texas was far enough removed from such activity to keep it from falling under the commercial music influence. Instead, it spread in a more organic manner, exchanging hands and evolving into different styles as it gathered influences from the ethnically diverse population of the Lone Star State.

No one captured the rise of Texas blues and jazz better than Henry Thomas, a songster born in 1874 who gained fame under the moniker of "Ragtime Texas." He was only sixteen years old when he left the cotton fields of Big Sandy to become a migratory musician, first playing the quills—an African folk instrument made from cane reeds that eventually would be replaced by the harmonica—and later picking up the guitar.

His propensity for playing rapid-tempo music is usually credited as the source of his nickname, although so little documentation exists that it's really just a theory. While less than half a dozen of Thomas's recorded songs are considered as true blues music, his work certainly paved the way for commercial blues performances. He rode the rail lines between Dallas/Fort Worth and Texarkana, singing songs and chronicling his experiences in verse. Like Joplin, he moved on to Missouri and Illinois and also was at the 1893 Columbian Exposition in Chicago. His movements are far more difficult to follow than Joplin's, however; he was constantly on the move and his music records a restless life spent traveling on the rails.

Ragtime Texas managed to provide a sort of bridge between the numerous early musical influences, utilizing everything from spirituals and coon songs to minstrel songs, square dance tunes, waltzes, and rags. His compositions contained such standard blues themes as laboring in the fields, the desire for escape, the role of the railroad in providing that escape, and the hard life of the jailhouse—something that blacks who traveled from town to town frequently found themselves far too familiar with, regardless of whether or not they actually committed a crime. Lost love and loneliness were also earmarks of his songs.

What is most noticeable about Thomas's tunes is that they had the basic instrumentation of what would later emerge as Texas blues. His songs "Texas Worried Blues," "Cotton Field Blues," and "Easy Street Blues" all carried the lighter, faster melody that would soon define the sound from the conventional blues of the day.

Between 1927 and 1929 Thomas made a series of recordings, only a handful of which are considered true blues numbers, even though many carried the word "blues" in their titles. The twenty-three songs he recorded for Vocalion Records in Chicago are the final exhibits of his abilities and the only enduring testament to his sound. He eventually wound up in Dallas, where the red light district of Deep Ellum had become a hotbed of activity for a budding blues scene, and he then vanished without a trace. It seemed a fitting departure for a man who, despite his legendary status, lived so elusively.

By the time Thomas made his recordings, the blues had become a viable music market, appealing to both blacks and whites. It is ironic that although Thomas was considered a major influence and innovator, he didn't make it into the recording studio until a year after country blues master Blind Lemon Jefferson.

By then both Dallas and Houston had found their own blues scenes; jazz was starting to swing, and record albums were transporting the musical message across state lines. A musical movement had been born, and the entire country would soon take note of it.

Recommended Listening:

Best of Joplin's Piano Rags – Josh Rifkin (Nonesuch)
Joplin's Greatest Hits – Dick Hyman (RCA)
Gems of Texas Ragtime – Richard Zimmerman (Webster Records)

Chapter Three

The Early Blues

If the birth of the blues was subtle, its childhood and adolescence was anything but. As the 1920s began, the fledgling recording industry tapped into the blues, and white audiences throughout the nation joined blacks in eagerly buying up what soon became known as "race records."

By the time the rest of the nation awakened to the sound of the blues, the music already was deeply entrenched in the Southern heritage. Early on, the sound had been borrowed by whites, who were fascinated by the black fiddle players and songsters performing at white dances in the late nineteenth century; the black and white minstrel shows touring the country during the Civil War further influenced the mix. Hispanic and country music both were noticeably influenced by the blues in Texas, not to mention the obvious intertwining of jazz and the blues.

In other areas of the South, the blues enjoyed similar success, even though, like the compositions of Henry "Ragtime Texas" Thomas, many of the songs were "blues" in name only. Yes, the blues were around long before published music ever appeared, but that doesn't mean the first published blues songs were actually what would qualify as "the blues." (This *is* the music industry, after all!) The word "blues" often was used simply because the word was recognized and understood by whites; initially it was more of a marketing concept than a truly defined sound.

The first published song with the word "blues" in its title appeared in 1912, with W.C. Handy's "Memphis Blues," a song Handy actually had penned three years earlier with a different title. (Initially, it was a campaign song for Memphis's black mayoral candidate E.H. Crump.) If Handy had originally given the song its lasting "Memphis Blues" title, the composition also would have been the first blues song ever to get a copyright. That honor went instead to a white musician from Oklahoma named Hart Wand, who wrote "Dallas Blues" and copyrighted the number in 1909—the first year that copyrights came into practice. (Ironically, "Dallas Blues" wasn't actually written about Dallas; it was so named because the chorus made one of Wand's hired hands long to go back home to Dallas.)

With the word "blues" bandied about so much in titles, it's almost impossible to track down the first "true" blues recording, so most music experts give that credit to Mamie Smith and Her Jazz Hounds. Smith's 1920 recording of "Crazy Blues," on the O'Keh Records label, is more blues-tinged than being an actual blues song, but it is significant because it became the first million-selling blues record and kicked open the door for the real thing.

Early on, women set the stage for the recorded blues, and until at least the mid-twenties, the male presence in the blues was felt more on stages and street corners than in the recording studio. Women dominated the recorded blues market, and it would take until the end of the decade for the men to catch up. Once they did, however, the male presence oftentimes overshadowed the efforts of their female counterparts.

Many of the women who rose to prominence in the blues recording industry were veterans of the vaudeville circuit and minstrel shows, already well versed in the ways of flashy performances and stage presence. That's the path that brought Texas blues legend Sippie Wallace to the forefront, although she was much more direct and down-to-earth than most of her sequin-clad predecessors, something largely attributed to her Lone Star roots.

Born in Houston in 1898, Wallace's music career was seemingly part of her birthright. Born to a Baptist deacon in a large, musical family, the young Beulah Thomas grew up singing gospel and playing the church organ. Her older brother, George W. Thomas, is considered her biggest influence in learning the blues. By the time George left for New Orleans, where he became a successful pianist, songwriter, and music publisher, young Sippie—so nicknamed because, as a child, she found it

Blues names

Ever wonder where blues artists got their names? Here's where a few Texas greats found their famous monikers:

Black Ace—Babe Kyro Turner made a recording in 1936 called "Black Ace," and the name stuck.

Blind Lemon Jefferson—Lemon was his given first name; the "blind" moniker is simply a matter of fact. Depending on who you ask, Jefferson was born blind or was nearly blind from his early days.

Blind Willie Johnson—This, too, came from the obvious. Johnson was blinded at the age of seven when he got caught in the crossfire of a domestic dispute between his father and stepmother, and the pan of lye his stepmother threw at his father splashed in his eyes.

Funny Papa Smith—John Smith supposedly got his "Funny Papa" nickname for his propensity for appearing in a stovepipe hat; that nickname became "Funny Paper" due to misunderstanding at his record label, which released "The Complete easier to eat soup by sipping it through the space between her teeth—already was enamored with the traveling shows that came through town. Sippie taught herself how to play the piano to accompany her singing and soon was invited to hit the road. She eagerly left home to pursue a life of show business as a traveling tent performer.

In 1915 she and her younger brother, Hersal, went to New Orleans to help their big brother, George, avoid the draft. In New Orleans ragtime was at its peak and jazz was beginning to find a foothold in the famed red light Storyville district. Alongside other artists like Louis Armstrong, King Oliver, Clarence Williams, and Sidney Bechet, the young singer polished her talent.

Recorded Works of J.T. "Funny Paper" Smith." Oof—that had to hurt. Smith originally called himself "Howlin' Wolf," a nickname that was lifted by Chester Burnett.

Leadbelly—A colorful storyteller, Huddie Ledbetter often said his nickname came after he took a belly full of buckshot; other reports claimed it was a name given to him by fellow prison inmates for his hard work and fast pace on chain gangs. Most likely the name came from a corruption of his last name.

Lightnin' Hopkins—Sam Hopkins went to Los Angeles in the mid-thirties to record with Houston musician Wilson "Thunder" Smith, and the record label gave him the nickname so they could promote the act as "Thunder and Lightnin'."

Ragtime Texas—Henry Thomas is believed to have earned his nickname from his fondness for playing quick-tempo music.

"Sippie" Wallace—This blues singer, born Beulah Thomas, said she got the nickname Sippie because, as a child, she enjoyed sipping soup.

T-Bone Walker—A play on Walker's middle name, "Thibeaux."

Sippie Wallace with Jim Dapogny's Chicago Jazz Band in 1982. Jim Dapogny (right)/Rod McDonald (left). *Photo courtesy Ron Harwood.*

With the closing of New Orleans' historic Storyville in 1917, the music scene there began to splinter. (The renowned red light district was shut down at the request of the U.S. Department of the Navy as World War I began; the military didn't want their young recruits corrupted.)

Meanwhile, Chicago had become something of a recording mecca, and so sometime around the early 1920s, George moved to Chicago to play with his friend Clarence Williams, where he hooked up with O'Keh recording rep Ralph Peer, who happened to be scouting for fresh new talent. Sippie, meanwhile, married Matt Wallace in Houston and was later summoned away from the tent shows to audition in Chicago. In September of 1923 she recorded a demo that was released within days, and the record "Shorty George" and "Up the Country" sold 100,000 copies in the first quarter following its release. She was dubbed "The

Texas Nightingale" by O'Keh Records, a nickname that would remain with her through the remainder of her life.

Sippie became the first true blues woman west of the Mississippi River to build a national reputation, and a string of other successful songs followed, including "Special Delivery Blues," with Louis Armstrong on trumpet, "Bedroom Blues," a tune written by her two brothers, and the highly suggestive "I'm a Mighty Tight Woman." Wallace's brand of blues was earthy and direct, often suggestive and delivered with a wink and a nudge—like a devilish dose of worldly-wise sisterly advice. Her songs lived on long after she quit performing; "Up the Country" and "Caldonia" were modified and re-recorded by artists including Louis Jordan, B.B. King, and Canned Heat.

Cut from similar cloth was Victoria Spivey, also a Houston native, who became another leading blues vocalist in the 1920s. Like Wallace, Spivey was more spicy than sophisticated; a far cry from the more cultured, cosmopolitan blues ladies who first set foot in the recording studio. Born in 1906, Spivey was witty and determined, something that made up for her less-than-refined vocals. Unlike Wallace, who got her start in the church, Spivey launched her career playing piano in saloons and brothels of their hometown. She made no apologies for her racy vocals, which, like those of many of her contemporaries, could be more than just a little risqué. (When she sang her "Black Snake Blues," it's safe to say she wasn't talking about reptiles.)

In her early years, Spivey cut her teeth on the Houston club and party scene then headed to Dallas where, at the age of twelve, she was performing in Lazy Daddy's Fillmore Blues Band and L.C. Tolen's Band and Revue. She spent her teens playing the club circuit, and by the early 1920s, she was in the right place at the right time—and had the right image and attitude to go along with it all. As the blues grew from a passionate, heart-felt form of musical expression into a full-blown industry, Spivey had the savvy and spirit to rise to the top.

Victoria Spivey, like Sippie Wallace, hailed from Houston. She lived for a time with Sippie's family in Houston's Fifth Ward and was no doubt influenced by the legendary blues players. *Photo courtesy John Meekings.*

She began working alongside the soon-to-be legendary Blind Lemon Jefferson, playing bars, brothels, and "gay houses" in Dallas, Houston, and Galveston. Her close association with the Thomas family helped her land a deal with O'Keh Records, and when she recorded her original composition, "Black Snake Blues," for the label in 1926, she gained a reputation not only as a powerful singer, but as a well-versed lyricist, too. Spivey soon began writing songs for the St. Louis Music Company, one of many hats she would wear during her long and varied career.

Although Spivey clearly enjoyed a nice racy romp through the fields of sexual innuendo, she also built a reputation as something of a moralist. The socially conscious anthems of the 1960s would seem like mere suggestions for change when held up to the kind of direct, no-holds-barred lyrics Spivey wrote and recorded. When accompanied by her rough wails and moans, the songs had the ability to paint a picture that chilled to the bone and left a lasting impression.

With "T.B. Blues," she took on the prejudices and discrimination rampant against those who were afflicted with tuberculosis in the late twenties. Her equally powerful "Dope

Head Blues" is the first song on record that warned of the evils of cocaine addiction.

Spivey, who recorded some thirty-eight songs for the O'Keh label, also was quite possibly the first female singer to address the issue of domestic violence. Her "Blood Hound Blues" brought up the theme that has re-emerged in countless Lifetime Television movies—a woman retaliating against her abusive husband. Not unlike the song "Goodbye, Earl" on the Dixie Chicks' 1999 album *Fly*, Spivey's song tells the tale of a woman who poisons her husband after he has blackened her eyes one too many times. Unlike the protagonist in the modern version, however, Spivey's heroine ends up in jail, finally breaking out and spending the rest of her life on the lam.

Wallace and Spivey joined the ranks of legendary ladies like Ma Rainey and Bessie Smith, who shaped the velvet-and-steel voice and image of the blues. Although the blues has always been largely dominated by those bearing the Y chromosome, women like Wallace and Spivey proved that women could also be great performers. At a time when prejudices against both blacks and women still were the norm, the early blues women created works that continue to reach across the barriers of time and also serve as a testament to their iron will and passion for the music.

Wallace's fame, like her life, was tempered with heartache and pain; in 1926 her nineteen-year-old brother Hersal, the piano-playing phenomenon, died of food poisoning. Ten years later she lost both her older brother George and her husband within months of each other. She had recorded some forty songs between 1923 and 1929, but now her blues muse appeared to have been silenced; she sought solace in her religious beliefs and spent the next four decades as a singer and organ player at the Leland Baptist Church in Detroit.

Victoria Spivey visited with Sippie in Detroit in 1965, and, with the help of Ron Harwood, her then-seventeen-year-old manager, was able to lure Wallace back on stage. In 1966 Harwood (who now is Wallace's biographer) teamed up with Willie Dixon to convince the "retired" blues lady to hit the road on the blues festival circuit. Wallace recorded another album in 1966, this time for the Storyville label, which included her wildly popular song, "Women Be Wise, Don't Advertise Your Man." "Women" saw her accompanied by Little Brother Montgomery, an old Chicago friend and a pal of Hersal, as well as New Orleans piano great Roosevelt Sykes. That song would so inspire a young singer named Bonnie Raitt to investigate the blues that she later toured with the legend, and their duet of "Women Be Wise"—recorded live in San Francisco in 1976—appears on the 1990 Warner Bros. release *The Bonnie Raitt Collection*.

Although Wallace endured a stroke in 1970, she refused to let that hinder her renewed career. Harwood, who managed Sippie during her "comeback years," promoted the great blues lady back into the national limelight. He organized The Little Chicago Jazz Band, led by famed music historian/piano player James Dapogny, to back her. The group played together for two years before cutting a demo for Atlantic Records. The resulting album, *Sippie* (which included Raitt's signature guitar work), earned Wallace her only Grammy Award nomination. It also picked up a W.C. Handy award for Best Blues Album and won Album of the Year and Album of the Month awards from various publications. She recorded only one more album—in Ann Arbor, Michigan, with Axel Zwingenber—which was released only in Europe. She died on November 1, 1986, at the age of eighty-eight—ironically, matching the number of keys on her piano.

Just as Spivey and Wallace had taken different roads to find success, they followed completely different paths once they found it. The ever-busy Spivey had gone on to appear in the 1929 film *Hallelujah*, which only broadened her popularity throughout America. She continued recording until sometime around 1937, married four times, and worked as a dancer, singer, and songwriter.

Spivey took a break in her forties, perhaps to catch her breath and gear up for the final productive years of her life. During the 1950s she gave few live performances and worked instead as a church administrator. In 1960 she apparently grew weary of the daily duties at the church and launched Spivey Record Company in New York. (The first album she released on the label featured Big Joe Williams on guitar and Bob Dylan on harmonica, performing under the name "Big Joe's Buddy.")

Her reunion with Wallace led to the album *Sippie and Victoria Spivey*, which came out in 1970 on Spivey's label. In addition to the album of old blues standards, Spivey was creating new music and, not surprisingly, taking on contemporary issues. The time was ripe for issues of drugs, sex, and violence, and Spivey's pen, as always, was poised to comment. She continued touring and also began contributing articles about the history of blues and jazz for various publications. Although it bears no consequence on her music career, Spivey fittingly also was the first person to subscribe to the magazine *Living Blues*. She continued making contributions to the world of music until her death in a New York hospital in 1976.

Two other Texas blues women of note to come out of that era included Maggie Jones, who was born in Hillsboro, and Wallace's niece Hociel Thomas (George's daughter), also a Houston native. While neither gained the status and legendary stature of Spivey and Wallace, both left their distinct fingerprints on the blues and, like their predecessors, blurred the lines between blues and jazz by recording with some of the early jazz greats. Most notably, all four women recorded with Louis Armstrong at some point; Thomas's 1925 recording session with the trumpet master featured her uncle Hersal on piano, just months before his death, and she later wrote the song "Go Down Sunshine."

As the blues continued to gain its toehold in the national market in the mid-twenties, the race was on for record companies to create "race labels," which featured rosters of all black artists. Labels such as Brunswick Columbia, O'Keh, Paramount, RCA, and Vocalion sent scouts to cities like Dallas and Houston in search of fresh talent for their records. It was on one such musical recognizance mission that Blind Lemon Jefferson was discovered and shortly thereafter became the top-selling country blues artist of his time.

By most reports, Jefferson was blind from the day of his birth in 1897 in Coutchman, although some claim he had partial vision—which could explain the eyeglasses he wears in the only known existing photograph of him, a publicity still for Paramount Records.

Lemon Jefferson discovered his talent for music early on and by the age of fifteen was performing on the streets of nearby Wortham and Mexia. Very little else is known about his early life; the self-taught musician was one of seven children, and his bread and butter in the early days came from playing at church picnics and country dances.

Sometime between 1915 and 1917, Jefferson moved to Dallas to join the street-level blues scene that was emerging there. It was during those days in Deep Ellum that a young Huddie Ledbetter—later known as Leadbelly—became one of Jefferson's lead men. In the cafes, saloons, and whorehouses of Deep Ellum, Jefferson found appreciative audiences for his original music, and within a year he earned enough money to take his show on the road. He bought a car, hired a driver, and traveled throughout the South and Midwest. After criss-crossing through Oklahoma, Georgia, and the Mississippi Delta, Jefferson eventually found fame back on the streets of Dallas.

It was there, nearly ten years after Jefferson had played his first note in Dallas, that a scout for Paramount Records first heard the music of Blind Lemon Jefferson. Jefferson's colorful,

Only one photograph of the legendary Blind Lemon Jefferson exists, and it portrays the mighty blues man with a guitar awkwardly propped on his lap. Blues lover/artist Neil Harpe re-created his own image of Jefferson as he may have appeared playing on the street corners of Dallas. *Photo courtesy Neil Harpe.*

charismatic style immediately caught the attention of the label rep, who shuttled him off to Chicago for his first recording session. Jefferson proved a prolific music machine, and during the next three years he laid down more than eighty tracks, most of them for Paramount. The recordings, almost all of which were originals, outsold any other black male performer of his time and established him as the first superstar blues man.

Jefferson's appeal was a combination of his music and his lyrics; his word-smithing oftentimes was simple, but it captured in startling, accurate detail the joys and hardships of life in the South for blacks in the early 1900s. His groundbreaking guitar style influenced everyone from Leadbelly and Lightnin' Hopkins to Bob Dylan and every white-boy blues player ever to put his fingers to the strings.

Jefferson didn't invent the guitar riff, but he certainly did his part to bring it into the spotlight. His imaginative use of guitar riffs heavily influenced the sound of the music of the day and provided inspiration for many artists to come. Much like Ragtime Texas before him, Jefferson used his guitar as a second voice, letting the instrument "answer" his two-octave-range voice. His first recording, "Long Lonesome Blues," came out in 1926 and set a new sound and standard for blues records. Jefferson exhibited a wide range of styles and ability and created a legendary body of work in just three years.

Under the name Deacon L.J. Bates, he recorded a number of spirituals, which were in direct contrast to his earthier offerings such as "Mean Jumper Blues," "Matchbox Blues," and "Black Snake Moan," something of a male answer to Spivey's "Black Snake Blues."

Very little is known about Jefferson's personal life, and what information is available generally contradicts itself. By some accounts, Jefferson was a hard-drinking womanizer, one who indulged in prostitutes and whiskey as a preferred form of payment for his musical performances. Other stories paint him as a devoutly spiritual man who was devoted to his wife and child and refused to perform on Sundays because it was "the Lord's day."

Jefferson's compositions ran the gamut of themes, not surprisingly hitting on many of the same topics as the work songs and field hollers of his ancestors. Although there is no evidence indicating he even spent so much as a single night in jail, many of Jefferson's songs carried the prison theme—"Prison Cell Blues," "'Lectric Chair Blues," and "Blind Lemon's Penitentiary Blues" all were obvious examples. His other songs touched on equally familiar songs of his heritage—life on the railroad, poverty, life in the fields, and of course, love and its easily mistaken companion, lust.

The large library of music he recorded belies Jefferson's short life. He died in 1929, and the cause of his demise is widely debated. He was found dead in a Chicago snow bank, and some stories have him freezing to death after being abandoned by a never-identified driver. Other stories say he had a heart attack and died on the street. Still more seedy stories have him meeting his end after being attacked and robbed on the street. No death certificate has ever been located for him, and the true cause of his death remains a mystery.

After his death Jefferson's body was returned to his hometown and buried in the Negro cemetery at Wortham. For years his grave, as well as that of his sister and mother, were unmarked, but in 1967 it was marked with a Texas historical monument. In 1996 concerned blues fans joined with the Texas Music Office to raise money for a proper headstone. Today a large tombstone marks the gravesite of this blues legend, borrowing a line from one of Jefferson's own songs for its inscription: "Lord, it's one favor I'll ask of you. See that my grave is kept clean."

The last five years of the twenties was a phenomenal and prolific time for recorded blues music. Eager to find new talent, record labels sent scouts and engineers to hotspots such as Dallas, hoping to mine the territory for future stars. Columbia Records discovered twenty-five-year-old blues singer Lillian Glinn on one such visit in 1927; the Dallas native was viewed as a brilliant new talent, and her rich, full voice embodied the spirit of the blues. The young singer showed a phenomenal range, but after only two years of recording, she ended her professional career and returned to the church. Her lasting contribution is the song "Shake It Down," which she recorded in 1928 and which still stands up against any other classic blues song today.

The recording bug also captured the all-but-overlooked talent of blues belter Bessie Tucker, who came seemingly from nowhere (well, East Texas, anyway) and disappeared almost as quickly as she had surfaced. A woman of tiny stature, she somehow possessed a voice that sounded twice her size, one that was captured during a recording session for the Memphis-based Victor record label in 1928. The recordings, made with piano accompaniment by K.D. Johnson, showcased a deep-pitched bluesy sound that is nothing short of astonishing.

Although her life is primarily a mystery, one thing seems clear—she knew her way around a prison cell. Her songs were largely about prison life, such as "Penitentiary," her most widely known song from the 1928 recording session. She recorded the following year in Dallas, again with Johnson pounding the ivories, but that's where her story ends; she then vanished from the musical landscape.

The late twenties saw a number of blues musicians come and go, most leaving too faint of a trace to ever be able to uncover their stories. Willard "Ramblin'" Thomas, an excellent blues guitarist and singer, was discovered by Paramount and Victor, who were impressed with his slide techniques. He made a number of recordings for both labels during that time, oftentimes relying more on his incredible voice than his finger work.

His younger brother, Jesse "Babyface" Thomas, never found the same level of success but did make a number of recordings for assorted labels, continuing his career into the forties. After cutting his teeth with Blind Lemon Jefferson and Leadbelly, Babyface eventually came into his own, developing his own style rather than borrowing so heavily from his heroes and their influences. Babyface's personal flavor of the blues was more upbeat and romantic than those favored by his older sibling, and where Ramblin' Thomas worked the slide technique, Babyface's method was more rhythmic. He frequently worked with Babe Kyro Turner, later known as "Black Ace," who built his own guitar while still a child and, as an adult, played the slide guitar "Hawaiian style"—with the guitar flat on his lap. Turner played at community events in his hometown of Hughes Springs in the twenties, working his way up to dances in Greenville by the thirties and later touring, recording, and even hosting a radio show on the Fort Worth station KFJZ in the late thirties.

Like Ramblin' Thomas, Blind Willie Johnson mastered a slide technique that gave him a lasting home in blues history, despite his brief recording career. Nobody can dispute Johnson's right to sing the blues; he was born into a tumultuous household in Marlin, although the year is widely argued. Records put his birth anywhere from 1890 to 1900, but what is known about the late great performer is that he brutally lost his sight while he was still a small child.

Johnson's father, George, was a farmer, and his mother died while Willie was still an infant. Willie was just seven years old when his stepmother suffered a beating at the hands of his father after he discovered her infidelity. She angrily threw a pan of lye at her husband but inadvertently hit Willie, blinding him for life. Those harsh terms of his life may have accounted for his fire-and-brimstone brand of blues, which fervently preached a message of repentance and screamed of certain and severe afterlife consequences.

Johnson used a pocketknife, rather than a bottleneck, for his slide work and created his own brand of blues. More gospel in its lyrics but definitely blues in its composition, Johnson's sound was perfected when he was a teenager playing for donations on the streets of small Texas towns.

He was twenty years old when he met his wife, Angeline, while playing on a Dallas street corner, and it was also in Dallas that he met Elder Dave Ross, who helped land him on the Columbia record label. He found success with such mournful but forceful tunes as "Dark Was the Night, Cold Was the Ground," about the crucifixion, and "Jesus Make Up My Dying Bed." Angeline joined him on his last set of recordings for Columbia, contributing a somewhat ethereal falsetto to his alternately gruff bass and his natural tenor vocals.

Whether Johnson willingly left his recording career or his record label abandoned him is another point of debate; most likely he was another casualty of the Depression. Regardless of the reason, he returned to his life as a street corner musician in 1930. Angeline continued serving as both his eyes and his sometimes-accompaniment, and they lived in Beaumont, singing and begging until his death in 1947. The blues man's exit from this earth was as tragic as his entrance; he died of pneumonia after his cabin caught fire and Johnson extinguished it, then wore the still-damp nightclothes to bed. But his legacy as one of the earliest and most powerful slide guitarists outlived him, and six decades later his Columbia recordings still serve as a testament to his powerful force both as a singer and guitarist.

Most blues musicians relied on two voices to convey their music—the second voice being the instrument that they played. Victoria Spivey and Sippie Wallace had their pianos, Blind Lemon Jefferson and Blind Willie Johnson had their guitars; but Texas Alexander hearkened back to the origins of the blues and made his voice the only instrument he ever mastered.

Born Alger Alexander in (depending on who you talk to) either Leona or Jewett sometime between 1880 and 1900, he modeled his vocal style after the field shouts and hollers that he undoubtedly heard as a small child. He landed on the O'Keh record label in 1927 and committed more than sixty tracks to glass, the majority of which were released by 1930. An older cousin of Lightnin' Hopkins, Alexander played with his then-fifteen-year-old cousin in 1927 at Houston's Rainbow Room, and the two also performed with Blind Lemon Jefferson in Dallas on more than one occasion. Alexander recorded with jazz greats like King Oliver and blues/jazz crossover Lonnie Johnson, but his life and times are perhaps best reflected in the songs he left behind, most of which have prison or work themes.

He lived the part of the mysterious drifter, who sometimes sang for migrant cotton pickers, and throughout the 1930s, he and his younger cousin often traveled around as hobos, playing for a living and occasionally landing in jail.

After spending time in prison in the first half of the 1940s for killing his wife, Alexander returned to his drifting, itinerant lifestyle. He performed on the streets with the up-and-coming musicians of that era, and after recording with Hopkins in 1947, he all but disappeared from the blues scene. His death in Houston from syphilis is placed in 1954 or 1955—again, depending on who you ask.

Texas Alexander wasn't the only blues master to base his prison songs on life experience; that common thread had been woven through songs from the very beginning. Few, however, lived that experience as fully as Leadbelly.

Born Huddie Ledbetter sometime around 1888 in Louisiana, to sharecropper parents, Leadbelly made his way to Dallas via Louisiana and East Texas. By 1916 he was said to have shared the stage with Blind Lemon Jefferson, who he claimed had a dramatic influence on his music. Leadbelly's style incorporated field hollers and Negro spirituals into his particular flavor of the blues; his music was something of a melting pot for traditional influences.

By the time he hooked up with Jefferson, Leadbelly had chosen the twelve-string guitar as his primary instrument (although the mandolin, piano, and accordion all were in his repertoire of instruments), a choice that landed him the title "King of the Twelve-String Guitar."

Perhaps the only thing bigger than Leadbelly's musical talent was his temper, and in 1917 he abruptly interrupted his musical career with a thirty-year sentence for murder. Leadbelly already had seen his share of altercations with the law and in his youth had spent some time in the Shaw State Prison. His crime in Texas earned him a bunk at the Huntsville Prison Farm. Apparently Leadbelly wasn't particularly pleased with his accommodations, and his attempt to escape added another six years to his sentence.

But the music that kept him out of prison detail proved to be his "get out of jail free" card. Six years into his sentence, he impressed visiting Governor Pat Neff with a song he improvised on the spot—begging for an early release—and miraculously won a pardon.

Within five years Leadbelly was back in prison, this time in Louisiana on charges of assault with intent to murder. Once again music proved to be the trump card that could set him free.

As part of their exhaustive search for blues and folk music for the Library of Congress in 1933, historians Alan and John Lomax visited prisons and stumbled upon Leadbelly. They were stunned by his knowledge of African-American folk music, and the father-and-son team petitioned the governor of Louisiana, O.K. Allen, seeking Leadbelly's release as a musical resource.

The guitarist was granted his freedom and split his time as a performer and a chauffeur for John Lomax. The elder music historian was determined to make Leadbelly a star and recorded countless numbers of the blues man's songs for the Library of Congress, as well as recording some tracks for the American Record Company.

Leadbelly left Texas in 1935 and moved to New York, where he found friendship and musical partnerships with the likes of

Pete Seeger, Woody Guthrie, and other stalwarts of the bohemian folk community. He found moderate success with his liberal politics and forward-thinking lyrics, which were reflected in songs like "Bourgeois Blues." But it was his song "Goodnight Irene" (originally titled simply "Irene") that found the most success—unfortunately, after his death, when it was recorded by the Weavers, led by Pete Seeger.

Despite his growing success, Leadbelly found it impossible to keep his temper under control, something that found him living for a time on Rikers Island in 1939, again on an assault charge. He continued recording after that final incarceration, laying down several tracks for Capitol Records in 1944.

He dreamed of being a true star and by 1945 had his own (short-lived) radio show on the West Coast. Leadbelly also tried, to no avail, to get Hollywood to capture his life story on film.

By now Leadbelly found himself plagued with problems from the development of amyotrophic lateral sclerosis, more commonly known as Lou Gehrig's disease. He continued touring and wasn't actually diagnosed with the disease until 1949, when he returned from a tour of Europe, where he had begun to find a following. He played his last concert on June 15, 1949, at the University of Texas in Austin, vowing to get well and come back for another show. He died less than six months later.

At the time of Leadbelly's death, the blues scene had changed dramatically from the days when he first began singing for his supper. The thirties brought with them the Depression, which slowed the production of race recordings but encouraged the live scene to evolve out of the limelight in which it had been incubated for more than a decade. The blues took a back seat to other forms of music as jazz began to swing, only to re-emerge in the postwar days with a new fire and energy. As proven time and time again, sometimes even the blues had to step back to catch its breath.

Last of the great country blues men

One of the last songsters to be discovered, Mance Lipscomb was a blues singer who was very nearly overlooked. In fact, the country blues master wasn't discovered until the age of sixty-five, when Arhoolie Records founder Chris Strachwitz committed the musician's rural sounds to recorded history.

Born Bowdie Glen Lipscomb in Navasota in 1895, Lipscomb borrowed his name from a friend named

Mance Lipscomb became a musical legend, but wasn't even discovered until the age of sixty-five. He enjoyed a fourteen-year career before retiring. *Photo by Chris Strachwitz. Photo courtesy of Arhoolie Records, Inc.*

Emancipation. His father was a professional fiddler who taught Mance how to play the violin and then the guitar; by the age of eleven, Mance was accompanying the elder Lipscomb.

Despite the fact that Dallas and Houston were rich with musical opportunities, Mance stayed close to his home, never leaving East Texas or trying to create a career out of his music. He performed at community dances or family gatherings but worked as a farmer to support his wife, their three adopted children, and a son named Mance Jr. Although uneducated, his ability was nothing less than brilliant. Not limited to blues songs, Lipscomb served as sort of a living musical history book, filled with a diverse and seemingly endless repertoire that he delivered with a high baritone voice. Blues ballads, gospel songs, shouts, and children's songs all found their way into his mental catalog and marked him as a truly unique artist.

When Arhoolie released Lipscomb's first recordings in 1960, the blues man went from being a buried treasure to a folk scene darling. In Austin, where he began playing frequently, he was welcome at any number of clubs and claimed to have taught Janis Joplin a thing or two about rhythm. He performed at folk festivals like Monterey and Newport and became a popular artist on the coffeehouse circuit across the country, where he would invite young up-and-coming artists to share the stage with him.

Lipscomb's long career spent only fourteen years in the spotlight. He quit performing in 1974 and two years later, at the age of eighty, died quietly at his home.

Recommended Listening:

Sippie – Sippie Wallace (Atlantic Records)

Blind Lemon Jefferson – Blind Lemon Jefferson (Milestone MCD)

Blues Masters, Volume 11: Classic Blues Women – (Rhino)

The Complete Recorded Works (1930-1931) – J.T. "Funny Paper" Smith (DCU)

Sweeter as the Years Go By – Blind Willie Johnson (Yazoo)

98 Degrees Blues – Texas Alexander (CTFS)

The Essential Recordings of Texas Blues – (Indigo)

Chicago Blues – Ramblin' Thomas (Biograph)

Huddie Ledbetter's Best – Leadbelly (Capitol)

King of the 12-String Guitar – Leadbelly (Sony)

Chapter Four

Boogie Woogie and the Rise of Jazz

Although jazz and the blues, as noted earlier, sprang from the same well, they were poured into different vessels and served up in distinctly individual ways. Just as ragtime set the tone for blues, the rise of boogie-woogie in the early 1900s made it possible for jazz to begin to swing in the twenties and thirties.

Although many historians place the breakthrough of boogie-woogie as sometime around 1927, it belonged to Texans long before that. Jazz historians have traced it back to the work camps and brothels along the Texas-Louisiana border as early as 1899. The development of the railroad no doubt enabled the music to spread to other areas; itinerant musicians followed the rail system from one lumber or mining camp to the next, taking with them the spontaneous style of boogie-woogie and barrelhouse music.

Originally played solo on the piano, boogie-woogie is characterized by the rolling bass played by the left hand and the synchronized melody played by the right. Using the musical call-and-response pattern of its predecessors, the music played by one hand evoked a response from the other, with an emphasis on the left (bass) hand. Closely related to barrelhouse piano, which is something of an extension of ragtime, boogie-woogie is a buoyant, uplifting, and energetic style easily given to the improvisation that later would appear in jazz.

The sound and style of boogie-woogie was initially viewed as something distinctly Texan—while most of the African-American pianists in Texas played their music in this rollicking style, the sounds in cities like New Orleans, St. Louis, and Chicago were decidedly slower. But as more musicians made their way from Texas into other areas, the music took hold in other areas as well. In fact, in the annals of history, boogie-woogie is most often attributed to the Chicago area, the city where it gained tremendous popularity in the late twenties and continued its hold throughout the thirties. Much credit is given to practitioners such as Clarence "Pinetop" Smith, Meade "Lux" Lewis, and Albert Ammons for popularizing boogie-woogie, but once again it was the Thomas family from Houston—the same family that gave Sippie Wallace to the world—who made such musical progress possible.

George W. Thomas was still living in his hometown of Houston when he composed "New Orleans Hop Scop Blues" in 1911, a boogie-woogie piece that wouldn't actually be published until 1916. The song features a powerful boogie-woogie bass line and generally is credited as being the first published work utilizing that style.

After George and his younger brother Hersal moved to Chicago in 1919, the brothers became instrumental in delivering boogie-woogie to the masses. The two young men collaborated on the song "The Fives," which was copyrighted in 1921 and became one of the most influential works of the era, followed closely by George's 1923 composition "The Rocks." (George recorded the latter song under the name of Clay Custer, as the practice of using pseudonyms was very common at the time, allowing artsts to work for multiple companies.)

Hersal, meanwhile, had become a piano prodigy, accompanying his sister, Sippie Wallace, on her recordings, including sessions with Louis Armstrong. He recorded "The Fives" in 1924, earning rave reviews from the critical press and leaving a lasting imprint on the face of the music. When he recorded "Suitcase Blues" one year later, he showed the full range of his talents, substantially raising the musical bar for pianists who would later record his works. His number "Hersal's Blues," which he wrote and recorded in the summer of 1925, provided an eternal legacy for the young pianist. It would be two years before Meade "Lux" Lewis recorded "Honky-Tonk Train Blues," the song that often is viewed as a break-through recording in the boogie-woogie movement. Clarence "Pinetop" Smith didn't record his "Pinetop's Boogie-Woogie"—the song credited with slapping the "boogie-woogie" label on the sound—until 1928. However, the music didn't truly find its stride until the late thirties, when a radio broadcast from Chicago's Sherman Hotel put Lewis, Smith, and Ammons in the spotlight and made boogie-woogie legends out of them. The boogie beat was picked up by contemporary blues men and, later, by rock bands of the sixties, but by the early forties, it had melted into the newer form of music called jazz.

As previously mentioned, jazz took hold in New Orleans in the early years of the 1900s, finding its main toehold in the famed Storyville red light district. In the open atmosphere provided by the area's pleasure seekers, young musicians felt free to experiment with the music and develop their own individual styles. Musicians like Ferdinand "Jelly Roll" Morton and Louis Armstrong were some of the area's first popular entertainers who honed their talent in the streets. Although the foundation for jazz (originally known as jass) was laid by African-American musicians, the credit for the first jazz recording goes to the all-white Original Dixieland Jass Band in 1917. As with ragtime and the blues, the music's originators were busy creating the music on the streets while the white-boy bands beat them to the history books and recording studio.

Storyville was closed the same year as that first jazz recording was released, which meant that much of New Orlean's thriving music scene was shut down as well. Jazz musicians spread the music to areas across the nation, with many of them gravitating to Chicago. Joe "King" Oliver left his familiar New Orleans environs to become one of the first to achieve success elsewhere, and as his Creole Jazz Band soared to fame, other jazz musicians left the Big Easy in search of success in the Windy City.

By the 1920s Chicago had replaced New Orleans as jazz's capital, while other musicians took the sound to Los Angeles and New York. Kansas City, meanwhile, was developing a scene of its own, and it attracted one of the first great jazzmen from Texas—trumpeter Lammar Wright. Born in Texarkana in 1907, Wright did the musical equivalent of running off and joining the circus at the age of fourteen. By his early teens he had joined the Bennie Moten Band, and in 1923 O'Keh Records recorded the band, which was then a six-piece ensemble featuring Wright on the cornet. One year later the outfit expanded to ten pieces and was back in the studio, this time in New Jersey.

Wright continued his tenure with Moten until 1927, when he left to play with a band originating from St. Louis called the Missourians. The band toured and recorded, and in 1930 it was taken over by Cab Calloway, who made Wright one of the group's primary soloists.

The growing popularity of jazz music brought with it the rise of the so-called "territory bands" in the mid-twenties. The bands typically were small, comprising unknown artists who traveled a circuit and earned just enough money to get them from one town to the next. Many of the "unknowns" in those territory bands later moved on to larger, more prominent bands, and many of them came from Texas. While it may be the names like Duke Ellington, Benny Goodman, Louis Armstrong, and Jelly Roll Morton that stand out in the minds of the casual listener, those names rose to the top thanks to a tremendous and bountiful crop of sidemen who took the songs and made them swing.

Territory bands in the twenties and thirties were nothing if not competitive. In sort of a mercenary twist on the old "if you can't beat 'em, join 'em" philosophy, band leaders often pillaged their competitors, luring away their best players—one of the most effective means of ensuring they wouldn't be outplayed by the other band. That practice caused more than one notable band to crumble, but it also yielded some of the strongest musical unions of the era.

It was in Chicago, New York, Kansas City, and St. Louis that the most popular territory bands of the twenties surfaced. Texas itself was never viewed as a hotbed for jazz bands, even though it produced a large number of artists and bands. Dallas was the city most responsible for polishing these young talents (thanks to its bustling Deep Ellum scene that stayed open twenty-four hours a day) and then turning them loose on an unsuspecting but eventually appreciative public.

Texas did produce a handful of bands, although none of them found the national recognition that was heaped upon many of the territory bands in the other cities. Ironically, the most acclaimed "Texas" territory band, the Alphonse Trent Orchestra in Dallas, rarely boasted a Texan in its lineup. The Trent orchestra actually came to the Lone Star State by way of Arkansas and became the first "colored" band to play for the white audiences of Dallas. That outfit also carved its place in music history by becoming the first black band in the nation to have its own regular radio program, which aired on Dallas's WFAA beginning in 1925.

While they may not have shared the same renown, bands like Gene Coy's Happy Black Aces in Amarillo and Johnson's Joymakers in Houston served as formidable training grounds for young, ambitious players. They yielded such talents as Carl "Tatti" Smith and Joe Keyes, who would rise to make instrumental contributions to the future of the jazz scene.

The Blue Devils became one of the first hot territory bands of the twenties, and it did so at the hands of some of Texas's top players. Although its home base originally was at the Ritz Ballroom in Oklahoma City, it was staffed largely with musicians from the nearby Lone Star State. When band member Walter Page took over as bandleader in 1927, the already thriving group picked up steam and became a serious musical threat to bands such as the one led by Bennie Moten, who ultimately looted the Blue Devils' wealth of players to staff his own ensemble.

Trumpeter Oran "Hot Lips" Page joined the Blue Devils in 1923, becoming the first Texan in its lineup. He was the younger half-brother of Walter Page, who already was in the band (although not leading it), something that certainly couldn't have hurt his chances of being invited to join. But even if he originally was given special consideration to be included in the group, he more than earned his right to stay there.

Born in Dallas in 1908, Page was clearly influenced by the works of Louis Armstrong and King Oliver; early on he played with such blues women as Ma Rainey and Bessie Smith. When he took a chair with the Blue Devils, he already was flexing his vast range of skills, which included a searing, sizzling style on the trumpet and proficiency as a blues and scat singer.

Unfortunately, Page's talents would never truly be given the recognition they deserved. In the Blue Devils he drove the brass section with a muscular musical force, and his contributions didn't end when he left the floor. Page was also responsible for bringing to the Blue Devils a talented young pianist named Bill Basie, whom the world would later know as Count Basie.

Page eventually left the Blue Devils to join Bennie Moten's outfit and played with the band until Moten's sudden death in a dentist's chair in 1935. When Moten's temperamental younger brother, Buster, took over the band, Hot Lips was among a number of musicians who fled the band. While many of the players faced unpredictable futures, it seemed certain that Hot Lips was about to grasp that elusive brass ring.

Trumpet great Louis Armstrong had developed a condition with his lip that made his future on the horn uncertain at best. His manager, Joe Glaser, was alarmed enough to realize he needed a backup superstar, and he signed a contract with Page that would have meant certain success if Armstrong's condition had not improved. When the master trumpeter recovered, however, Page found himself trapped by a contract that would forever leave him in Armstrong's shadow.

That didn't prevent him from making his living doing what he loved; in August 1937 his new band opened in Harlem, but the group had dissolved within a year. He went on to make a number of admirable solo recordings but never achieved the credit that many believe was due him. Critics have frequently called him "the most underrated [jazz] trumpeter," and he proves this on his recorded works with Billie Holiday's orchestra in the late thirties and Joe Turner's Fly Cats in 1940. He went on to work with Thelonious Monk in the forties and also ended up on the stage at Carnegie Hall on more than one occasion.

Hot Lips played with Artie Shaw and Fats Waller and ultimately recorded no less than 116 songs that serve as a lasting testament to his often overlooked skills. His work in the forties with Pearl Bailey saw the singer go on to become a star, while Page continued living the life of a sideman—one who achieved lasting respect in lieu of fame—until his death in November 1953.

At the time the Blue Devils were beginning, no one could guess which of its young musicians would use the band as a training ground and which would find it the high point of their musical careers. Among the most promising young talents to join the mix was a self-taught musician named Henry "Buster" Smith, who joined up with the Devils in 1925 at the request of Hot Lips Page.

Smith, who was born in Alsdorf in August 1904, grew up in a musical family and had picked up the organ by the age of four. Afraid that this natural talent would lead him to a life of sin, Smith's grandfather gave the organ away. (Certainly, he was neither the first nor last boy in the Bible belt to be chastised for playing with his organ.)

That act couldn't halt Smith's interest, it merely enticed him to explore his abilities further. By the time he was eighteen, Smith's family had moved to Dallas and he had taught himself to play not only the organ, but the clarinet, alto saxophone, and guitar as well. He launched his career at the bustling Tip-Top Club on Central Avenue but left a year later to play in medicine shows until being recruited by Page.

The young sax player's presence in the band undoubtedly helped propel it into a more competitive position with other bands—something that eventually led to it being looted by Bennie Moten, but not before Smith had put in a full decade with the Blue Devils. Smith's departure from the Blue Devils in 1933, which came after many of the band's best known players left and coincided with the departure of tenor sax star Lester Young, spelled the end of the legendary Blue Devils. After a stint with Moten, Smith created a new band with one of his Blue Devil alums, forming the Buster Smith-Count Basie Band of Rhythm.

Together, Basie and Smith pioneered a new, fatter jazz sound that used heavier reeds and before long became known as "the Texas Sax Sound." Smith left the band in 1936, right before Basie hit the big time. Although Smith might have regretted that lost opportunity, he made his own mark on jazz history, moving to Kansas City and forming a new band.

One of the first additions to the new lineup was a seventeen-year-old alto sax player named Charlie Parker, who had grown up listening to Smith in the Blue Devils and Bennie Moten bands. The future sax legend's sound was very much influenced by Smith's playing, and his influence on the life and career of "Bird" reached even farther once Parker joined the band. Smith became a father figure in Parker's life, in addition to a strong musical mentor. When Smith left K.C. for New York in 1938, Bird quickly followed and ultimately found fame.

In New York, Smith turned his attention to arranging, working with former band mates Count Basie and Hot Lips Page. He made a few recordings, including reuniting with Page for eight tunes in a 1940 recording session. By 1942 Smith was in search of a quieter life and slower pace, so he returned to Dallas and didn't record for another seventeen years. He organized small combos and played in the area and became a teacher for many young musicians. His 1959 recording for Atlantic records marked his first 33 rpm LP, and also his last. In the early sixties a car accident ended his days as a sax player, but Smith turned his talents to the bass guitar and continued leading a dance band until 1980. Eleven years later he died of a heart attack in his adopted hometown of Dallas.

The third Texas wheel that helped set the Blue Devils in motion came from San Marcos. Eddie Durham was born into a large musical family in 1906 and by the age of ten was a member of a band that included one brother and a cousin. His older brother, Joe, played the cello on a brief stint with Nat King Cole and, after taking a correspondence course, taught Eddie and his other brothers to read and write music.

Durham was all of eighteen years old when he took his show on the road, playing the circus circuit with the 101 Ranch Brass Band. Proficient on the trombone, he also picked up the guitar—after first mastering the banjo—and was invited to join the Blue Devils in 1928.

Bringing prowess in all three areas, Durham excelled in each and soon was arranging songs for the Blue Devils. Within the year, Bennie Moten had started pilfering the Devils, and Durham became the first to switch teams. In addition to providing stand-out solos both on the trombone and the guitar, Durham did arranging work for Moten and began taking the band in a new direction. The ensemble soon included Hot Lips Page and Count Basie, among other former Blue Devils, and became a highly polished, high-profile band. Durham's scores moved the band in the direction of swing, a sound it would perfect in later recordings.

Durham left the band in 1934, one year before Moten's death and the beginning of the band's downward spiral. After Basie formed his own band (in his post Buster Smith-Count Basie Band of Rhythm days), Durham returned to the fold and created some of the most memorable works of the band's early career. "Swingin' the Blues," "Time Out" and "Every Tub" show Durham at his swinging best, giving Basie's boys a hard-hitting big-band sound. With a heavy nod to the blues, Durham's compositions—unlike those by Buster Smith, which also were recorded by Basie's bands—created a jazz texture that strayed from the Texas-based sound, creating a livelier sound that left ample room for various sideman soloists to stretch their creative limbs.

As powerful as Durham's talents were in arranging music or playing the trombone, perhaps his most overlooked contribution to the jazz world is the introduction of the electric guitar.

Although he is most remembered for his arrangements and his trombone prowess, music owes a debt to Durham for being the first jazz player to plug in.

In the early thirties musicians already were experimenting with ways to amplify their sound, launching the eternal "bigger, louder, faster" quest that never seems to be satisfied in the music world. Les Paul, the renowned guitar inventor, had tried a number of methods for getting wired; he even tried inserting a phonograph needle into the top of his acoustic guitar to create an electric sound.

But it was Durham who is credited with introducing the electric guitar solo; in 1935 he dissected his acoustic instrument and inserted a plate under the strings in an attempt to bounce the sound back to the audience. With a microphone held to the guitar, the electric sound made its debut at Durham's fingertips. (Later that same year, Gibson introduced its first electric guitar, opening the door for an entirely new sound.)

Durham's career continued to be multifaceted, juggling his talents as an instrumentalist with his abilities in front of the band. He arranged music for many of the white big bands of the forties, including Artie Shaw and Glenn Miller. One of Miller's best-known compositions, "In the Mood," was one of Durham's projects. He went on to form his own band in the forties then directed an all-female orchestra. His performance schedule slowed in the fifties and sixties, although he continued working on arrangements for a number of groups, and he released albums in 1974 and 1981 in England. He toured with the Harlem Blues and Jazz Band in the eighties and died in New York in 1987.

Durham influenced a number of musicians, including jazz guitar great Charlie Christian, but perhaps no one was more affected by the accomplished performer than his cousin, Herschel Evans. The Denton-born Evans was on his way to mastering the alto sax when his cousin persuaded him to switch to the tenor sax. That proved to be a masterful move; he went on to play with the Troy Floyd band in San Antonio and Lionel Hampton and Buck Clayton in Los Angeles before joining his cousin in Count Basie's band in late 1936.

The combination of Durham's well-muscled musical arrangements and Evans's high-energy sax proved a formidable one. He was an acclaimed soloist, and the combination helped elevate the stature of Basie's band, particularly important as Basie went about rebuilding his troops following the amicable departure of soloist/arranger Buster Smith. Evans rose to an enviable stature, recording with notables like Harry James and Lionel Hampton. Although he died of heart disease in 1939, at the age of thirty, his fingerprint left a lasting impression on the jazz world and influenced generations of tenor players that followed.

The territory bands of the twenties and thirties were heavily populated with Texans, such as trombonist Dan Minor, a Dallas native who became the main trombone soloist for Count Basie's orchestra in the late thirties. Like many of Basie's players, he played in the Blue Devils in the late twenties and was among the players recruited by Bennie Moten before Basie took over. Although Minor was eventually overshadowed by more powerful players during the swing era, he played music for the rest of his life and died in 1982.

Trumpet players Joe Keyes of Houston and Carl "Tatti" Smith of Marshall both were mainstays of Basie's brass section, and Smith also led his own band in Kansas City. He recorded with Basie's band before all but disappearing off the musical landscape, supposedly moving to South America in the late forties and continuing to play into the fifties, which is when he seemingly disappeared.

Texans are quick to claim Austin-born pianist Teddy Wilson as their own, even though his family moved to Alabama not long after his birth in 1912. Wilson made his name in Chicago as a pianist and arranger, performing with Jimmie Noone and Louis Armstrong before joining Benny Carter's band in New York. He later toured with Benny Goodman and then launched his own big band in 1939, touring internationally and polishing his reputation as pianist. He taught piano at Julliard School of Music from 1945 until 1952 and during the sixties worked as a solo pianist. Wilson created a style that was often called "elegant," and it's only fitting that his last recording, in 1980, was called "Gentlemen of Swing."

John Dickson "Peck" Kelley was born in Houston in 1898, and the proficient pianist ultimately found his fame as a band leader. Peck's Bad Boys, a territory band that was a training ground for many jazz greats, including Jack Teagarden and Pee Wee Russell, was only the beginning. He led various bands until the late forties then worked as a solo pianist. Attempts to get the reclusive Kelley to travel or record were largely unsuccessful, and despite his powerful reputation, there is little to document his legendary ability. Unfortunately, he left behind only two recordings as a testimony to his skill, and he died in 1980.

Like many Texans in the jazz industry, Dallas's Budd Johnson was a talented force whose work was largely behind the scenes. He and his younger brother Frederic "Keg" Johnson grew up in a musical family and launched their careers playing in Kansas City in the late twenties then moving on to Chicago where they played with Louis Armstrong. Budd gained attention for his multiple talents as a tenor sax man and arranger, but he also could play the drums, clarinet, and baritone and alto sax. After Armstrong, Budd arranged for such greats as Buddy Rich and Woody Herman, and in the forties he played with Dizzy Gillespie and Billy Eckstein.

Budd managed to translate the standard jazz sound of the thirties and forties into the rock 'n' roll rage of the fifties, where he found work as a producer and arranger, even though his heart stayed firmly planted in jazz. He performed with a number of his own combos throughout the rest of his life and appeared at international jazz festivals until his death in 1984.

Keg's ability on the trombone saw him playing with Benny Carter and Fletcher Henderson after ending his tenure with Armstrong's outfit; he logged fifteen years with Cab Calloway before going on to play with Ray Charles and, until his death in 1967, often reunited on stage with his older brother.

The noticeable absence of Texas bandleaders in the national circuit had one very notable exception, which came from Vernon, near the Texas-Oklahoma border. Weldon Leo "Jack" Teagarden, born in 1905, also landed in a rather musical family. Three siblings: Charles (trumpet), Cub (drums), and Norma (piano) also became renowned jazz performers, however none found the same degree of fame as their brother. Although their father was an amateur cornet player, much of the credit for the family's musical inclinations is heaped upon their mother, Helen, who was a piano teacher and church organist. She started all of her children off as piano students, but the boys branched out to other areas. By the time he was seven, Jack had picked up the baritone horn and within another two years was playing trombone. His earliest performances were the duets he played with his mother at the Vernon Theatre as accompaniment to silent movies.

His father's death in 1918 was a pivotal point in Teagarden's life and launched his somewhat nomadic lifestyle. The family moved to Nebraska then to Oklahoma City. Late in 1919 Teagarden returned to his Texas roots, living with an uncle in San Angelo and playing trombone in local bands.

He hooked up with a San Antonio quartet for about a year then joined Houston's best-known jazz band, led by pianist Peck Kelley. He stayed with Peck Kelley's Bad Boys for a couple of years before signing on with R.J. Marin's Southern Trumpeters and then joining Doc Ross and his Jazz Bandits.

Although he was white, Teagarden's music was steeped in the tradition of the black blues singers he studied and listened to at every opportunity. Obviously stirred by the blues tradition, he fit it into a jazz framework and brought a fresh approach to what had been a rather straight-laced white jazz scene. His sensational style reframed the way jazz bands viewed the trombone, making it a viable solo instrument for the first time.

Teagarden's music caught the ears of bandleaders in states as far away as California and New York, who tried unsuccessfully to recruit the young trombonist. He finally headed for the Big Apple in 1927, hoping to play with Paul Whiteman's orchestra but landing instead in an outfit led by Ben Pollack—after beating out Glenn Miller for the first trombone chair. Later that year he recorded with Pollack's Kentucky Grasshoppers, the first of more than one thousand recordings that would chronicle his prolific career. He went on to share the studio with such legends as Louis Armstrong, Benny Goodman, and Red Nichols, as well as backing his idol Bessie Smith and providing a smooth, fluid backing track for a rising young jazz singer named Billie Holiday. The recording sessions also gave the trombone player a chance to showcase his vocal abilities, and his blues singing might well have made him famous had it not been so overshadowed by his prowess on the trombone.

In 1933 Teagarden finally got his chance to play with Whiteman's orchestra, and he signed on for a five-year stint with the rather straightforward outfit, thus putting his improvisational urges on ice, at least temporarily. Although his tenure with Whiteman provided Teagarden with financial stability, it handcuffed him creatively, and much time has been spent debating whether Teagarden could have gone on to find even greater success if he'd not been bound by that obligation.

When his time with Whiteman ended in 1938, Teagarden finally formed his own band. The ensemble was a critical success but a financial disaster, and after struggling for nearly nine years, Teagarden finally folded it and joined with Louis Armstrong's All-Stars from 1947 until 1951. He then formed another group, the Jack Teagarden All Stars Dixieland Band, which lasted five years; a series of other bands that he organized included one that toured Europe in 1957 and another that toured Asia in 1958 and '59. In the meantime he had appeared in three movies and had won a number of music awards and even was the featured performer at the 1957 Newport Jazz Festival.

On stage, Teagarden was unmatched; off stage, his life was marred by heavy drinking and failed marriages. His fourth marriage proved to have the most longevity, lasting more than two decades and yielding three children as well as one foster child. But the drinking eventually took its toll, and in 1964, at the age of fifty-eight, bronchial pneumonia forced Teagarden to cut short his performance at the Dream Room in New Orleans. He was found dead the next afternoon in his hotel room, and doctors cited his chronic alcohol consumption as a contributing factor to his premature death.

While Eddie Durham was the first musician to put the electric guitar on a jazz record, Charlie Christian was the man who took it to an art form. Christian, who was born in Bonham in 1916, spent most of his childhood in Oklahoma City with his father, a blind musician who worked as a singer/guitarist. The younger Christian played bass and guitar in a number of small groups before heading back to Texas in 1934 and playing bass with the Alphonse Trent band in Dallas.

Although no one will dispute his talent, it was also a series of good breaks that allowed Christian to explore his abilities. When he was overheard playing a guitar, the bassist was switched to a guitar chair in Trent's outfit. His career took further leaps when he met his mentor Eddie Durham in Oklahoma City, where Durham was playing with Jimmie Lunceford's orchestra. Durham showed him the way to play an amplified guitar, and before long Christian had mastered intricate solos previously reserved for saxophones. His reputation as a guitarist soared, and over the next two years he played throughout the Midwest and Southwest, stunning audiences with his masterful, emotional fingering on the strings.

He was playing at the Ritz Café in Oklahoma City when he so impressed jazz critic John Hammond that the critic recommended him to Benny Goodman. Goodman, however, had little interest in allowing Christian, an African American, into his all-white band. When Hammond flew Christian to Los Angeles for an audition, the famed bandleader was immediately appalled by the guitarist's green suit, purple shirt, and yellow shoes, and he made it clear he wanted nothing to do with Christian.

The persistent Hammond, with the help of two of Goodman's sidemen, slipped Christian onstage during a break, giving the bandleader no choice but to listen to the twenty-two-year-old guitarist. His energized forty-five-minute performance of "Rose Room" easily won him a spot with the band, and by the end of the year, Christian recorded that song as a member of Goodman's sextet. His single-string solos and down-stroke technique set a new standard for jazz musicians and marked a completely different approach to the music and the instrument on which it was played.

The volume of recordings that Christian produced over the next three years is nothing short of prolific. He proved himself a master of improvisation, finding room for riffs where no one else could imagine they'd exist. Christian's exquisite jams with such up-and-coming jazz artists as Dizzy Gillespie and Thelonious Monk are proof of his trailblazing style that would stand untouched for at least the next two decades, and he walked a razor-thin line between blues and jazz, attracting fans of both genres.

In 1941 Christian contracted tuberculosis but continued a rigorous playing schedule and a routine of hard living after hours. Refusing to give up his vices or allow his body to heal, the legendary guitarist died early in 1942 in a Staten Island sanitarium at the age of just twenty-six.

Christian was the most widely recognized guitarist of his era to come out of Texas, but he wasn't alone. Austin's greatest contribution to the strings was Oscar Moore, who was born in 1912 and, like most guitarists of the era, was heavily influenced by the Christian's guitar work.

Moore's talent took longer to incubate, but by the 1940s he had become a valuable part of the Nat King Cole Trio. He spent ten years as part of that combo, perfecting the interplay between guitar and piano and providing solos reminiscent of Christian's fancy finger work.

He left Cole's fold in 1947 and recorded with Art Tatum and Lionel Hampton, among others, before joining his brother, Johnny, in the band Three Blazers. For four consecutive years, *Down Beat* readers voted him Best Guitarist, but his career came to an end when, for reasons unknown, he quit the band to become a bricklayer. He occasionally returned to the stage or the studio until his death in 1981.

Jazz in the forties began to gravitate toward the bebop movement, moving away from the big band swing that had dominated the scene since the rise of territory bands. A dispute over royalties put a ban on recording from 1942 to 1944, and the scene was further splintered by World War II, which had drafted both fans and musicians away from their passion. Although jazz appeared to be in a state of chaos, it would soon regain its footing and resurface with revolutionary new sound and style.

Recommended Listening:

Hot Lips Page and His Band, 1938-1940 – Oran Page (Classics)

The Legendary Buster Smith – Henry "Buster" Smith (Atlantic)

Budd Johnson and the Four Brass Giants – Budd Johnson (Prestige)

Jack Teagarden 1928-1943 – (Best of Jazz)

Solo Flight – Charlie Christian (Topaz)

The Oscar Moore Quartet – (Tampa)

Chapter Five

Cowboy Songs and Country Music

Of all the music to come out of the Lone Star State, country music is the one most readily identified with Texas tradition. From the outside looking in, Texas is prime cowboy country, and the widespread modern-day presence of Stetsons and boots does nothing to dispel that notion. Regardless of what sounds might have come out of the state before and since then, cowboy songs and country music remain one of Texas's earliest and most enduring contributions to the national soundscape.

By the late 1800s cowboy songs were as much a part of American heritage as the cowboys themselves. Although the songs, which were rooted heavily in the folk tradition, were sung just about anyplace you could find a man on a horse, their style was widely associated with Texas. The early settlers in America brought with them their traditional songs from England, Scotland, and Ireland but found that many of the lyrics didn't translate into life in the Old West. So like the preachers before them, cowboys often borrowed the melodies of these traditional songs and supplied them with more relevant themes. "The Unfortunate Rake," a song about an English soldier dying of syphilis, took on much more meaning to cowboys when it was transformed into "The Streets of Laredo." And instead of "The Ocean Burial," a ballad about a sailor being buried at sea, early cowboys sang, "Bury Me Not on the Lone Prairie."

Much of the credit for the preservation of those old ballads belongs to John Lomax, who chronicled cowboy songs the same way he later would preserve blues and prison work songs—by going directly to the source. Born in Mississippi in 1867, Lomax grew up in Bosque County, where he became fascinated with American folk songs. He tracked down the history of the Old West directly from cowboys and ranch hands, creating lasting documentation of the early songs such as "The Old Chisholm Trail" and "Git Along Little Dogies." While attending the University of Texas, he made his first attempt to point out the literary value of the lyrics, but he found his efforts ridiculed.

Lomax took his passion to Harvard a decade later, where he found the support—financial and otherwise—to publish what would become an invaluable snapshot of American musical history. His book *Cowboy Ballads and Other Frontier Songs* was published in 1910, and although it would take another twenty years for the public fascination with cowboy songs to truly catch on, it played an instrumental role in capturing the musical legacy that predated recorded music.

The Texas cowboy tradition began in the 1860s, when cattlemen drove their herds northward and took their music with them. By far the most popular cowboy song—both in Texas and beyond—was "Home on the Range," which became even more renowned when composer David Guion included it in his New York production *Prairie Echoes* in 1930.

Guion, who was born in Ballinger in 1892, was a child prodigy who began studying music at the age of five, first in San Angelo and later in Fort Worth before studying at the Royal Conservatory of Music in Austria.

By the early 1920s Guion was already on his way toward becoming an important figure in chronicling the folk and cowboy songs of early America; he was one of the first composers to transcribe early music, from folk songs to Negro spirituals, and transform them into concert pieces. Among his contributions were "Turkey in the Straw," "The Yellow Rose of Texas," and "Arkansas Traveler," although his best-known work remained the 1908 arrangement of "Home on the Range." Guion's handiwork did a remarkable job of representing the early days of Texas with songs like "The Bold Vaquero" and "Texas Fox Trot."

Although his roots were obviously and firmly planted in Texas, his boots frequently were elsewhere. In New York City he hosted a weekly western-themed radio show for a time, penning both the scripts and the music. He wrote commissioned pieces for the 1936 Texas Centennial and for the Houston Symphony Orchestra fourteen years later; in all, he composed more than two hundred published works that comprised both religious and secular music.

During the course of his career, Guion also was active as a teacher, devoting six decades of his life to guiding young musicians and colleges and conservatories nationwide until his death in Dallas in 1981 at the age of eighty-nine.

Guion played into America's fascination with the Old West and cowboy songs, and by the time the 1920s rolled around, country music was well on its way to becoming a musical staple. It was in the hands of Amarillo's Eck Robertson that country music crossed the threshold into the commercialized world, as Robertson became the first performer to promote his music on the radio.

Born Alexander Robertson in Arkansas in November 1887, the legendary fiddler embodied the popular Lone Star adage, "I wasn't born in Texas, but I got here as fast as I could." He was only three years old when his parents moved to the Texas

Panhandle, and he was raised in a family where fiddling was just part of growing up. His father, grandfather, and uncles all were accomplished fiddle players, often entering competitions and contests.

By the time Robertson left home at sixteen, determined to pursue a career in show business, he had become proficient on the guitar, banjo, and fiddle. He first peddled his talents with a traveling medicine show through the Indian Territory (now known as Oklahoma), but as silent films entered the entertainment world, he left the circuit to provide live "background" music at theaters. Dressed in western clothes, Robertson built his reputation as the "Cowboy Fiddler."

Eventually Robertson returned to Amarillo and, after marrying his childhood sweetheart, Nettie, in 1906, he took a job tuning pianos. To satisfy his musical urges, he performed at fiddle contests and also at vaudeville theaters with his wife. But it was an Old Confederate Solders reunion in Virginia that immediately changed the path he was on.

The son of a Confederate soldier, Robertson made it a point to attend the annual reunions. In 1922 he met former Confederate soldier and fellow fiddler Henry Gilliland and played a duet with the seventy-six-year-old man for the opening ceremony of the reunion. Astonished by how well their talents blended, Robertson convinced the older player to drive to New York City and record an album.

They arrived in the Big Apple without an invitation and still wearing their unlikely outfits—Robertson dressed in cowboy garb, Gilliland in his Confederate uniform. Driving to the Victor Talking Machine Company, Robertson convinced the studio to record them on the spot. The date was June 30, 1922, and it became the acknowledged birth date of recorded country music. The duo chose two David Guion selections, "Arkansas Traveler" and "Turkey in the Straw," for their recording, and the studio invited them back the next day to lay down six more tracks, two of which were never released.

Victor released the recording of "Sallie Gooden" and "Arkansas Traveler" in September of 1922, but the other four recordings wouldn't come out until 1923 and 1924. Riding on the popularity of the first release, Robertson became the first artist to promote his recording on the radio, taking it to Fort Worth's WBAP and hawking it on the air. At the time there was no such thing as "country music." Instead, within months of Robertson's recordings, what were termed as "hillbilly bands" were playing live on radio stations well beyond Texas.

While he had access to a radio station, Robertson's location didn't lend itself to a recording career. He had, however, opened the door for country music, and many fiddlers eagerly followed him through that portal. In the years following his first recording session, more than a dozen fiddle players from Texas made their own records, although Robertson still was seen as the standard by which fiddlers were judged.

Finally, seven years after his first session, Robertson recorded again for Victor, this time with his musical family—son Dueron ("Eck Junior"), daughter Daphne, and wife Nettie—and with Dr. J. B. Cranfill on second fiddle. The stock market crash of 1929 and ensuing disputes with the Victor Company are largely blamed for the failure of his second endeavor, but it couldn't mar his regional fame.

Back in Texas, Robertson still reigned supreme among fiddle players, appearing as both a contestant and a strong drawing card at fiddler contests. He enjoyed a radio career performing for WBAP and other small stations and went to Hollywood in 1937 to play in a hillbilly band for the movies. That move ended in a dispute with his employer, and three years later he recorded some one hundred songs for Sellers Transcription Studio in Dallas, hoping again to jump-start his recording career. The songs, however, were never released, and the recordings have never been found.

Although his place as midwife to the birth of country music was secured in that New York studio in 1922, the fame Robertson had so hoped for eluded him, and he spent his final years living quietly in Amarillo, dying in a Texas nursing home in 1975. Disappointed by the dismal financial results of his musical ventures, he often blamed the record company's unfair practices for robbing him of the commercial success that was due him.

Instead, it was another Texan, Vernon Dalhart, who turned the country music industry on its ear and proved that commercial success was possible.

Born near Jefferson in 1883, with the heavy metal-friendly name of Marion Try Slaughter, Dalhart was raised on a ranch in Marion County and earned the honor of releasing the first country music hit. But it was an unusual and unlikely path from the family ranch to country music fame.

Dalhart discovered his singing ability early on and was performing publicly by the time he was twelve years old. When his father was stabbed to death by a drunken brother-in-law in the late 1890s in a fight no doubt worthy of Jerry Springer's "best-of" television episodes, Dalhart found himself working as a cowboy, which is where he learned many of the traditional cowboy songs and ballads that would later make him famous. Whatever else the experience may have added to his life, his time as a cowpuncher also gave him his recording name—he borrowed his famous moniker from the towns of Vernon and Dalhart, two of the burgs in the Texas Panhandle where he worked during the summer.

Dalhart's mother moved from the dusty plains to the more cosmopolitan regions of Dallas shortly after the turn of the century, and Dalhart began studying at the Dallas Conservatory of Music. By 1910 he was working as a soloist at the First Baptist

Church and moved to New York City to find additional instruction. There, he found work singing in operas and operettas, including a role in *Madame Butterfly*—not something that most country music artists past or present can add to their resume.

By the mid-teens, Dalhart had landed parts in a handful of stage productions, but his career as a tenor wasn't exactly going great guns. About that time, Edison cylinder discs had become popular, and he started recording for Columbia—and Edison Diamond Disc and Victor and, it seemed, anyone else who would listen. Although at the time it wasn't unusual for artists to perform under other names—usually as a means of sidestepping some of the limitations of their recording contracts—Dalhart took the practice to an extreme.

Using some 110 pseudonyms, he sang everything from pop tunes to patriotic ditties to operatic numbers to spiritual selections. Taking something of a schizophrenic musical approach, he recorded in a number of ethnic styles, at one point even adopting a thick Southern Negro dialect for his recording of "Can't Yo' Heah Me Callin' Caroline."

Dalhart finally stumbled into extreme success in 1924. Having tried virtually every other style of music on the face of the planet, he decided to record some of the country songs he had heard during his cowhand days in the Panhandle. "Hillbilly" music, as it was still called at that time, had become popular, so, having nothing to lose, Dalhart recorded the song "The Wreck of the Old '97" with a B-side offering of "The Prisoner's Song" for Victor Records.

Neither Dalhart nor his struggling record company could have predicted the public response; released in November of 1924, the B-side song became an instant hit, selling more than a million copies—a first for the fledgling country music scene. Overnight, Dalhart went from an unknown to an unparalleled success; that song alone eventually sold more than 25 million copies during Dalhart's lifetime.

His career renewed, Dalhart wasted no time in trying to hold on to that slippery brass ring. He not only recorded additional songs for Victor, but he gave his first successful song a bit of competition by recording "The Prisoner's Song" for a number of different labels under various aliases.

Using his Dalhart nom de plume, the Texan became America's best-selling artist from 1924 to 1928 and found his biggest hit with 1927's national bestseller, "Home on the Range." He had a number of other million-sellers, including "The Convict and the Rose," "The Death of Floyd Collins," and "My Blue Mountain Ridge Home." And while his fame proved to be lasting, fate was more fickle with his fortune.

Like Robertson, Dalhart's recording career was one of the casualties of the Great Depression, and the musician lost most of his money in the stock market crash of 1929. Record sales suffered across the board as the country struggled with the Depression, and Dalhart faded into obscurity. Although he had recorded some 1,000 songs during his career, Dalhart's final years were spent working jobs such as night watchman, voice teacher, and night checkout clerk. By the time he died of a heart attack in 1948, Dalhart had all but vanished from the consciousness of the American listening public, and it wasn't until the 1960s that his music was rediscovered and dusted off for public consumption. He was elected into the Country Music Hall of Fame in 1981.

Dalhart's success may not have given him the life he had envisioned, but it served as a tremendous source of inspiration for a struggling young music industry. It also gave country or hillbilly music something it had lacked until that point—respectability—and, in doing that, opened the door for other forms of country and western music to swing into the public's consciousness.

Carl Sprague was one of the first to follow Dalhart's lead, and in 1925 he recorded the cowboy song "When the Work's All

Done This Fall." Many point to this as the first true recorded cowboy song, and as other artists jumped on the bandwagon, Sprague stood out as one of the few singers who not only sang about the cowboy life, but had actually lived it.

Sprague, who had grown up on a ranch near Houston, went on to make twenty-eight recordings with Victor Records, and the company was doing well in the cowboy market, thanks largely to Dalhart's contributions. Victor went on to build an entire catalog of cowboy singers, but Sprague bowed out of a commercial career. Instead, he coached football at Texas A&M University and became a major in the United States Army. He occasionally performed in public and had a weekly radio program at Texas A&M for a time, but he was ultimately lost in the crush of singing cowboys trying to round up their own fame.

Texas, of course, had no shortage of such performers. Waxahachie produced Jules Verne Allen, another singing cowboy who had worked on ranches in Texas and Montana since his childhood. He obviously preferred the "singing" to the "cowboy" part and built a strong following by performing on radio stations in the Southwest beginning in the late 1920s. On San Antonio's WOAI, Allen performed as "Longhorn Luke," romanticizing rodeos and roundups and borrowing heavily from Lomax's treasury of cowboy songs. His successful career continued into the thirties, and he even wrote a book, *Cowboy Lore*, in 1933 to further expound upon his reflections of the cowboy lifestyle that had served him so well.

Perhaps the most enigmatic of all the singing cowboys of the era was Goebel Reeves, best known as "The Texas Drifter." Born in 1899 to a successful middle-class family in Sherman, Reeves shunned the comfortable trappings of his parents and instead chose the life of a drifter. The experience added a new dimension to cowboy music, and he penned such now-classic songs as "The Cowboy's Prayer" and "Hobo's Lullaby."

Reeves's commitment to the hobo lifestyle included rejecting the commercial success that was due him. Even after his recording of "Big Rock Candy Mountain" brought him national acclaim, he downplayed the musical success and stuck to life on the rails. He died in California in 1959 after enjoying a diverse career, thanks to the combination of his original lyrics and distinct yodeling style. The highlight of that career, he often claimed, was teaching a young man named Jimmie Rodgers how to yodel.

Rodgers was not a Texan by birth, but he adopted the Lone Star State as his own, and it was in the South that he found his most devoted fans. Born in 1897 in Mississippi, Rodgers lost his mother and his chance at a stable childhood at the age of four. He tagged along on the job with his father, a railroad worker, and by the age of fourteen was working on those crews himself. He worked the line between Meridian and New Orleans, which is where Reeves apparently met up with the future star in 1920.

Rodgers was learning a lot more than railroad work; he picked up the trainmen's ballads and learned to play a number of stringed instruments. His yodel often was used to imitate the train's whistle, and it fit perfectly with his drawn-out, melancholy vocals. Rodgers perfected his skills by entertaining his fellow workers during breaks, playing either the guitar or banjo.

The hard life of a railroader took its toll on Rodgers' health, and after a bout with tuberculosis in 1924, he was told he needed to find less strenuous working conditions. He joined a trio and played at fairs and political rallies and finally left the rails in 1925 to track down a career as an entertainer.

His first gig, as a blackface entertainer in a medicine show, was short-lived and followed by a fling as manager and owner of a roadside café. He briefly returned to the railroading life until it once more threatened his health, so he left the career for good when he landed a job on the police force in Asheville, North

Carolina. There, he formed the Jimmie Rodgers Entertainers, a four-man troupe that played for WWNC radio and saw Rodgers billing himself as "The Singing Brakeman." In August of that year he landed a record contract with Victor Talking Machine Company and introduced his signature yodel on "Sleep, Baby, Sleep," an old lullaby. By the end of the year, his star was beginning to rise, and Rodgers was asked to return to the recording studio.

With the recording of "Blue Yodel No. 1" (also known as "T for Texas"), Rodgers found his first hit. It was the first of a dozen blue yodels he would record, all of them simply named with a number, as in "Blue Yodel No. 2." He quickly became the music business's hottest property, and despite his frail health, he recorded some 111 songs and sold more than 20 million records in the next six years.

His health often interfered with live performances, but it couldn't stop his career. He couldn't answer the demand for shows in England, Canada, and South America, but he continued with radio performances and vaudeville appearances as often as he could find the strength to do so. A Washington radio announcer named Ray McCreath dubbed him "America's Blue Yodeler" after seeing him perform live, and the title stuck.

By 1929 Rodgers was earning as much as $100,000 a year, but most of it was eaten up by medical bills and a lawsuit with his first wife. He moved to Kerrville, where he had built a $50,000 mansion called Blue Yodeler's Paradise, and limited himself to a few performances a year that allowed him to stay in the South or Southwest.

He was named an honorary Texas Ranger in 1931, which prompted him to write "The Yodeling Ranger," and even as his health diminished, he continued working on plans for an extensive tour. By 1932 he was forced to sell his beloved mansion and move to a much less extravagant home in San Antonio with his wife and daughter. He began making twice-weekly appearances on KMAC radio in San Antonio and toured East Texas in the spring and summer of '32.

Rodgers' ill health sidelined him in January of 1933, sending him to a Houston hospital for a month and earning him stern directions from the medical staff to take a six-month rest. Perhaps knowing the end was at hand, Rodgers ignored the doctors' orders and traveled to New York in May for a recording session. His health had deteriorated so badly that Rodgers had to rest on a cot between takes just to gain enough strength to record the next song.

On May 26, two days after he finished his recordings, Rodgers died in his New York hotel room. He is largely recognized as "The Father of Country Music," and in 1961, by unanimous vote, he became the first person ever named to the Country Music Hall of Fame.

The loss of Rodgers was huge, not just to a country that had fallen in love with his sound, but to a recording industry that had come to depend upon it. The search for a replacement would never prove successful. Although no one could fill his boots, many performers followed in his tracks and were fascinated by the sounds he created. Among his most ardent admirers was a young Gene Autry, who gained both fame and fortune as the first full-blown singing cowboy.

Born in Tioga in 1907, the firstborn of four sons was saddled with the very un-showbiz moniker Orvon Gene Autry. Like most everything else in his early years, it couldn't possibly hint at the promising future that lay ahead of him.

From his father, a livestock dealer and horse trader, Autry learned much about the cowboy traditions, while his mother completed the other half of the singing cowboy picture by teaching him to play the guitar. His grandfather, a Baptist preacher, was the first to recognize Autry's ability and put him in front of an audience; the future superstar was singing in the choir by the age of five.

His family bounced between Oklahoma and Texas, following his father's uncertain occupation and giving the younger Autry plenty of chances to hone his cowboy skills. He worked alongside his father or with his uncles, stacking and baling hay and learning the ins and outs of a farmhand. It was enough to make him determined to escape the grueling and often unrewarding lifestyle, and he began performing in both of the states he called home by the time he was in high school. Although he longed to find success either as a musician or as a baseball player, he hedged his bets by taking accounting classes through a correspondence school and also by learning Morse code.

He landed a job at a railway station, where he passed time by singing and playing his guitar. When noted humorist Will Rogers stopped by to telegraph his newspaper column, he encouraged the future star to pursue his talent. Autry did just that, landing his first "showbiz" job in 1928 as "Oklahoma's Singing Cowboy" for radio station KVOO in Tulsa. A year later he headed to New York City, where he recorded his first two songs for Victor Records, which also happened to be Jimmie Rodgers' musical home. He spent the year recording for Victor and a number of other labels, sometimes using a pseudonym. Even as the stock market crash took hold and the Depression set in, Autry still managed to find success. He signed with the American Recording Company (ARC) and in 1931 had his first million-selling hit with "That Silver-Haired Daddy of Mine," a duet with Jimmy Long.

Hollywood was starting to develop an interest in the phenomenon of singing cowboys and went looking for a star to put in its saddle. Autry, of course, with a built-in audience from his recording work, fit the bill perfectly. Technically, the first cowboy to sing in a movie was Ken Maynard, a Texan who sang four original cowboy songs in the 1930 film *Songs of the Saddle*. Maynard, however, was known mostly as an actor who could sing; it wasn't until Autry landed a singing part in Maynard's

1934 movie *In Old Santa Fe* that singing cowboy movies became a hot new film genre.

Although he had no film experience, Hollywood decided to take a chance on him because he was selling a tremendous number of records at a time when the entire country was in the grips of the Depression. His role in that first movie was small, but Autry quickly became a huge movie star, and a string of successful films—averaging about eight a year—followed.

When he wasn't filming, Autry stayed true to his first love and recorded a seemingly endless parade of hits that often romanticized his Texas heritage. "The Yellow Rose of Texas," "Mexicali Border," and "South of the Border" were just a few of the songs that kept Autry on the charts and on top of the world. In 1940 he took on a radio program, "Melody Ranch," a half-hour show that continued for sixteen years, despite a "break" in broadcasts when Autry served in the Army Air Corps during the Second World War. When he returned from his military service, he broadened his involvement in the entertainment world by becoming a successful businessman, buying radio and television stations while maintaining a rigorous pace of recording, broadcasting, and filming.

In between he found time to produce programs for the hot new media of television. By the time he hung up his spurs in 1956, he had made more than ninety films, recorded 653 songs, and had expanded his cowboy repertoire to include children's classics like "Here Comes Santa Claus" and "Peter Cottontail."

He made history in 1949 by becoming the first person to record the Christmas song, "Rudolph the Red-Nosed Reindeer," a song that Autry disliked and, initially, didn't want to record. His wife encouraged him to record it for his younger fans, and it later won Autry a Hall of Fame award at the 1985 Grammys.

Autry was able to combine his enterprising business skills with his love of baseball in 1960 when he bought an expansion team, the California Angels, later known as the Anaheim Angels. That same year he formed his own record label, Republic. But it was his fame as a singing cowboy that overshadowed his reputation as a savvy businessman and real estate mogul. His recording days may have been over, but his name continued to be recognized internationally. He opened the Gene Autry Western Heritage Museum in Los Angeles in 1988, displaying such memorabilia as guns owned by Wyatt Earp and Annie Oakley and costumes worn by television's Lone Ranger and Tonto. Autry died at his Southern California home in October 1998, just two days after his ninety-first birthday.

Other singing cowboys followed closely in Autry's trail, and by the early thirties, cowboy songs had captured the nation's fascination. They also had caught the attention of a young University of Texas student named Woodward Maurice Ritter, who would become one of the very few singing cowboys to come close to finding the superstar status of Autry.

Ritter was born in Murvaul in 1905 and was the youngest of six children. During high school he moved to Nederland to live with a sister and graduated from South Park High School in Beaumont.

Even though Ritter went to the University of Texas at Austin in 1922 to study law, he had already developed an interest in music, and it was the sound of the authentic cowboy songs that truly became music to his ears. His UT professors included John Lomax, J. Frank Dobie, and Oscar J. Fox, all of whom doubled as noted folk music historians and had an obvious and tremendous impact on Ritter's future.

During his five years at UT, he was president of the Men's Glee Club, but Ritter didn't officially begin his singing career until 1929, when he landed work singing for KPRC radio in Houston. By 1930 he was traveling throughout the South and Midwest with a musical troupe, playing one-night shows that eventually led him to New York a year later. In the Big Apple he joined the Theatre Guild and launched his career with a role in the Broadway show *Green Grow the Lilacs*—a production that later grew into the hit musical *Oklahoma!*

Although he was not a cowboy, Ritter embraced the cowboy music and quickly became known as a "cowboy singer"—thus the new moniker of "Tex," something he picked up in the East. The combination of his southern drawl and his encyclopedic knowledge of cowboy songs and history was too powerful for New Yorkers to resist, and Ritter became the Texas toast of the

Tex Ritter went to school to study law, but professors like John Lomax and J. Frank Dobie piqued his interest in music. Instead of a legal counselor he became a much-loved singing cowboy, starring in Broadway shows and films and enjoying a successful recording career. *Photo courtesy of Tex Ritter Museum.*

town. He was sought after for lecture recitals at schools throughout the East, and he became the featured performer at the Madison Square Garden Rodeo in 1932. That same year he landed a record contract with ARC and scored his first big hit with "Rye Whiskey."

Ritter appeared in five Broadway shows during the early thirties, which only served to further captivate those Yankee audiences. As radio began embracing the cowboy mystique, Ritter found himself in the right town at the perfect time. New York City's station WOR launched "The Lone Star Rangers," one of the first western-themed radio shows, with Ritter in the saddle. He spent the next four years in guest-star slots on radio stations throughout New York, building his reputation as one of the most popular singers of the emerging cowboy genre.

By 1936 the trail that Gene Autry had blazed for singing cowboy films was becoming a well-traveled one, and it seemed inevitable that Ritter would ride down that path as well. His first movie, *Song of the Gringo*, gave the public exactly what it was looking for—a handsome cowboy hero with authentic Texas roots to fill his Hollywood boots. Never mind that his hands had never worked on a real ranch; he fit the bill of exactly what America wanted to see, and hear.

As Ritter's movie career took off, he began recording for other labels and in 1942 became the first cowboy artist to ink a deal with Capitol Records. He gave the label its first major star and went a long way toward replacing the public's perception of backwoods "hillbilly music" with the more easily romanticized notion of "western music."

By the time of his first Capitol release, "I've Got Spurs That Jingle, Jangle, Jingle," in 1942, western music had finally started finding acceptance and even respect within the industry, which was taking note of its commercial viability. Ritter did his part to boost the genre's commercial success, releasing a string of hits, including "Boll Weevil" in 1945, "You Are My Sunshine" in 1946, and "High Noon" in 1952.

Like Autry, Ritter eventually took his talents to the small screen. Although he made some eighty-five movies during his career—seventy-eight of them westerns—he moved to television in 1959 with the musical variety show "Ranch Party," which ran until 1962. Two years later he became the fifth person elected into the Country Music Hall of Fame, and he was president of the Country Music Association from 1963 to 1965. Ritter later tried his hand in politics, making an unsuccessful bid for the U.S. Senate, and is also the father of television actor John Ritter. The legendary singing cowboy died of a heart attack in 1974 in Nashville.

The national fascination with cowboys gave anyone from Texas a leg up, which is why many non-Texans began identifying themselves as being from south of the Red River. The Sons of the Pioneers, for example, began in California, not the Lone Star State as was often implied, and included a Canadian group member. Likewise, Roy Rogers (born Leonard Slye) rode to Hollywood out of Ohio, although he often was identified as a native Texan. However, Rogers later earned a Texas connection by marriage when he got hitched to Dale Evans, who was born in Uvalde in 1912. She entered show business in the early forties as a singer-actress and married Rogers in 1947. By the fifties the duo had made movies and recorded songs together, and they starred in the popular television program "The Roy Rogers Show," whose theme song was written by Evans.

Not only did the cowboy ideal help to popularize cowboy music, it also crept into the instrumentation and wardrobe of performers who strayed from the cowboy genre and merely adopted the image. Even though Bill Boyd and His Cowboy Ramblers found their biggest success with jazz-oriented tunes, the image of this fiddle-driven dance band remained true to the highly romanticized cowboy. The name "Tex" certainly didn't end with Ritter, and in the cowboy-crazy thirties, many who bore the name had never even seen the state.

One who earned the name was Doie Hensley "Tex" Owens, who came from a large musical family in Killeen and created Cowdell's Wagon Show, a traveling musical variety show. He performed music mostly as a sideline until 1931, when friends convinced him to take advantage of the burgeoning popularity of radio acts. That led to a ten-year stint as co-host of the "Brush Creek Follies" in Kansas City, which featured his group The Original Texas Rangers.

Owens had a number of hit songs but found huge success with "Cattle Call" in 1935. That same song later became a crossover pop hit for Eddy Arnold. Meanwhile, Owens' sister, Ruby Agnes, went on to claim her own piece of fame as the popular radio and recording artist Texas Ruby.

Despite his success on the air, which included appearances on radio shows around the country, Owens went back to the oilfields after the end of World War II. He eventually returned to the entertainment arena, this time as a movie cowboy, but that career ended in 1950, when a horse fell on him and broke his back during the filming of John Wayne's *Red River.* He died in 1962 at the age of seventy.

Much of the success enjoyed by country music in the thirties and forties can be attributed to the proliferation of radio stations. While many industries foundered in the throes of the Great Depression, radio boomed, and most of its programming was country music. Country radio programs were part music, part miraculous promises, hawking hillbilly bands and magic cure-alls in the same breath. The salesmanship proved so successful that soon evangelists got into the act and on the air.

The link of country music and a Christian message proved a lucrative one. Country stars expanded their repertoire to include gospel themes, becoming the first crossover artists in history. Oftentimes the lines between country and gospel music blurred, and the radio became a part of religion in many areas of the state. It was, however, not without corruption.

One of the most notorious names in Christian radio's early days is Dr. John R. Brinkley, who took radio broadcasting nationwide and became one of the country's leading entrepreneurs. Brinkley, a shrewd but not particularly scrupulous businessman, launched his first radio station, KFKB, in Kansas in 1923. The station not only became extremely popular, but it gave Brinkley some political muscle as well. Although his bids for the governor's seat in 1930 and 1932 were unsuccessful, he became the first politician to use bands along the campaign trail to draw crowds of supporters—a political tool still used today. Brinkley also used the wattage to plug his medical practice, including his own special precursor to Viagra: implanting goat glands in impotent males. That was enough to get his medical license pulled, but it didn't stop the good doctor from practicing.

If the public was adoring of Brinkley's broadcast genius, the Federal Radio Commission was anything but. When they refused to renew his license, Brinkley moved to Del Rio, Texas, and forever changed the way the country listened to music. He built a hospital and then built an empire.

In 1931 the U.S. limited the power of radio stations to no more than 50,000 watts. Just across the border in Mexico, Brinkley discovered, he could lease stations with 100,000 to 150,000 watts and get a signal reaching as far as Canada. He launched XERA, the first of the so-called X-stations, and began a new trend that gave advertisers incredible access to those who walked the tightrope between finding salvation and being suckered in. On the air, Brinkley pushed cures, country music, and Christianity, sprinkled with a liberal dose of far-right politics. The X-stations proliferated, and within seven years, eleven stations filled the airwaves with advertisers offering pictures of Jesus that came in both the autographed and glow-in-the-dark varieties, prayer cloths, and even live baby rabbits blessed by your favorite singing gospel star.

It became harder for listeners to actually find a song on the air, but the stations still managed to produce some real musical value. In Dallas, KRLD touted the talents of the StampsBaxter Quartet, a product of the StampsBaxter Music and Printing Company. The brainchild of V.O. Stamps, the company opened its doors in Dallas in 1924, and by the early thirties, Stamps and his partner J.R. Baxter had three offices devoted to song writing and publishing. As an innovative twist, Stamps also found talent and created powerful gospel music quartets to perform that music, which made KRLD, the publishing company, and the quartet itself more successful than they could have ever been individually.

Other notable gospel groups found radio to be the perfect catapult to stardom as well. In Houston the Campbell Family got its start on the airwaves, and Lubbock produced the Chuck Wagon Gang. One of the biggest country-gospel groups to come out of the Lone Star State was The Herrington Sisters, a trio from Wichita Falls who took their talent beyond state lines to become national radio singing stars.

The country gospel tradition continued to prosper and thrive on into the fifties, yielding scores of new acts. Western swing, meanwhile, had taken cowboy songs and hillbilly sounds in another direction and dominated the scene during the forties. As the fifties began, America had embraced a more urban approach and spurned much of the rural appeal of the traditional country music sound. Folk music was becoming a movement that would hit its peak in the sixties, and many country acts landed on folk festival bills.

As western dance bands won out over reflective ballads, a number of Texans continued churning out eventual classics. Charlie Walker, a San Antonio DJ, had a string of hits that began with “Pick Me Up on Your Way Down” and continued with such songs as "My Shoes Keep Walking Back to You" and "Don't Squeeze My Sharmon." Riders of the Purple Sage, a Texas trio that actually hooked up in California, did their part to hold on to the western feel and scored a hit with the single "Ghost Riders in the Sky."

But it is Johnny Horton who had one of the biggest impacts on country music of the fifties, performing songs that are inextricably linked with the era. Born in Tyler in 1929, Horton spent his childhood picking cotton and later attended Baylor University in Waco on a basketball scholarship.

He was working for the fishing industry in California in 1950 when he began singing country music for radio station KXLA. Under the moniker "The Singing Fisherman," he launched his career as a barn dance performer five years later on the Louisiana Hayride. His first hit, in 1956, was a swinging rockabilly-flavored number, "Honky-Tonk Man," but it would be three years until he helped spur on country music's next revitalization.

"When It's Springtime in Alaska" launched the trend of "saga songs" and returned to a more traditional country sound. A spin-off—or perhaps a natural extension—of the folk music movement, saga songs told the stories of historically significant events and fictionalized episodes. The songs returned to the art of storytelling, which was the very place that country music had begun.

Hard-core country fans were thrilled and kept "Springtime" at the top of the charts for several weeks. Other artists, such as Johnny Cash and Eddy Arnold, followed suit, but it was Horton's 1959 recording of "The Battle of New Orleans" that carved his place in music history. The song, released in June, was a smash hit with both country and pop audiences, and country music again found crossover success. It also won Horton a Grammy Award in the category of Best Country Western Performance.

By the end of the year, the saga song enthusiasm had dwindled, although it has resurfaced several times, briefly, through the years. Marty Robbins, Jimmy Dean, and Lefty Frizzell all adopted the same narrative style (at least momentarily) during the early sixties long enough to earn a hit record or two.

As the saga song hit machine slowed down, Horton remained true to his first love, country music, but never had the chance to realize the full potential of his talent. He was en route to Nashville on November 5, 1960, when he was killed in an automobile accident. The accident made a widow of his bride, Billie Jean, for the second time; she had previously been the wife of Hank Williams. Even more ironically, both men played their final gigs at the same club—The Skyline Club in Austin.

Horton's place in history might have been to popularize the saga song, but he didn't invent it. Long before Horton stepped up to the microphone, Red River Dave McEnery had led the way there.

Born in San Antonio in 1914, McEnery's career began in the early thirties on his hometown radio. He picked up a guitar early on, and it was his frequent strumming of the song "Red River Valley" that earned him his name.

He originally found his fame in New York, where the natives enjoyed his songs and his colorful wordsmithing. Borrowing from the style of ballads found in his native San Antonio, McEnery showed an incredible and sometimes irreverent knack for translating current events into cowboy songs.

He ended up in a number of cowboy movies in the early 1930s and became among the first of the singing cowboys to land his own radio show. Original tunes like "The Battle of the Alamo" and "Pony Express" were early saga songs that made him popular, but it was his extremely topical 1937 song "Amelia Earhart's Last Flight" that truly put him in the spotlight.

As the rest of the country struggled with the pilot's mysterious disappearance, McEnery put those feelings into words. Two years later he was at the New York World's Fair to perform that song live for the debut of commercial television.

Red River Dave left New York in the late forties and returned home to San Antonio, where he still lives and occasionally performs. He began broadcasting his songs on the border radio station XERF, selling both himself and his songbooks to the rest of the nation.

Although he appeared in a number of western films, it has always been McEnery's ballads that have made him most memorable. He has covered everything from the Ayatollah to Watergate to Patty Hearst in his ballads, and he continues to document history within the confines of just a few bars and chords.

McEnery's saga songs were able to survive the change in the musical climate, but most in the late forties and early fifties weren't so fortunate. By the time the fifties rolled around, Nashville was becoming a dominant force and country music was in a state of flux.

The rural, often simple sound that had been country music's trademark now was being rejected in favor of a slicker pop sound. Steel guitars and fiddles were being pushed aside in favor of a more heavily orchestrated sound. Few people were able to make that work for them as well as Jim Reeves.

A native of Galloway, Reeves was born in 1923 and grew up in Carthage, where he fought boredom with music and baseball. By the age of six he was playing guitar and even joined in some neighborhood jams.

He played baseball for the University of Texas and then pitched for the Class C East Texas League before retiring in 1946 following a leg injury. One year later he launched his radio career as both a singer and a disc jockey, performing under the name Sonny Day. Later he would be known as Gentleman Jim.

Although he signed with a small Houston label, Macy, in 1949, it wasn't until he inked a contract with Abbott Records three years later that Gentleman Jim found success. He found national acclaim with his second recording, 1953's "Mexican Joe," and subsequently landed in Shreveport, where he was an announcer for KWKH and made frequent appearances on Louisiana Hayride, one of the leading forums for discovering new talent.

Too smooth to be honky-tonk, Reeve's resonant vocals helped spearhead the new pop Nashville sound. His initial success was followed up with the second well-received recording, "Bimbo," and RCA Victor signed him to their roster in 1955, the same year that the Grand Ole Opry brought him into its fold. Reeves became a phenomenally popular performer, touring Europe and South Africa multiple times and starring in the film *Kimberly Jim*.

Among his biggest recordings were "Four Walls" and "He'll Have to Go," which showcased his rich baritone voice and somehow bridged the gap between hillbilly music and Nashville pop. He discovered a young songwriter named Dottie West and helped launch her career when he scored a No. 3 hit with her composition, "Is This Me?" in 1962.

Although he died in a plane crash on July 31, 1964, his songs have lived on, with some recordings being released posthumously and generating a surprising volume of fan mail for Reeves, who was inducted into the Country Music Hall of Fame in 1967. He continued hitting the charts into the eighties, including some releases that were electronically turned into duets after his death.

Country music in Texas at the time of Reeves' death was in a state of flux. Rock 'n' roll music had invaded, and many feared the final demise of country music. But the strong folk roots of the sound mandated that it could never die out, it could only change. Honky-tonk music found its savior in George Jones, a singer who was born in Saratoga, near Beaumont, and never lost touch with his musical roots.

Jones emerged as one of the most prolific and successful country music performers of the sixties and seventies, recording over 150 albums and keeping his East Texas twang intact. Growing up listening to gospel and country music, he started

George Jones became one of the most important figures in country music during the sixties and seventies, invigorating honky-tonk music with a fresh breath and recording more than 150 albums.

playing the guitar at the age of nine, and when he was sixteen he began singing on a radio station in Jasper, Texas. A short-lived marriage and a stint in the military briefly interrupted his career path.

Jones's discovery is largely attributed to Pappy Dailey, who became one of the most important record producers in the years following World War II. Dailey created Starday Records in 1953 with partner Jack Starnes and was building one of the most successful independent labels in Texas when he signed Jones. The label already had enjoyed its first hit with Arlie

Pappy Dailey built one of the most successful independent labels in Texas with Starday Records, which he founded in 1953 with partner Jack Starnes. The label most notably launched the career of George Jones and eventually relocated to Nashville from Beaumont.

Duff's number seven song, "You All Come" in 1954. One year later Jones would take the label up the charts to the number four spot with "Why Baby Why."

By this time Starnes had left Starday, and Don Pierce stepped in, turning most of his attention to the promising career of George Jones. They relocated to Nashville, which was becoming the capital of country music, where they believed they would find a major label home for their efforts. The singer found a place on the bill alongside Elvis Presley at the Louisiana Hayride and then joined the cast of the Grand Ole Opry.

Jones's distinctive vocals seemed made for country music, blending perfectly with the steel guitar. By 1957 Mercury Records wanted Jones on its roster and took the Starday production team along with it.

For the next four years, Jones enjoyed a respectable career, but it was his 1962 song "She Thinks I Still Care" that shot him all the way to the top. The single became the number one record of the year and led to his first County Music Association Male Vocalist of the Year honor, something he would repeat three more times in the next two decades. The sixties were a mixed bag for Jones, who publicly battled an alcohol problem but also enjoyed a number of musical home runs, including "Tender Years," "White Lightning," and "Walk Through This World With Me."

As the sixties ended, Jones began a partnership both on stage and off with Tammy Wynette, whom he married in 1969. At about the same time, he split from Pappy Dailey, his long-time mentor, and he moved from his hard-core honky-tonk image toward a softer image, one that was enhanced by the duets he and Wynette sang. They became the First Couple of country music and played out their love story on stage with songs like "We Can Make It" and "Loving You Could Never Be Better." By 1974, however, the tune had changed and Jones was finding hits with songs like "The Grand Tour," which tells the story of a marriage in shambles, and "The Door." The couple divorced in 1975.

The seventies were a troubled time for Jones, but he rebounded near the end of the decade and in the eighties enjoyed several top ten hits, although his growing problems with drugs and alcohol grabbed most of the headlines. He cleaned up after his 1983 marriage to Nancy Sepulvada and enjoyed a few more visits to the top ten, the last time being in 1988 with a remake of the Johnny Horton hit "One Woman Man." Jones reunited with Wynette in the studio in 1995 then published his autobiography, *I Lived To Tell It All*, in 1996. The release of his 1999 album, *Cold Hard Truth*, was overshadowed by his well-publicized car accident just a few months earlier, when Jones smashed his car into a Nashville bridge. Tests showed he had been drinking, and Jones returned to rehab.

Jones played a significant role in keeping the honky-tonk sound alive and has been one of the most prominent performers in the Nashville scene. As the music moved toward a pop sound, traditional country music found its leaders in such crossover singer-songwriters as Roger Miller, Ray Price, and Willie Nelson. That would later spawn the progressive country sound and forever put Austin, Texas, on the map as more than the state's capital. The new sound brought together rock and country and, in doing so, united unlikely audiences who found a common love.

Recommended Listening:

Sing, Cowboy, Sing! The Gene Autry Collection – (Rhino Records)

Blood in the Saddle – Complete Recordings, 1932-1947 – Tex Ritter (Bear Family Records)

The Early Years – Jimmie Rodgers (Rounder)

Johnny Horton's Greatest Hits – (Columbia)

Album Number Two – Red River Dave McEnery (Bluebonnet)

16 Greatest Songs – Jim Reeves (RCA)

Heartaches and Tears – George Jones (Mercury)

Nearly Nashville

Were it not for a tragic freak accident, many believe that Dallas, not Nashville, would have become the country music recording capital of the world. In fact, the city was well on its way to becoming just that back in the fifties.

Most of the country music recording business in Dallas was concentrated around one particular site—Jim Beck's Recording Studio. Beck nurtured and recorded much of the talent that was growing in Texas, discovering such artists as Floyd Tillman, Billy Walker, Lefty Frizzell, Marty Robbins, and Ray Price. It was Beck who saw Roy Orbison performing with his band, the Wink Westerners, and invited the boys to record at his studio in 1955.

Dallas was working on becoming Music City in 1958; the activity at Jim Beck's Recording Studio had captured the attention of Decca Records A&R head Paul Cohen, who thought it would be more affordable to record country artists out of the Texas studio than in Tennessee. But then Cohen became head of Coral Records, and Owen Bradley, bandleader at Nashville radio station WSM-AM, filled Cohen's shoes at Decca's Nashville office. Intent on keeping the business in Nashville, Bradley decided to build a recording studio on 16th Avenue to compete with Beck's studio. However, it took one more twist of fate—this one much more cruel—to secure Nashville's toehold on the boot-scooting market.

Back at his Dallas studio, Beck was alone, cleaning the recording heads on his studio equipment. The windows were closed, and Beck inhaled too much carbon tetrachloride, which sent him into the hospital for several weeks. He never recovered, and his death marked the end of Dallas's opportunity to become the country music capital.

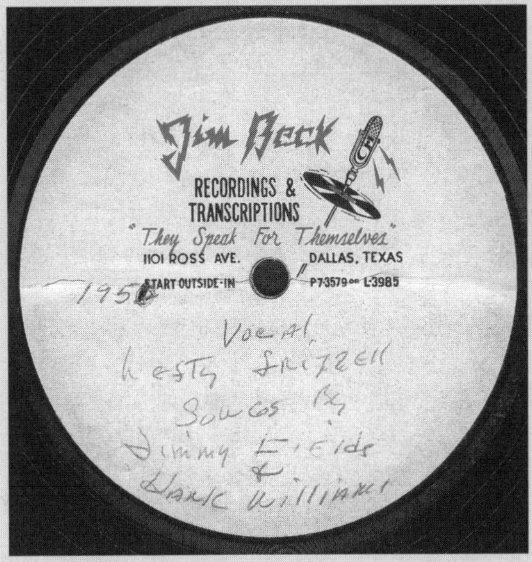

Jim Beck's recording studio set the pace for country music in the fifties, with up-and-coming artists such as Lefty Frizzell, Marty Robbins, Ray Price, and Roy Orbison cutting their teeth—and some of their records—at the studio. *Photo courtesy of David Dennard*

Bradley's 16th street studio, meanwhile, became one of the anchors of what would become Music Row, and Texas artists like Marty Robbins, George Jones, and Johnny Horton headed to Nashville for their recording endeavors.

Chapter Six

Western Swing and Honky-Tonk

Long before anybody knew what to call it, western swing was making a name for itself. Brewed in the musical melting pots that could only have been crafted in the multicultural climate of Texas, the sound borrowed influences from country, Tex-Mex, blues, cowboy, folk, and polka music but was played with an undeniable jazz flavor. Easily the most adventuresome music of its time, western swing defied genres and ultimately redefined musical boundaries, setting the stage for the inevitable onslaught of rock 'n' roll.

At the time western swing was emerging, white musicians were still something of an anomaly in the big band jazz scene. Their presence became even more curious when they began interpreting the upstart jazz feeling on stringed instruments and fitting it into the context of cowboy songs and hillbilly music. Some who played it called it jazz, others called it hot string music, which is the term that was widely used to describe western swing until after World War II. What they didn't call it was "country," and greats like Bob Wills protested that his band never played country music. Even so, western swing remains a spin-off of country music while managing to maintain an identity and history of its own.

Pinpointing the exact arrival of western swing is close to impossible, but the rise and reign of the fiddle-driven sound began sometime in the late twenties and gained tremendous momentum in the early thirties. And the man at the forefront of the musical revolution was Bob Wills, the Texan whose name has become synonymous with western swing.

Born in 1905 near Kosse, James Robert Wills seemed destined to pick up the fiddle. Both of his parents' families boasted fiddling skills, but it was his father, John, who was most widely recognized for his ability on the strings. "Uncle John," as the elder Wills was known, had earned his reputation as a fearsome fiddler at countless competitions and dances, including showdowns with renowned fiddler Eck Robertson. The accomplished player passed his secrets on to his son, and the younger Wills played his first dance, alongside his father, when he was just ten years old.

But Wills's musical influences reached beyond genetics and family tradition. His family moved to West Texas when "Jim Rob" was only eight, and the future legend was fascinated with the country blues of the black Texans who populated the cotton fields. He began working some of those sounds into his white-boy fiddlin' and during his teen years became one of the hottest acts in the Texas Panhandle.

In 1929, when Wills was twenty-four, he moved to Fort Worth and signed on to perform in a traveling medicine show, where he played a blackface minstrel. It was there that he met Herman Arnspiger, the guitarist who would help Wills shape the future of music.

The duo began playing house parties under the Wills's Fiddle Band moniker and went on to get their own radio show. At that time radio bands often took on the names of their sponsors, and when Arnspiger and Wills were joined by vocalist Milton

Bob Wills grew up playing the fiddle and went on to change country music with a multi-cultural sound called Western Swing. *Photo courtesy of Denton Record-Chronicle.*

Brown in 1930, their sponsorship by Aladdin Mantle Lamp Company on Fort Worth's WBAP radio made them the Aladdin Laddies. Unsure of what to call the new sound, many simply referred to it as "western jazz."

One year later the trio's sound had caught the ears of Wilbert Lee "Pappy" O'Daniel, general manager of Burrus Mill. O'Daniel lured the Laddies away to advertise Burrus' Light Crust Flour on KFJZ, with live performances every day at 7 A.M. and noon. When they weren't performing, the trio wore other hats for the mill, including those of truck driver and salesman. The new sponsorship gave them a new name, one that is still alive and well today—the Light Crust Doughboys.

The Doughboys enjoyed a quick rise to fame and soon were playing nights at the Crystal Springs Ballroom in Fort Worth, a club now legendary for being a favorite party place of the infamous duo Bonnie and Clyde. The band was finding unprecedented popularity, so O'Daniel furthered their cause by launching the Texas Quality Network, a string of radio stations that allowed the Light Crust Doughboys to be heard not just in their hometown of Fort Worth, but in Dallas, Houston, and San Antonio as well. The sound proved just as successful outside of its home turf, and the broadcasts built a following as big as Texas.

The band's popularity wasn't the only thing that was growing; the size of the group itself was expanding as well. Steel guitarist Leon McAuliffe, tenor banjo master Sleepy Johnson, singer/yodeler Leon Huff, Milton Brown's younger brother,

The Light Crust Doughboys began in 1931 as a radio band that was primarily a promotional tool for the Burrus Mill's Light Crust Flour.

Durwood, and Bob's brother, Johnnie Lee Wills all were brought into the musical powerhouse. With an emphasis on instrumentals, the band presented a previously unheard array of sounds, including Tex-Mex, Hawaiian, Cajun, cowboy, and jazz. Listeners could not get enough of the sound, and the Doughboys became the true trailblazer in the salad days of western swing.

Beneath the swinging, upbeat surface of success, however, trouble already was brewing. By all accounts, O'Daniel had an affable radio presence and public persona that he later would parlay into a successful bid for governor of Texas. As announcer for the Light Crust Doughboys, O'Daniel managed to find fame of his own, and he slapped his name on as many Doughboys projects as he could. He wrote a number of the songs recorded by the band, and his name appeared on all of the group's record labels. But his actions often were heavy-handed and controlling, and as the band's success grew, so did the conflict.

As more listeners tuned in to hear the music, O'Daniel began spending much of the Doughboys' airtime reading his own poems or furthering his personal political ambitions. He also wanted control of the band outside of the radio studio, and when he demanded that the band stop playing the lucrative dance circuit, it was the final straw for vocalist Brown. Brown signed off from the Doughboys and created his own western band, the Musical Brownies.

Whatever misgivings Wills might have had about staying in the group surfaced just a few months later, when a wage dispute prompted him to walk out of the Doughboys ranks and begin forming what would soon become the legendary Texas Playboys. This group included his younger brother and McAuliffe from the Doughboys, as well as Tommy Duncan on piano, Kermit Whalen on bass and steel guitar, and June Whalen on rhythm guitar. Moving outside of Doughboy territory, the group landed in Tulsa, where in 1934 it found a home on radio station KVOO and stayed there for nine years.

It was there, in Tulsa, that the Texas band found its first taste of commercial success. Not only did the audience love the original numbers that the Playboys performed, they also couldn't get enough of the standards, which were transformed in the hands of Bob and the boys. Driven by Wills' fiddle-playing and trademark vocal yelps and by McAuliffe's jazz-tinged steel guitar, the tired traditional songs were transformed into exciting dancehall fare that became American classics. Wills became the first country-flavored act to put a drummer in the lineup, seating Smokey Dacus on the throne. In addition to playing daily on the radio, the band toured relentlessly, playing several nights a week at Tulsa's Cain Academy as well as playing dances throughout the Southwest. Although the dance band remained primarily a fiddle outfit, Wills began adding horns and reeds in the mid-thirties, something that allowed the band to put the swing in the western dance band sound.

Wills took an unusual approach to his live shows, playing each song twice—once so that dancers could catch the rhythm, the second time so they could move to it. The Texas Playboys were, above all, a dance band, and during the tough economics of the Depression, this ever-expanding outfit created a much-needed upbeat soundtrack for a generation that badly needed a reason to dance.

The success of Bob Wills and the Texas Playboys has never been touched by any other western swing band, nor has his legacy. Wills' 1940 recording of "New San Antonio Rose" remains a classic, as do "Take Me Back to Tulsa," "Time Changes Everything," and the uncharacteristically sad "Faded Love." His band churned out numerous musicians who then struck out on their own, creating western swing outfits that emulated but never overshadowed the success of the Playboys. In fact, as western swing's popularity spread, bands popped up throughout

Flour Power

Few bands—western swing or otherwise—boast the kind of longevity enjoyed by the Light Crust Doughboys. Since it was formed in 1931, with the powerful lineup of fiddler Bob Wills, vocalist Milton Brown, and guitarist Herman Arnspiger, the group has grown from a little fiddle band into a Lone Star treasure. The Doughboys got their start on radio station KFJZ in Fort Worth, primarily as a promotional tool for Light Crust Flour, which gave the band its name.

The Light Crust Doughboys built one of the most enduring bands of all time. Formed in 1931 with future stars Milton Brown and Bob Wills, the band still performs today and was named Official Music Ambassador for the State of Texas in 1995. *Photo courtesy Denton Arts & Jazz Festival.*

For the next year and a half, the Light Crust Doughboys were one of the hottest tickets in the Southwest. W. Lee "Pappy" O'Daniel, manager of Burrus Mill, was so impressed by the band that he became manager-announcer and the

Doughboys were heard throughout Texas and Oklahoma. Their ranks grew with legendary players such as banjoist Sleepy Johnson, yodeler Leon Huff, and steel guitar master Leon McAuliffe.

By 1933 both Wills and Brown had left due to disputes with O'Daniel. He took the band on the road, which eventually led them to Chicago, where they recorded an album for Vocalion Records. One year later banjo player Marvin "Smokey" Montgomery joined the crew and became it's most enduring member.

O'Daniel and the Doughboys parted ways in the mid-thirties, but the group didn't suffer from his absence. From 1935 until 1937 the Doughboys were at the peak of their popularity, which was bolstered by their appearance at the 1936 Texas State Fair, the same year they appeared in the Gene Autry movies *Oh Susanna* and *The Big Show*. By the time World War II temporarily halted their radio performances, the band could be heard on more than 170 radio stations in the South.

After the war, Montgomery reassembled the band and resumed the radio broadcasts, which continued until 1952. As television became more popular, the Doughboys focused on live performances and began appearing as the house band at the Big D Jamboree in 1951 under the name Country Gentlemen. In 1954 they beefed up the lineup and temporarily changed the name to The Texas Stompers.

For seven decades the Light Crust Doughboys have maintained their popularity. Their albums released in 1998 and 1999 were nominated for Grammy Awards. In 2000 the group released its first Christmas album. Montgomery continues managing the Light Crust Doughboys, which in 1995 was designated as the Official Music Ambassadors for the State of Texas by the Texas Legislature.

Texas and Oklahoma, giving the country such acts as Dallas's Roy Newman & His Boys, which featured Gene Sullivan on vocals, and Fort Worth's Crystal Springs Ramblers. From San Antonio, Adolph Hofner and His Texans weighed in with German and Czech-influenced western swing, while Houston

First Lady of Western Swing?

When recounting the legends of western swing, the history books make it clear that the genre has always been a man's world. But the feminine footnote that all too often is overlooked is the role of Laura Lee Owens McBride, a powerhouse vocalist who was born in Oklahoma in 1920 and grew up singing.

Her father, D.H. "Tex" Owens, was a mechanic by trade but quit his job to pursue his dream of becoming an entertainer. That paid off with his own radio show in Kansas City, where he became a well-known radio cowboy singer and wrote the classic country tune "Cattle Call." His daughter became one of his featured performers and was a regular on the air by the time she was ten.

Whether it was in her blood or her upbringing, she picked up a love for the musical lifestyle. Shortly after she graduated from high school in 1938, she formed the Prairie Pioneers in Kansas City but moved the group to California a year later. The move proved to be a successful one; the group ended up filming more than a dozen movies with cowboy star Gene Autry.

A marriage to her father's guitarist ended during her California years, and she moved to Tulsa after the divorce, where she began working with a retooled version of the old band, this time called Sons of the Range. When the band landed a spot on KVOO radio, her vocals attracted Bob Wills, who hired her as yielded a handful of acts that included Ted Daffan and His Texans, The Village Boys, and Shelley Lee Alley and His Alley Cats.

The same year he released "New San Antonio Rose," Wills threw his hat in the Hollywood arena, appearing with Tex Ritter

the first woman to sing with his band. If Wills was destined to become the king of western swing, Laura was about to be crowned its queen.

With the Playboys, Laura appeared in a number of B movies and also married Cameron Hill, one of the band's guitarists. Her recordings with Wills in the early forties included "I Betcha My Heart I Love You," which would become her signature song.

Laura's life changed again in 1945 when her husband landed a job with bandleader Dickie McBride. Not only did it mean a move to Houston, but a new gig and a new husband for Laura. She began singing with McBride's outfit on KTRH radio and one year later divorced her husband and married the bandleader.

The union proved successful both on stage and off. The couple had one daughter, Sharon, and developed a devout following that extended beyond state lines and into Louisiana.

In addition to singing, Laura tried her hand at other careers, including selling real estate and being a disc jockey. When Dickie died in 1971, she began performing with Ernest Tubb and returned to the Texas Playboys for several reunion engagements. She also recorded a solo effort, *The Queen of Western Swing*, and worked through the seventies as a disc jockey and manager of a resort and dinner theater. She had returned to Texas and was living in Bryan when she died of cancer in 1989.

in *Take Me Back to Oklahoma*. The following year he and his entire band were featured in *Go West, Young Man* with Glenn Ford, and the dashing bandleader went on to appear in nearly twenty films, most of them B-movie westerns.

Wills had a string of unsuccessful marriages before marrying his final partner, Betty Anderson, in the fall of 1942. Later that year he signed up for a stint in World War II and after the war found continued success touring and recording with an ever-changing lineup of talent. Heart attacks in 1962 and 1964 slowed the great fiddler but couldn't stop him. After the war, though, the big bands of western swing broke into smaller groups and gave way to a new sound called "honky-tonk." By the 1950s only a handful of western swing bands still played, and the music would lay still for nearly two decades before it was resuscitated.

Even though he claimed never to have played country music, Wills was elected into its Hall of Fame in 1968, rightfully joining such greats as Roy Acuff and Johnny Cash. Less than one year later, on May 31—the day after he was recognized by the governor of Texas for his contributions to American music—a stroke sidelined him, nearly permanently. He never completely recovered, but the Texas Playboys still met one last time, in 1973, to record a memorial album. Wills suffered yet another stroke during that session, prompting fellow musician and ardent admirer Merle Haggard to step in and complete the project. *For the Last Time: Bob Wills and His Texas Playboys* became the biggest seller of Wills's monumental career and earned him his first and only Grammy Award. Wills died in Fort Worth on May 13, 1975.

Although Bob Wills was easily the King of Western Swing, his one-time partner Milton Brown is recognized as the father of the sound. Scholars of the western swing era are quick to note that Brown developed the music's characteristic sound and style long before Wills perfected it. And Brown's departure from the Light Crust Doughboys was one of the most significant moments for western swing, opening the door for scores of musicians to follow and allowing him to further explore the music's many possibilities.

Before hooking up with Wills in Fort Worth, Brown was a salesman for a cigar company. Born in Stephenville in 1903, the aspiring vocalist had moved with his family to Fort Worth at the age of fifteen. Working days selling cigars, he began singing for dances at night, backed on guitar by his twelve-year-old brother, Durwood. When the Depression hit and the older Brown lost his job, he began pursuing his music career in earnest.

What made Brown's situation so unusual is that he became a bandleader who didn't play an instrument—something that was practically unheard of until he came along. But his instincts on stage were natural, and when teamed with Wills's fiddling talent and the guitar ability of Herman Arnspiger, the results were nothing short of remarkable, opening a new chapter in the musical history books.

Brown's departure from the Doughboys in 1932 gave him the chance to shine as a bandleader. A ladies' man who owned an enticing husky voice, Brown raised the bar for western swing musicians. The Musical Brownies sidestepped traditional country, putting an emphasis on jazz that crystallized with the addition of Bob Dunn on steel guitar in 1934. Dunn became the first steel guitarist to go electric, which allowed the Brownies to swing harder than any of its contemporary competitors.

Assembling a top-notch cadre of musicians, Brown stepped outside the standard pool of musicians to pull in jazz pianist Fred "Papa" Calhoun and renowned fiddler Cecil Brower, who was classically trained and had previously played with the Dallas Symphony Orchestra. But it was Dunn's presence that pushed the Brownies to new heights and helped make them the hottest band in the Dallas/Fort Worth area.

The Musical Brownies found a warm reception on Fort Worth radio station KTAT and before long were regulars at dances, including a regular slot at the Crystal Springs Ballroom. Within two years of forming the band, Brown had found success beyond state lines, and from 1934 to 1936, the group recorded more than a hundred tracks for the Victor and Decca labels. The band was still looking for its big hit when its leader met an untimely end.

In April of 1936 Milton Brown was returning from a gig at Crystal Springs when his tire blew out and sent the car spinning into a pole. The crash immediately killed his sixteen-year-old female passenger, and although Brown survived the impact, he never left the hospital. Five days later, at the age of thirty-two, Brown died of pneumonia.

Exactly where Brown could and would have taken the music is something that can only be imagined in retrospect; he had just begun finding his sound and undoubtedly would have pushed western swing in new directions. Many suspect he would have overshadowed even Bob Wills, and Wills likely never would have worn the crown as the reigning king of western swing.

Even though Brown's brother and longtime collaborator, Durwood, tried keeping the Brownies intact, the group never recovered from the loss of its dynamic leader. The Brownies held one more recording session for Decca in March of 1937, but already members had begun drifting away and starting their own projects. While the assembly of innovative players didn't remain intact following Brown's death, their talents didn't exactly go to waste.

Fiddler Cliff Bruner was among the most enduring performers ever to come out of the Brownies; he picked up the instrument at the age of twelve with the sole intent of escaping a life spent picking cotton. The Texas City native spent his teen years as a traveling musician and landed in the Musical Brownies when he was twenty.

After Brown's death, Bruner went to Houston to form The Texas Wanderers, which included fellow ex-Brownies Bob Dunn on steel guitar and Ocie Stockard on tenor banjo.

Dunn later formed his own band, The Vagabonds, and he and Bruner drew from the same pool of musicians, making their lineups appear basically interchangeable. But it was Bruner's band that found the most success in the Texas Gulf Coast region. Driven by Bruner's sizzling, brilliant fiddling, the Wanderers enjoyed commercial success during the World War II years. He attracted a number of legendary players through the next fifteen years, including monster pianist/singer Aubrey "Moon" Mullican, who became famous for his signature two-finger piano playing style that later influenced such players as Jerry Lee Lewis and Mickey Gilley.

It was Mullican's vocals that helped the Wanderers find their first big hit, "It Makes No Difference Now," written by a young Floyd Tillman and recorded by the Wanderers in 1938. The following year the band made history by recording the first truck-driving song ever. The Ted Daffan composition, "Truck Driver's Blues," sealed the band's place in country music and launched the career of the young songwriter, who later would earn a slot in the Nashville Songwriters' Hall of Fame.

By the time western swing's popularity hit a decline in the early fifties, Bruner had put down the fiddle and picked up a career selling insurance. Although he occasionally played, it wasn't until the western swing resurgence of the seventies that the world heard from him again. Bruner once again dazzled audiences with his fiery fiddling style, both on stage and on Johnny Gimble's 1980 album *Texas Swing Pioneers*. He died of cancer on August 25, 2000, at his home in Houston.

Bob Dunn continued to play western swing even after he and Bruner parted ways. The pioneering steel guitarist, who

Aubrey Mullican launched his career playing the pump organ in church, then moved on to bars and brothels, where his late nights earned him the lasting nickname "Moon." He became one of honky-tonk's leading pianists, and his career enjoyed a resurgence with the rise of rockabilly in the fifties. *Photo courtesy of David Dennard.*

had come to the Lone Star State by way of Oklahoma, was a traveling musician before teaming up with Bruner in the Musical Brownies in 1932. His experience in jazz bands was evident in his steel guitar style; he played the strings like a horn, with short staccato bursts that were a far cry from the traditional chords played on the Hawaiian instrument.

Although he formed his own bands and played in countless sessions after relocating to Houston, he unplugged his steel guitar for good in 1950 and opened a music store, which he ran until his death in 1971 from lung cancer.

Johnny Gimble, meanwhile, emerged as one of country music's most impressive fiddlers and also should receive some sort of honor for his amazing longevity. Born in 1926 in Tyler, John Paul Gimble picked up the fiddle when he was about nine and by the age of twelve was playing in a band with his four brothers. He formed the Rose City Swingsters with his brothers in the early thirties and found success on local radio, but when he graduated from high school in 1943, he moved to Louisiana to play with Jimmie Davis.

Most of what Gimble played in his early days was a direct reflection of what he heard on the radio, and that led him directly into western swing territory. He hooked up with Bob Wills in the forties and found most of his early success as a member of the Texas Playboys. He found his own group in 1951 and later returned to the Playboys' lineup, but when western swing started losing ground in the early sixties, Gimble put down his fiddle for a time. He worked as a barber until he "got enough nerve to sell everything and move to Nashville," where he found session work throughout the seventies. Among his most notable performances were the 1970 Bob Wills tribute album by Merle Haggard and the final recording by Bob Wills and the Texas Playboys, released in 1974. It was also in 1974 that he released his first solo effort, aptly named *Fiddlin' Around*.

Eventually Gimble returned to his home state and has stayed in demand both as a session performer and a bandleader. He has earned a number of Best Instrumentalist and Best Fiddle Player awards and in 1993 was nominated for a Grammy Award for his work on *Heroes*, a fiddle tribute album by Mark O'Connor. That same year he released *Under the X in Texas*, and he continues popping up on programs like "Austin City Limits." Today Gimble continues to give the fiddle a workout and recorded several tracks at a studio in Waco in 2000, which he expects to release as an album in 2001.

As the western swing movement began losing momentum, the music already was wandering off in a new direction. The western swing spin-off known as honky-tonk took music in an entirely new direction and proved to be the perfect country soundtrack for the WWII generation. And the Wurlitzer Company had created the perfect machine for playing that soundtrack.

Although the company put its first coin-operated phonograph on the market in 1928, it wasn't until the repeal of Prohibition and the ensuing proliferation of bars and taverns that the jukebox found success. Picking up its name because of its presence in "juke joints," the jukebox became the perfect stand-in for live music acts. But suddenly the old cowboy songs and country crooning didn't fit the high-octane environment of the roadhouses and bars where the music was played, and changing times demanded a change in the music.

The term "honky-tonk" officially surfaced in 1936 at the hands of Al Dexter, the man typically credited with giving rise to the movement. Prior to Dexter's landmark recording "Honky-Tonk Blues," the word "tonk" was used, primarily by southern blacks, as slang for beer joints. Dexter's adoption of the phrase and adaptation of it to music created a new sound and a new lyrical approach, one that looked at lives where the lovin', drinkin', workin', and livin' were always hard.

Dexter had been born Clarence Albert Poindexter in Jacksonville, Texas, in 1902. If ever a man was badly in need of a stage name, it was Clarence Albert Poindexter. In what no one can deny was a brilliant career move, he had shortened his moniker to Al Dexter by the time he started performing in bars and clubs in the early thirties. Working as a housepainter by day, he assembled a band and was playing on the outskirts of

Longview at night when he landed a contract with American Recording Company in 1935.

Although by then he already had released some recordings on the Vocalion label, it was shortly after signing with ARC that he released "Honky-Tonk Blues" and scored his first big hit. In a case of life imitating art, he opened his own honky-tonk, a place in Turnertown, Texas, called the Roundup Club. He gleaned plenty of experiences from his tavern ownership, enough to inspire a second hit, "Pistol Packin' Mama." Although its lyrics garnered controversy ("They were blood and thunder and sometimes women came looking for their men with guns..."), the song shot to the number one spot on the *Billboard Magazine* bestsellers chart and stayed there for eight weeks. Dexter suddenly found himself in demand for national tours, and he quickly scored another number one hit with "Rosalita," which spent a week in *Billboard*'s top spot.

From 1944 through 1948 Dexter penned a handful of other hits, including "Too Late to Worry," "Wine, Women and Song," and "Calico Rag." He toured with big bands and racked up several hits throughout the forties, but none could top the success of his anthem to gals with guns.

By the beginning of the fifties, Dexter's success was beginning to play itself out, so he opened the Bridgeport Club in Dallas and focused on his business interests. He occasionally took the stage of his club and even recorded for King, Decca, and Capitol, but he concentrated more on investments than entertainment. He was inducted into the Nashville Songwriters' Hall of Fame in 1971, and thanks to his honky-tonk success, when he died on January 28, 1984, at his home on Lake Lewisville in Texas, he was a very wealthy man.

Dexter's first hit might have fired the first honky-tonk shot, but many others charged eagerly into the musical revolution. Among the first to the front was Floyd Tillman, who already had polished his skills on the strings before finding his place in the honky-tonk world.

Born in Oklahoma in 1914, Tillman was raised in rural Post, Texas, where he learned to play the banjo, mandolin, and guitar. By the age of eighteen, he had joined Adolph Hofner's German-Czech swing band, and he went on to play in the Mack Clark Orchestra before trying his hand at songwriting.

Tillman could turn a country-western phrase easier than most, and his song "It Makes No Difference Now," as previously noted, became a major hit for Cliff Bruner's Texas Wanderers. Even before the western swing craze completely gave way to the honky-tonk movement, Tillman joined a group led by fiddler Leon "Pappy" Selph, featuring ex-Wanderers pianist Moon Mullican, steel guitarist Ted Daffan, and guitarists Chuck Keeshan and Dickie McBride. Together this lineup became the Blue Ridge Playboys, the era's first true honky-tonk band. Although the group formed in 1935 and was initially considered a western swing outfit, its members soon embraced both the honky-tonk sound and sentiment.

Tillman's songwriting skills were in good company; Daffan, who would later pen the first song about truck driving, wrote a number of classics, including "Worried Mind," "I'm a Fool For You," and "Born to Lose." Mullican, readily considered the band's most versatile player, became honky-tonk's leading pianist but brought with him a suitcase full of influences that allowed the music to soar. Cajun, blues, ragtime, jazz, and country swing all were worked into his scorching piano style, and he went on to score a huge hit in 1950 with "Jole Blon," written by fellow Texan and hardcore Cajun Harry Choates.

In the Blue Ridge Playboys, Tillman perfected the singing and songwriting skills that would earn him a permanent spot in the history books. His West Texas drawl made him the perfect pitchman for the honky-tonk lifestyle, and his songs about cheatin' hearts and hurtin' fools eventually set the standard for jukebox fare.

Tillman served in the Army Air Corps during World War II then resumed his musical career and found a Number One hit with 1944's "They Took the Stars Out of Heaven." The years following the war saw Tillman's career take off, with the slow honky-tonk dance hit "I Love You So Much It Hurts" and the landmark 1949 song, "Slippin' Around." That tale of infidelity was the first to openly sing of adultery, and at the time it created enormous controversy—but still became a million-selling hit. The classic has been covered numerous times through the years and prompted Tillman to later pen an answer song, called "She's Slippin' Around," which looked at the hypocrisy of the double standard.

Even though his last hit was 1960's "It Just Tears Me Up," Tillman and his tunes have remained favorites of honky-tonk fans worldwide. He was inducted into the Nashville Songwriters Hall of Fame in 1976 and was elected to the Country Music Hall of Fame in 1984. Tillman's songs have not only inspired other great artists such as Lefty Frizzell and Willie Nelson, his songs were also hits for them. His 1982 album, *Floyd Tillman and Friends*, saw him teaming up with collaborators and fans like Nelson and Merle Haggard. Tillman, who rarely performs these days, now lives in Marble Falls, Texas.

Although band mates Ted Daffan and Moon Mullican didn't share the long-term commercial success that Tillman enjoyed, they were part of a powerful trio that made significant contributions to country music. Daffan may have built a formidable reputation as a songwriter, but his steel guitar prowess was just as fearsome.

The Louisiana-born Daffan was raised in Houston, where he developed an early and insatiable affinity for two things that would change his future: the Hawaiian guitar and electronics. He proved to be a pioneer in the amplification and electrification of instruments; Daffan ran a radio repair shop where he modified instruments and built homemade amps.

He joined the Blue Ridge Playboys in 1934 but also began writing songs to supplement his income. His music topped the charts before he did; Cliff Bruner scored a number one hit with "Truck Driver's Blues" a year before Daffan signed with O'Keh Records.

The 1940 record contract marked the launch of his own band, Ted Daffan and His Texans. He immediately picked up his first big hit with "Worried Mind," and three years later his band topped record sales for the year. He continued playing with the band until the latter years of the fifties, while simultaneously getting hit records from the numerous other artists who recorded his songs.

Daffan created a publishing company in 1958 with Hank Snow and three years later opened a solo publishing venture. He continued writing hit songs and was inducted into the Nashville Songwriters Hall of Fame in 1970. He died in Houston on October 6, 1996, at the age of eighty-four.

Moon Mullican's skill as a pianist not only landed him in the same bands as Tillman and Daffan, but put him alongside his band mates in the Nashville Songwriters Hall of Fame. Born in Polk County in 1909, the future pianist honed his talents on the family's pump organ and was a church organist in his formative years. As a teenager he began playing for dances and moved to Houston when he was sixteen to pursue his musical career.

His work in Houston was a far cry from the church scene; he played primarily at brothels, which is where he is believed to have picked up his signature barrelhouse style of pounding the keys. (His late-night work schedule earned him the nickname "Moon.") He took that style to Cliff Bruner's bands before joining the Blue Ridge Playboys and then went solo in 1946. That proved to be a successful move; he signed with King Records and enjoyed success both as a singer and a songwriter. As the forties drew to a close, he joined the cast of Nashville's Grand Ole Opry and stayed there until 1955, when he left to enjoy a successful career as a singer, songwriter, recording artist, and even as a nightclub owner.

Mullican savored the advent of rock 'n' roll, finding it a perfect vehicle for his two-finger piano pounding. Unable to break into the young rock market, he still was able to influence some of its greats, not the least of whom was Jerry Lee Lewis. He recorded the novelty song "I Ain't No Beatle (But I Want to Hold Your Hand)" in the mid-sixties, and even though his health was suffering, Mullican continued performing. He died of a heart attack on January 1, 1967, one day after vowing to cut back on pork chops. Nine years later he was posthumously inducted into the Nashville Songwriters Hall of Fame.

If artists like Tillman and Mullican set the stage for the honky-tonk sound, Ernest Tubb was the man who gave it a voice. With a friendly, folksy sound, Tubb's voice was simply unmistakable. Born in 1914 on a cotton farm near Crisp, this Texan was heavily influenced by his talented musical mother, who played both piano and organ and instilled in her son an interest in music and poetry. By the time he was a teenager, Tubb had moved to San Antonio where he earned his living as a soda jerk. But the music of his mother was never far from his heart; he taught himself to play the guitar and soon was playing a regular nonpaying gig for KONO radio station.

Tubb's main musical inspiration was Jimmie Rodgers, the "Father of Country Music," whom Ernest discovered when he was just fourteen years old. Tubb bought every Rodgers album he could find and soon set his sights on becoming a country singing star, even trying to master the yodeling that Rodgers made famous.

Rodgers had settled in Kerrville for health reasons in 1929 but died just four years later. Ernest never got the opportunity to meet his idol, but Rodgers' widow, Carrie, heard Tubb in

Ernest Tubb, shown here in the early 1960s, became the first star to take an electric guitar on stage at the Grand Ole Opry. His association with the Opry, which began in 1942, lasted more than four decades. *Photo courtesy of David Dennard.*

1935, and the two struck up a friendship. She was so taken with the young performer that she even bestowed the late Rodgers' treasured guitar upon Tubb and helped him land a recording contract with RCA Victor a year later.

Tubb's music initially emulated the yodeling and singing style of his hero, but the more he played, the more he developed his own voice. He was forced to give up yodeling when his tonsils had to be removed, and initially Tubb feared that it would be the end of his singing career. Instead, he found a new sound that obviously did just as well.

Paying his dues on the Texas radio circuit, Tubb supported himself with a variety of nonmusical jobs but finally landed a paying gig in 1940—the same year he signed with Decca

Records. At KGKO radio in Fort Worth, Tubb was finally getting paid for what he loved to do. However, the modest $75 a week salary wasn't enough to make ends meet, and within a year he was contemplating hanging up his guitar for a job in the defense industry. Just as he was about to call it quits, his success finally took flight.

"Walking the Floor Over You," released in the fall of 1941, became Tubb's first hit. It also won him a sponsor for his radio program, something that was vital to his financial well-being. As his first single climbed the charts, Gold Chain Flour signed on as his official sponsor, saddling him with the nickname, "The Gold Chain Troubadour." (In later years that moniker wisely was changed to "The Texas Troubadour.")

Tubb's years of hard work paid off in a big way and in quick fashion once he found his first hit. He continued making live appearances, frequently playing rowdy honky-tonks. It was his inability to be heard over the honky-tonk crowd that turned out to be an important factor in further shaping his distinctive sound. Tubb decided he had to add electric amplification to his lead guitar simply to be heard. By the end of 1942 he was appearing on the stage of the Grand Ole Opry and became the first artist ever to take the electric guitar into such a venerable country institution. Wearing his tailored Western suit and ten gallon hat, he exuded a more dignified persona than the "hillbilly" handle that was so closely associated with country music. His association with the Opry extended across four decades, making him a regular performer there in between his live club shows and his blossoming movie career. Hollywood came knocking shortly after "Walking the Floor Over You" found its way onto the charts, and Tubb appeared in numerous movies.

Still, it was music that made Tubb a legend, and his string of hits seemed endless. In 1948, the same year he ended a fourteen-year marriage, Tubb had three songs on *Billboard*'s Top Ten; the next year he more than doubled that number. His second marriage, to Olene Adams Carter in 1949, proved more successful, and the couple eventually had five children.

During the course of his forty years as a recording artist, Tubb sold more than 30 million records and recorded more than 250 songs. He played more than 300 live shows a year, touring tirelessly and always ending his performances by flipping over his guitar to reveal the message "Thanks" on the back.

Wanting to share his good fortune with other performers, Tubb opened a record store in Nashville that bore his name and supported a number of up-and-coming artists by presenting them on the live in-store broadcast that immediately followed the Grand Ole Opry on WSM. That show, the "Midnight Jamboree," gave a boost to such then-unknowns as Hank Williams and Loretta Lynn, and through his band, the Texas Troubadours, he launched the career of many young musicians. His devotion to the honky-tonk style and culture was evident in such songs as "Walking the Floor Over You," "Thanks a Lot," and "Two Glasses, Joe," but he also showed his range by having hits with songs like "Goodnight Irene," the moving war ballad "Soldier's Last Letter," and even a waltz—"Waltz Across Texas." Tubb also became the first country artist ever to headline a show at Carnegie Hall.

For proof of Tubb's place of honor among his contemporaries, one need only glance at his 1979 album *Legend and Legacy*, which attracted a stellar lineup of country music greats who wanted to show their gratitude for the man who had done so much for the music. Willie Nelson, Johnny Cash, Conway Twitty, Charlie Rich, Waylon Jennings, George Jones, Marty Robbins, and Loretta Lynn were just a few of the stars to stop by to lend their voices to the project and thank Tubb for his music and its influence on their careers.

His rigorous performance schedule helped boost his fame but also undermined his health. Tubb stayed on the charts through the sixties and in 1965 became the sixth person elected into the Country Music Hall of Fame. He returned to the silver screen in 1980 to play himself in the movie *Coal Miner's Daughter*, but it would be his last film appearance. A bad case of emphysema, no doubt exacerbated by endless miles and too many nights in smoke-filled honky-tonks, eventually sidelined the great performer, who died on September 6, 1984, at the age of seventy.

Tubb was neither the first nor last artist to be so heavily influenced by Jimmie Rodgers. Rodgers can also take posthumous credit for Lefty Frizzell throwing his hat into the honky-tonk ring. Lefty began as an almost slavish follower of the great yodeler, but he quickly developed a sound and style that made him a legend in his own right.

Born in Corsicana, Texas, in 1928, William Orville "Lefty" Frizzell was raised in the oil fields of Texas and New Mexico, where the scratchy records of Jimmie Rodgers made a tremendous and lasting impact on him. He was twelve when he picked up his first guitar, and it only took about two years for him to start making money out of his talent. He entered a songwriting contest in Dallas and earned a whopping five dollars and the first-place title.

But Frizzell clearly had bigger things in store for him; he was playing live by the time he was sixteen, and at twenty-two he signed on with Columbia Records, beginning an alliance that would last until 1973.

Although rumor and lore passed on through the years has the singer picking up the nickname of "Lefty" from his days as an amateur boxer, in reality, that was nothing more than a complete fabrication of an overeager press agent. What is most unbelievable, however, is his phenomenal rise to the top. By the time he inked his contract with Columbia, Frizzell had found a following at the Ace of Clubs, a dance hall in Big Spring, Texas. It was there he perfected his unique vocal style of dragging his southern drawl across the words, lingering as long as

Lefty Frizzell scored his first hit with demos he recorded in Jim Beck's Recording Studio in 1950, selling more than two and a half million copies in less than two months and landing him a deal with Columbia label.
Photo courtesy of David Dennard.

possible on each one as if he were reluctant to let it go. That vocal caress of each word would later become standard for honky-tonk fare, and monosyllabic words would eventually be slurred into multiples as the style took hold. In Texas, perhaps, where the word "yes" often comes off as a three-syllable word, the sound couldn't have been that unusual. But never had it been so well captured in song, and the music world would never be the same after that.

Frizzell's growing popularity caught the ears of a Dallas recording studio owner by the name of Jim Beck, who invited the singer to his studio and then took the demos to Nashville, which was quickly becoming a hub for country music activity.

Beck recorded a number of the country artists of the day, including Ray Price, Johnny Horton, and Floyd Tillman, and his studio became a place where local country music artists hung out, looking to make contacts or get a record deal. The demos from Beck's studio landed Frizzell the Columbia contract, and his first recording, "If You've Got the Money, I've Got the Time" backed with "I Love You a Thousand Ways" was released in September of 1950.

It took less than two months for that record to sell more than two and a half million copies, and each side of the single took its turn at number one for three weeks. Realizing the hit machine it had on its roster, Columbia had Frizzell back in the studio within three weeks to record more songs.

Nothing could have prepared the label or the singer for Frizzell's impending catapult to the top. He spent more than half of 1951 atop the *Billboard* music chart, with three of his seven singles holding the top spot. He toured with Hank Williams and then, at the age of twenty-three, was invited to join the cast of the Grand Ole Opry. In October he found even further cause to celebrate when four of his singles made it into *Billboard's* Top Ten country chart in the same week—a feat that has yet to be repeated.

In 1952 Frizzell left the Opry and headed to California, appearing on such television shows as "Town Hall Party" and "Country America." His hits continued to tumble out, and by 1954 he had charted fifteen consecutive hits, a streak that ended with the release of "Run 'Em Off." He would not return to the top ten again until 1959, nor did he ever again enjoy the kind of runaway success he saw in the first four years of his career, but his influence in the honky-tonk genre continued to be enormous. His 1964 hit, "Saginaw, Michigan," was the last time he made it to number one—or even into the top ten—again, but that didn't keep his influence from being felt in musicians around the world. And it wasn't just music that he changed.

Shortly after moving to California in 1953, Frizzell became the first country artist to appear on stage wearing rhinestones. The fashion statement was made by Nudie Cohen, a lingerie-designer-turned-western tailor who included Frizzell's initials in rhinestones on the artist's lapel. Although the singer argued that the jewels would make him look less than manly, Cohen won the argument by insisting that only a real man could get away with wearing rhinestones. Not only did Frizzell's studded appearance earn rave reviews, it started a flashy new trend in the industry.

Although his later years weren't spent in the glaring spotlight that he enjoyed early on, Frizzell continued to have an influence on the country music scene. He returned to Nashville in 1962 and continued recording, signing with ABC records in 1973 and finding moderate success with the songs "I Never Go Around Mirrors" and "Lucky Arms." Like many honky-tonk artists, however, Frizzell practiced what he preached, and the hard drinkin', hard livin', honky-tonk ethic took its toll both on his health and his marriage. Although he suffered from high blood pressure, he refused to take his medication, and in 1975, while preparing for a tour, he suffered a massive stroke. Lefty Frizzell died on July 19, 1975, just as his last single, "Falling," was hitting the charts. Seven years later he was inducted into the Country Music Hall of Fame.

Where Frizzell slurred through the Texas sound, Hank Thompson clearly and carefully enunciated his vocals and also melded modern lyrics with traditional melodies. Born in Waco on the Brazos River in 1925, Henry William Thompson began his career on the radio as "Hank the Hired Hand" after winning a weekly Kiddie Matinee contest. Like Ted Daffan, Thompson was an electronics expert and was one of the few early musicians to build a home studio.

Hank Thompson gave honky-tonk a modern sound, adding a jazzy feel to his steel guitar-driven repertoire. *Photo courtesy of Hank Thompson Enterprises.*

He served a stint in the Navy during World War II then returned to his hometown and began performing with his band, the Brazos Valley Boys. When Thompson's outfit shared the stage with Tex Ritter, the singing cowboy was so impressed that he took one of the band's recordings to Capitol Records, which immediately led to a record deal.

Thompson's song, "Humpty Dumpty Heart" took him all the way to number two on the *Billboard* charts and spent thirty-eight weeks there. His distinctive steel guitar garnered a handful of hits for the group, which was growing both in size and popularity. By the early fifties he began developing the western swing aspect of his repertoire, straying away from Bob Wills's territory but infusing his honky-tonk sound with the swinging, jazzy beat. His song "The Wild Side of Life" was one of the biggest hits of the era, spending fifteen weeks at number one. (If the song doesn't ring a bell, that might be because most people know the song by its opening line, "I didn't know God made honky-tonk angels.")

Thompson defined and redefined honky-tonk music with such songs as "Waiting in the Lobby of Your Heart" and "A Six Pack to Go." Bridging traditional and modern music, Thompson polished the honky-tonk ethic and dressed it up to suit mainstream America. In 1989 the Country Music Hall of Fame made him its own.

The honky-tonk style peaked in the forties and early fifties, and as Nashville's slick pop packaging surfaced, it replaced the hard-core country sound that dominated the honky-tonk era. Ray Price was one of the few country artists who managed to successfully bridge both styles. Not only was he one of the last great honky-tonkers, he also managed to adapt his sound and image to suit the new commercialized, smooth country pop sound that emerged in the late fifties and early sixties.

Born in 1926 near Perryville, Ray Noble Price was, like his honky-tonk predecessors, raised on the music of Jimmie Rodgers, but he also got a hefty dose of Ernest Tubb thrown in. By the time he was a teenager, he was living in Dallas and had learned to play guitar and sing, but he studied veterinary medicine at what is now the University of Texas at Arlington. World War II interrupted his studies in 1942, but after serving four years in the Marines, he resumed his studies.

It was during that time that Price began playing in clubs and honky-tonks and landed on radio station KRBC. Within three years he was invited to join the Big D Jamboree, a popular live music showcase broadcast from Dallas.

The Big D Jamboree both discovered new talent and gave stage time to the big names of the day, from western swing to rockabilly to the modern country sounds that were taking over the radio. It was signing up with the Jamboree that turned Price's attention from animal medicine to music.

Not long after Price joined the cast of the Jamboree, CBS began televising the show and helped him find a record deal with the Nashville-based Bullet label. By 1951 two pivotal changes had occurred in his life: He had become friends with the legendary Hank Williams, and he had signed with Columbia Records. With Williams' help and mentoring, Price was signed to the Grand Ole Opry early in 1952, and by the middle of that year, he had his first hit, "Talk To Your Heart." The song climbed to number eleven, and later that year his single "Don't Let the Stars Get in Your Eyes" made it all the way to number four. He continued releasing top ten hits and in 1956 found his first number one disc with "Crazy Arms," which stayed on the charts for forty-five weeks.

Price's initial sound reflected Williams' influence, and his 1954 band, the Cherokee Cowboys, even included members of the Drifting Cowboys, which had been Williams' band before his sudden death from a heart attack on New Years' Day of 1953. Price eventually replaced those members with his own players, which through the years included Johnny Paycheck, Willie Nelson, and Roger Miller. The change in his sound was evident with the release of "Crazy Arms," and it brought a more electrified style to honky-tonk music. Driven by a hard fiddle and the pedal steel guitar of Ralph Mooney, Price popularized the 4/4 country shuffle beat that became his trademark and continued honky-tonking into the early sixties.

Ray Price set out to study veterinary medicine, but when he landed a spot on the roster at the Big D Jamboree, his career path took a new direction. By 1952 he had signed on with the Grand Ole Opry and had scored his first hit, "Talk to Your Heart." *Photo courtesy of David Dennard.*

By the time Price rebooted the honky-tonk ethic, country music, western swing, and honky-tonk all were taking a different course. Nashville's continuing rise as a country music mecca brought with it a slick country pop sound, one which Price also ventured into. He became a huge crossover act, releasing songs like "Make the World Go Away" in 1963 and

"Burning Memories" in 1964, something that alienated some of his hardcore honky-tonk fans but made him a household name. In 1970 he hit the top of the charts with his cover of Kris Kristofferson's "For the Good Times," and the next three years saw three consecutive number one singles with his name on them.

The fifties and sixties completely and permanently changed the musical landscape, and for better or worse, country music was never the same again. Nashville and rock 'n' roll had moved to the forefront of the scene and left western swing laying dormant until the early seventies, when Texas bands like Asleep at the Wheel and Alvin Crow and the Pleasant Valley Boys reminded the American consciousness of the legacy of Bob Wills and western swing. By then the retired sound had become wired and electrified, making way for the "progressive country" sound that followed and opening the door for the inevitable infusion of rock into the country genre.

Recommended Listening:

Anthology (1935-1973) – Bob Wills and His Texas Playboys (Rhino)

Texas Music, Vol. 2: Western Swing & Honky-tonk – Various artists (Rhino)

The Complete Recordings of the Father of Western Swing – Milton Brown and the Musical Brownies (Texas Rose)

Roy Newman & His Boys – (Origin Jazz Library)

Jive & Smile: Kings of Western Swing – Various artists (Charly)

Under the 'X' in Texas – Johnny Gimble & Texas Swing (Tejas Records)

Country Music Hall of Fame, 1984 – Floyd Tillman (King Records)

Waltz Across Texas – Ernest Tubb and the Texas Troubadours (Bear Family)

The Best of Lefty Frizzell – (Rhino)

The Essential Ray Price (1951-1962) – (Columbia)

Chapter Seven

The Blues Bust Loose

If the 1930s were something of a resting time for the blues, the forties saw its rebirth. That ground-breaking renaissance regained momentum in the sixties, setting the stage for some of Texas's most formidable blues legends to emerge, while at the same time laying an electrified foundation for rock 'n' roll. The influence of such legends still resonates through the music today, heard in the sounds of such contemporary Texas blues greats as Jimmie Vaughan, Angela Strehli, Anson Funderburgh, Jim Suhler, Lou Ann Barton, and Bugs Henderson.

The blues heyday that began in the late forties ultimately gave birth to such modern-day Texas-born blues-rock legends as Janis Joplin, Johnny Winter, and the phenomenal Stevie Ray Vaughan. But before it was able to build the bridge between blues and rock, the music first had to plug into a whole new sound. And for many of Texas's most high-profile artists, that success would not be found in their home state, but in California.

Without a doubt, the electrification of the blues changed both the way it was played and the way it was heard. The late thirties saw Gibson manufacturing the first mass-produced electric guitar, and it gradually found a presence in jazz bands and western swing outfits, as well as turning the heads of a few blues players.

Future blues great Johnny Winter performs with his band, Johnny and the Jammers, at the Big D Jamboree in Dallas. *Photo courtesy of David Dennard*

At the same time, music was becoming more accessible to mainstream America. Following the end of World War II, independent record labels began to surface, meaning artists no longer had to depend upon landing a deal with the major labels in big cities like Chicago and New York. The jukebox, which had become a controversial mainstay in clubs by the early forties, took the music to urban areas and introduced new sounds to the people who congregated there. That created something of a double-edged sword for musicians, who, on the one hand were now having their music heard by new audiences but, on the other hand, saw the machine as a threat to their livelihood.

But it wasn't just the musical landscape that was witnessing a significant and permanent change; the cultural climate was experiencing dramatic changes as well, and together they helped alter the attitude of the blues.

Even more noticeably than their white counterparts, Texas's black population faced uncertain and anxious futures as the thirties ended and the next decade began. War was on the horizon and, while they no longer lived in servitude, conditions were harsh and wages were meager. Many left the South to head to the promised land of the North, looking for jobs in the

T-Bone Walker got his start as a guide for Blind Lemon Jefferson and, by the age of fifteen, had joined a traveling music show. When he electrified his sound, he changed the blues for good. *Photo courtesy of John Meekings.*

developing industries of steel mills and assembly lines. Those who stayed in their familiar southern territory viewed the mechanization of America as a threat; it actually eliminated many of the jobs that southern blacks had counted on. As a result, these rural Americans sought new lives in urban communities, and during World War II, they entirely redesigned the face of urban America. By the war's end, about one-third of America's black population lived in the cities, and the country blues had found a city sound.

The faster pace of urban life was reflected in the music, creating something that eventually would come to be known as rhythm and blues. The music became flashier, the energy became infectious, and led by T-Bone Walker, the sound became nothing short of electrifying.

Born Aaron Thibeaux Walker in Linden on May 28, 1910, Walker frequently is acknowledged as one of the most important musicians in music history, particularly in the area of rhythm and blues. Even though he was a blues man, and a monumental one at that, his influence spilled into so many other styles, including rock 'n' roll, that he forever changed the sound of modern music far beyond the scope of the blues. That's an accomplishment his mother never could have predicted when she took her young son to Dallas to escape the strict church-going surroundings of rural Linden.

A guitarist herself, his mother, Movelia, certainly deserves some of the credit for Walker's achievements. It seems that both genetically and environmentally, she managed to pass on her love of music and her passion for the open road, and nearly every known step of his early years was taken in a musical environment, from his own home to churches to the bustling street scene of Deep Ellum.

It was in Dallas that the future legend learned the guitar firsthand from the first great Texas blues man, Blind Lemon Jefferson. Jefferson was a friend of the family, and the young

Walker spent about three years, beginning in 1920, as the blues great's guide. He led the blind man around the streets of Dallas, holding the tin cup for Jefferson's tips, and the youngster began to pluck at the strings himself. Movelia gave her son a banjo when he was twelve, and he played church socials on the weekends to raise money to buy the instrument he truly coveted, the one that would become his trademark instrument—the guitar.

Walker's musical gifts weren't limited to stringed instruments; his voice was equally impressive, and even as a child he sang in the family string band run by his stepfather, Marco Washington. The weekend shows also gave the future star the chance to polish his showmanship skills as he danced while he passed the hat for his stepfather and uncles at the end of their performances. He proved to be a natural-born performer, and his energy and passion for the stage appeared to be surpassed only by his amazing abilities on stringed instruments.

Walker was just fifteen years old when he struck out on the road for the first time after landing a spot with Dr. Breeding's B Tonic Medicine Show, where he worked as a guitarist and dancer in the touring act. He spent the next four years playing in bands and at carnivals throughout Texas and even toured the South with the great blues lady Ida Cox, before winning an amateur talent contest that landed him in Cab Calloway's band playing banjo for a week. There, he showed off a bit of what was to come, presenting an act that included doing the splits while playing his spotlight solo.

Not surprisingly, in the Oak Cliff section of Dallas where he had been raised, the guitarist was already a local legend by 1929. Under the moniker of Oak Cliff T-Bone, he recorded two songs for Columbia that year, "Wichita Falls Blues" and "Trinity River Blues," both of which hinted at the greatness that was to come but didn't quite capture it.

Like all Texas blues artists in the Great Depression, Walker found that money was scarce in the early thirties, and he took whatever work he could, often playing with small combos and jazz orchestras. He was fronting a quartet at Fort Worth's Gem Hotel in 1934 when he met his wife, Vida Lee, and became determined to find a better way to make a living. The rural South in the thirties offered little support for a musician and his family, so he followed the black migration from Texas to California. While most Texas blacks headed to the Golden State to take jobs in munitions plants and shipyards, Walker found work with a number of Los Angeles bands, and his career began to find a foothold in places like Club Alabam and Little Harlem.

Crowds were mesmerized by Walker's multiple offerings as a singer, dancer, and guitarist. He began drawing the first racially mixed crowds to high-dollar clubs in L.A. and also renewed a friendship with fellow Texas native Charlie Christian, the first artist ever to take the electric guitar into the jazz world. Christian and Walker had played together in Texas bands in the thirties, crossing paths as early as high school.

T-Bone wasted no time in trying his hand at the electric guitar, experimenting with a prototype as early as 1936. He wouldn't commit the electric sound to record for another three years, but he forever changed the sound and spirit of the music from the moment he first walked on stage with an electric instrument.

Walker did much, much more than simply plug in and play; he created a new tone and texture of blues music. His 1940 recording of "T-Bone Blues," cut with the Cotton Club Orchestra in New York City for Varsity Records, became a classic and kick-started the most successful time of Walker's career. The next few years would see him zigzagging the country and recording for a number of different labels, including Capitol, Black and White, and the house label of Chicago's popular Rhumboogie Club. Recordings like "Call It Stormy Monday," cut in 1946, and "T-Bone Shuffle," which quickly followed, became essential, classic blues songs as well as landing on the Hit Parade.

All the while, Walker's stunning, flamboyant showmanship added yet another pack-'em-in element to his performances. Leaping, doing the splits, playing the guitar behind his head or between his legs while doubling up a shuffle beat, Walker literally played the hell out of his instrument. He undoubtedly affected the exuberant style of those who would follow in his sizeable footsteps, an influence most obviously seen later in performers like Chuck Berry and Jimi Hendrix.

The post World War II days gave way to the fifties, and Walker's career slowed, although he maintained—as he does to this day—his legendary status. His live performances continued to prove his superstar abilities, but at the same time, his record sales began tapering off. Rock and roll and soul music were pushing the blues out of the record charts, and at one point Walker resorted to recording teen tunes like "Bobby Sox Baby," in which he sounds displaced and uncomfortable.

Fortunately, the downturn of the blues didn't last long; by the time the sixties began, Americans and Europeans were rediscovering the blues. T-Bone became a regular on the blues festival circuit, particularly in Europe, touring with names like John Lee Hooker, Brownie McGee, and Memphis Slim. Reinvigorated, he recorded his first album in years, this time on the Polydor label. That effort, "Good Feelin," earned him a Grammy in 1970 and encouraged him to step up the pace of his touring.

Years of hard living and too much nightlife had taken their toll on the blues great, and he suffered from chronic stomach problems even before a car accident sidelined him temporarily in 1972. Despite his health problems, he toured for almost two more years until a stroke on New Year's Eve of 1974 ended his career and put him in a nursing home. He died on March 15,

1975, and was recognized by the Rock and Roll Hall of Fame in 1987 for his contributions to music, which undoubtedly helped shape the sound that today is known as rock.

Walker was far from being the only Texas musician who packed up and headed to California to find fame in the footlights, but he certainly was ahead of his time. The true musical gold rush from the Lone Star State to the sunny coast didn't happen until the forties, and Walker beat most artists there by nearly a decade. But among the handful of other musicians who beat the rush was Pee Wee Crayton, although he went to the coast in search of much less glamorous work.

Pee Wee, born Connie Curtis Crayton on Dec. 18, 1914, in Rockdale (near Austin), shared much in common with Walker; both cut their musical teeth on the banjo, with Crayton adding the ukulele, guitar, and trumpet to his repertoire early on. Both men moved to California in 1935 to make a living, but while T-Bone headed for the stage, Pee Wee found work in the shipyards. The basic playing skills that Crayton had developed while growing up in Austin initially did little for him on the West Coast. Whereas T-Bone Walker had devoted his life to his musical calling, Crayton's flirtation with the blues was sporadic—until he saw Walker perform in Oakland in 1944.

That performance proved life changing for Pee Wee, who was immediately convinced he could become a guitar-playing hero in his own right. His hunch proved true, and while he was clearly influenced by Walker, Crayton worked hard to create a sound that would stand apart from his fellow Texan's talent.

Walker and Crayton became friends, and Crayton learned as much as he could from his newfound mentor. The friendship paid off handsomely, and within two years Crayton had mastered the electric guitar. He had quickly become so well known as a sideman that he was recording with such greats as pianist Ivory Joe Hunter, and in 1948 he signed with the Modern label and recorded the chart-topping single "Blues After Hours." He followed it up with the 1949 hits "Texas Hop" and "I Love You So" and began touring the country on the success of his singles, while building an even larger following on the strength of his live shows.

Despite the fact that he had a high, clear tenor voice, many of Crayton's hits were instrumentals. His early work paid tribute to the obvious jazz influences in his life, with smooth ballads and fluid pieces that later gave way to more aggressive jump-blues sound, only to return in the fifties to his original, smoother style.

As mentioned earlier, the fifties proved to be a challenging time for the blues, even in the music's most electrified and flamboyant form. Performers like Chuck Berry, Sam Cooke, Gene Vincent, and Jerry Lee Lewis were stealing the spotlight from the blues, and the gigs became harder to come by. Too many blues artists and not enough fans led Crayton to get dropped from the Modern label, which was finding more success with the recordings of an up-and-coming artist named B.B. King.

Pee Wee found himself on a number of smaller labels over the next few years, and despite the fact that he made some fine recordings during this time (such as 1957's "I Found My Peace of Mind"), he slipped out of the spotlight seemingly for good. From his home base of Los Angeles, Crayton began working odd jobs to supplement his failing musical career and playing the occasional live show.

The blues resurgence of the sixties eventually got around to paying Crayton his due, and by 1971 he was back in fine form, playing festivals and performing with greats like Big Mama Thornton and Big Joe Turner. His voice had changed, becoming lower and rougher, but his playing continued to showcase the flamboyant playing style that he had first emulated from T-Bone Walker and later expanded to make his own. He recorded new material as late as 1983 and continued performing until his death in June of 1985, when he suffered a heart attack just weeks after performing at the Chicago Blues Festival.

About the time things were taking off for Pee Wee Crayton, the musical migration from Texas to California was in full swing. While Texas guitarists like Charlie Christian and T-Bone Walker were blazing new musical trails, the Lone Star State's musical contributions didn't stop with the strings.

Perhaps one of the best non-guitar-slinging examples of Texas blues heroes is Charles Brown, who enjoyed a career at the keyboards that lasted more than half a century. Born in Texas City in 1920, Brown grew up studying classical piano but pursued a career in science, earning a degree in chemistry from Prairie View State College and performing in the college band.

He moved to Los Angeles in 1943 but not for the music. His planned employment at a research facility there didn't pan out, and Brown began working as an elevator operator and started playing piano gigs on the side. He won a local talent contest and soon found himself in demand for his skills on the ivories, which led to a union with Johnny Moore and Ed Williams to form the Three Blazers.

Led by Brown's smooth, laid-back vocals and jazz-imbued keyboard, the Three Blazers became one of the hottest R&B acts of the era. They introduced a new sound in blues, providing a smoky, mellow come-on that hinted at sounds of Nat King Cole but remained firmly rooted in the blues. "Driftin' Blues," the trio's first release, was a song that Brown had written when he was just twelve years old, and it stayed on *Billboard*'s R&B charts for almost two dozen weeks. For the next two years, the Three Blazers frequented the charts, including releasing the much-covered classic "Merry Christmas, Baby" in 1947.

Deciding to try a solo career, Brown left the Blazers and found himself on the R&B top ten charts at least ten times between 1949 and 1952, remaining a hot touring act through the mid-fifties. But as the story went for so many blues artists, rock rhythms soon swallowed up his sound. He found a place on the charts once again in 1960 with the holiday hit "Please Come Home For Christmas," which has been covered by everyone from The Four Tops to The Eagles.

He continued touring and recording throughout the sixties and seventies, but it was his 1986 album *One More For the Road* that resuscitated his career and reminded listeners that his velvety vocals were still alive and well. After his 1990 release "All My Life," he went on tour with Bonnie Raitt, delivering his brand of blues to thousands of new young fans and revitalizing his career. Brown concluded his impressive career with the release of the 1998 album *So Goes Love* and died on January 21, 1999.

The line that separated the blues from jazz was a fine and often blurred one. In the thirties and forties, no one straddled that line better than Eddie "Cleanhead" Vinson, a big band shouter with a powerful command of the alto sax. (His nickname, whose origin became obvious upon seeing Vinson's hairless scalp, was the result of an ill-fated attempt at using a lye-based hair straightener.) His music hopscotched from jump blues to jazz and back again, but his distinctive vocals won him a devoted blues following.

Vinson, a Houston native who was born there in 1917, grew up in a family that included piano-playing parents who encouraged their children to pursue music. By the time he was in high school, Vinson had picked up the sax and joined a band that included T-Bone Walker on guitar. By 1936 he had become part of the powerful horn section in Milt Larkin's big band, which also included such notables as Arnett Cobb and Illinois Jacquet, who later would excel in the areas of R&B and jazz.

He spent five years polishing his skills in Larkin's outfit before he left Texas and headed to New York, signing on with the Cootie Willliams Orchestra in 1941. The band found great success, thanks in part to Vinson's vocals on songs like "Somebody's Got to Go" and "Cherry Red."

By 1945 Vinson was ready to blaze his own trail, and he formed a band, landed a deal with Mercury, and immediately found a double sided hit with his first recording. Both "Old Maid Boogie" and "Kidney Stew Blues" were the kind of rollicking numbers that would become his signature. His immediate chart-topping success wouldn't be repeated; he joined the King Records roster from 1949 to 1952 but found only moderate success.

As the popularity of the blues stumbled in the fifties, Vinson explored his jazz interests, and his band lineup at one point included a young upstart by the name of John Coltrane. Cleanhead also penned a couple of classics made popular by Miles Davis, "Four" and "Tune Up," before moving back to Houston in 1954. From that time on, Vinson managed to balance his love of jazz and blues, playing the R&B circuit but also picking up work with the Count Basie band. Throughout the end of the fifties and into the sixties, he continued playing both sides, releasing albums both for blues and jazz labels.

Vinson's career enjoyed something of a revival in the seventies after an appearance at the Monterey Jazz Festival, and he continued recording and touring into the eighties, dazzling crowds with his own hybrid of jazz and blues. He was still performing regularly when he died of a heart attack in 1988.

While California became the musical promised land in the forties, not all the blues artists found it necessary to leave Texas to find their voice. Although not nearly as profitable or nationally high profile as the ones in California, Chicago, or New Orleans, Dallas and Houston continued to develop their own blues scenes.

Austin, which today is both the capital and the music center of the state, was slower to find its blues voice, something that is generally attributed to its small black population at the time, which made it an unlikely magnet for nightclubs and record producers. When the Austin scene began bustling in the 1960s, a number of new artists emerged to give the state capital a strong blues presence. With names like Stevie Ray Vaughan and Kim Wilson, and with the support of the renowned Antone's nightclub and record label, Austin later established itself as a prime source of white-boy blues. But in the early forties, the only way to find the blues in Austin was to head to the east side of town, where the majority of the black population was located and a small handful of clubs gave traveling blues musicians a stage on which to play.

The center of blues in Dallas shifted late in the 1940s as the railroad tracks that once defined Deep Ellum were torn up to make room for more modern roadways. But the city still offered a showplace for blues acts with clubs like The Rose Ballroom, which later became the Rose Room and then, in the 1950s, was known as The Empire Room. Regardless of what it was called, the Dallas club drew some of the top blues names of the day to its stage, bringing home greats like T-Bone Walker and Pee Wee Crayton and, later, Zuzu Bollin.

In Houston the scene was slower to develop than in Dallas, at least in terms of recording and national recognition. All that changed after World War II, when several independent labels sprouted to help spread the blues. The local labels made little effort to appeal to northern listeners, black or white, but still found some hits north of the Red River.

Gold Star, a label previously devoted to recording hillbilly music, changed its focus in 1947 when founder Bill Quinn decided to record Lightnin' Hopkins.

Hopkins, who was born with the much more subdued given name of Sam, was born in Centerville on March 15, 1912. Like so many of his fellow blues men, he was born into a musical family, and in this case, he learned the guitar from his older brother Joel. Hopkins was just eight years old when he made his performing debut at a country church picnic with none other than Blind Lemon Jefferson. The incident obviously had a profound and lasting effect on Hopkins, who set his sights on becoming a performer and by the time he was a teenager, was traveling throughout East Texas, accompanying his singing blues cousin Alger "Texas" Alexander on guitar. The two lived as hobos, often landing in jail and performing for a living in between.

Sam 'Lightnin'' Hopkins began his career accompanying his cousin, Texas Alexander, on guitar in the thirties, but didn't find widespread recognition until the sixties. Photo by Chris Strachwitz. *Photo courtesy of Arhoolie Records, Inc.*

The touring life was cut short in the mid-thirties when Hopkins earned an extensive stay in prison for an offense that no one seems able to recall. But after he'd served his time on the work farm, he moved to Houston and teamed up with a musician named Wilson "Thunder" Smith, and the two landed a deal with the Los Angeles-based Aladdin Records label. It was during his debut recording session that Sam Hopkins became Lightnin'—the record label wanted to bill the duo as Thunder and Lightnin'.

Despite the images conjured up by his stage name, Hopkins was a raw country blues player who told the story of his life in song with a slow drawl. His music was as real as any ever written, before or since, and his improvisation skills promised that he never told his musical stories quite the same way twice. As personal as his songs were, they struck a universal chord, with themes of women, hard living, and hard work. And while he experimented with the electric blues, it was in the gritty urban sound of the country blues that he did his best work. Even unplugged, Hopkins' guitar work was electrifying and moving.

Hopkins recorded for Aladdin in Los Angeles but continued to work out of Houston, which is where Gold Star's Quinn found him and convinced him to record for the hometown label. Lightnin' recorded some of the same songs for Gold Star as he'd done for Aladdin, but he found much better success with the Texas label. His first release for Gold Star sold some 40,000 copies and launched his reputation as a blues man, although it would take a couple more decades for him to find more widespread acclaim. While his music never sold as well as that of his musical contemporaries, the next couple of years saw him release singles whose sales more than doubled the volume of his original Gold Star issue.

Hopkins wasn't limiting himself to releases for Gold Star and Aladdin, however. Between 1946 and 1954 he recorded for a handful of labels, something he continued throughout his career. Sporting one of the most diverse discography in blues music, Lightnin' recorded for more than twenty labels during the course of his musical life, leaving behind an estimated eighty-five albums to his credit. But it wasn't until the blues resurgence in the sixties that he truly found an audience beyond the streets of his hometown.

Less than a year later he was "discovered" again by blues historian and record producer Sam Charters. Charters recorded Hopkins on the Folkways label, and about the same time, the guitarist was spotted in a Houston nightclub by Chris Strachwitz, who promptly launched the Arhoolie Records label on which Lightnin' also began recording. Within a year his career had been resurrected, and he was on his way to finding his place in history as one of the most enduring blues masters, enjoying a career that spanned some six decades.

By 1965 he had played Carnegie Hall with Pete Seeger and Joan Baez, was featured on the England/Europe tour of the American Folk Blues Festivals, and also held a slot on the Newport Folk Festival. His sound even found a following in the rock arena, and he performed with the Grateful Dead and headlined a bill that featured Jefferson Airplane.

Hopkins' success continued throughout the sixties and into the seventies, when he even appeared in a command performance for the Queen of England. He continued to record and perform live, although he began playing smaller clubs in Houston after an auto accident in 1970. He was featured in blues documentaries, contributed music for film scores, and continued being a much-sought-after performer for international blues festivals and Carnegie Hall appearances. In 1980 he was inducted into the Blues Foundation Hall of Fame, and he died of throat cancer in 1982.

Texas Alexander wasn't Hopkins' only famous musical cousin; Hopkins played a major influence in the life of his cousin Andrew "Smokey" Hogg as well. Hogg, born in the tiny community of Westconnie on January 27, 1914, was encouraged by Lightnin' to pursue his musical heritage.

Smokey was a simple man with a known penchant for at least two things—alcohol and the blues. It's unclear when he discovered the former, but the latter became an important part of his life early on. By the time he was thirteen, the young guitarist had run away to perform in a minstrel show, and he continued working throughout the state of Texas until he was discovered in 1937 by a talent scout for Decca.

That landed Hogg a record deal and a trip to Chicago, where he began to find a following for his unique, percussive style of blues. In 1947 he joined the slew of artists heading to Los Angeles and spent the next several years recording for a number of labels, including Exclusive, Bullet, and Modern. He had a couple of minor hits, but he died in 1960, at the age of forty-six, missing out on the blues music revival that many think would have made him a big name.

Gold Star's shift from hillbilly music to race recordings sparked something of a musical revolution in Texas back in 1947, creating a new competition among blues artists and spawning a number of other local labels. Within five years Houston had become a hotbed of recording activity for the blues, with labels like Macy's and Freedom entering the market and eventually attracting the attention of larger labels. But no other local label found the kind of success that was enjoyed by Peacock Records, a label started by Don Robey in 1949.

Robey, who was born in Houston on November 1, 1903, was a notorious and influential figure in the blues scene. He had dropped out of high school to become a professional gambler but later started a taxi business. His heart, however, was in music, and in the mid-thirties he began promoting ballroom dance events in the Houston area. By the end of the decade, he headed to California and opened the Harlem Grill nightclub in Los Angeles before returning to his hometown and opening the

Bronze Peacock Dinner Club, a jazz venue that pulled in some of the top bands and orchestras of the time. Robey had expanded his entrepreneurial pursuits to include a record store and talent management before he launched his record label, and it was seemingly by chance that the label was born at all.

One of Robey's first discoveries was Clarence "Gatemouth" Brown, a guitarist who was born in Louisiana on April 18, 1924, but whose parents moved to Orange, Texas, shortly afterward. His father was a musician who played a number of different styles, including country, bluegrass, Cajun music—just about everything but the blues. The younger Brown also was raised with a healthy dose of big band jazz influences, listening to the sounds of Duke Ellington and Count Basie and picking up the violin by the age of ten.

His "Gatemouth" nickname came from a high school teacher, who claimed the young man had "a voice like a gate," and it was one that served him well from the very beginning. By the time he left high school, he had added the guitar, mandolin, harmonica, and drums to his personal musical arsenal.

He was drafted in 1946 but by his own account, spent less than six months in the service because he felt "imprisoned." So he told his commanding officer he couldn't stay there, and the CO complied with an honorable discharge. Brown returned to Houston, where he worked to spread his music and finally earned his big break.

Brown was in Robey's Peacock club one night, watching T-Bone Walker play to a packed house, when Walker left the stage with a stomach ailment. Brown, who has since then maintained he had no idea what came over him, jumped on stage, picked up Walker's guitar, and improvised a tune on the spot, a song he called "Gatemouth Boogie." The crowd went wild, began shoving money at the stunned musician, and in fifteen minutes he went from being flat broke to having $600 in his pocket.

While the crowd was impressed with Brown's prowess, Walker was less than pleased with Gatemouth's actions, and while many stories claim Gatemouth completed the gig, Brown's version of the story says Robey intervened, pulled Brown into his office, and signed him under contract. The next day Brown was on a plane to California to record with Eddie Messner at Aladdin Records.

Robey was dissatisfied with the two singles that came from the Aladdin recordings and subsequently launched his own label, Peacock Records, to record Brown. Gatemouth's first pop out of the box, 1949's "Mary Is Fine," went to number eight on the R&B charts and was backed with the number nine-ranking hit "My Time Is Expensive."

Brown knew how to generate heat on stage, and he showed his eclectic musical background in each performance. He could take the music from blistering riffs to horn-driven rockers and then slow it down with Texas flavored blues. He proved he was more than just a blues man, incorporating his fearsome fiddling skills into his shows and pouring his far-reaching musical roots into the sound to break the blues mold.

Gatemouth's career stumbled in the sixties, a time which saw him moving to Nashville and dabbling in country music before returning to Texas. He resurfaced briefly in 1966 as the house bandleader for "The Beat," a Dallas-based syndicated R&B television program. Brown regained some ground in the seventies and landed a deal with Rounder Records, which eventually led to winning the 1982 Grammy Award for Best Blues Album. He marked his fiftieth anniversary as a recording artist with 1997's *Gate Swings* on the Verve label, and his latest album, *Guitar in Hand*, was released in February 2000.

Robey became significant for a number of reasons, not the least of which were his questionable business practices, which left him with much of the credit and rights to the works of the artists who recorded for him. But he also became one of the first African Americans to own a successful record label, something that was practically unheard of at the time. Robey's label preceded Berry Gordy Jr.'s successful Motown venture by a full decade, and Robey, regardless of what anyone might have thought of his tactics, was a true pioneer in the world of rhythm and blues and, later, pop music.

Despite his heavy-handed approach—or maybe because of it—Robey was able to build an impressive slate of artists on his roster who began generating a string of hits for the young label. Floyd Dixon scored a number eight single in 1950 with "Sad Journey Blues," and Marie Adams gave Peacock a number three hit with 1952's "I'm Gonna Play the Honky-Tonks." The label scored its first number one record when Willie Mae "Big Mama" Thornton recorded "Hound Dog" in early 1953 and stayed atop the R&B charts for seven weeks. Three years later Elvis Presley would cover the tune and stay on the R&B chart one week less than that, although his version stayed in the top spot of the pop charts for eleven weeks.

Thornton was an anomaly in the blues scene of the forties; whereas the earlier days had brought forth talent like Sippie Wallace, Ma Rainey, Victoria Spivey, and Ida Cox, the 1940s were notably void of female blues artists. Perhaps, then, it took a woman with a voice and stature as big as Thornton's to fill that void.

The religious background that Thornton was born into on Dec. 11, 1926, in Montgomery, Alabama, provided the perfect musical training ground for Willie Mae. The daughter of a minister and a vocalist in the church congregation, Willie Mae and her six siblings found plenty of musical inspiration in their environment. But the rigid religious rules collided with her love of the blues, which she discovered early on. At the age of fourteen, she was spotted in an amateur talent show (which she won) by Sammy Green, who invited the little girl with the big voice to join his Hot Harlem Review. She left Alabama and went

Big Mama Thornton and the Chicago Blues Band. Thornton landed on Don Robey's Peacock label in 1951 and, although she found great success, saw little financial return. Her career caught a second wind in the late sixties when Thornton's song "Ball and Chain" was recorded by an up-and-coming artist named Janis Joplin. *Photo by Jim Marshall. Photo courtesy of Arhoolie*

to Atlanta, where she spent seven years with Green's troupe. By the time she was twenty-one, Thornton had polished not just her vocal skills, but was accomplished on the harmonica and drums as well.

Houston, which was developing its own reputation as a blues center, seemed like the next logical step for Thornton, and she spent three years playing in clubs before signing with Robey's Peacock record label in 1951. She was working with Peacock label mate Johnny Otis on the West Coast when she picked up the "Big Mama" nickname, one that she lived up to both in sound and stature. Thornton was a big woman in every sense of the word—tall, broad, and possessing a big, coarse, and powerful voice that could simply drop jaws. When she recorded "Hound Dog," with Otis' band backing her, the single sold almost two million copies. (The flip side of the record was the autobiographical "They Call Me Big Mama.")

Although the success of "Hound Dog" permanently chisled her place in blues history, it did little for her in terms of financial success. Like many Peacock artists, Thornton saw little return on the two million copies, with some historians noting that she only received one check for the successful song in her entire life, and it was for five hundred dollars.

Still, what the song failed to do for her financially it certainly made up for with fame. Thornton found herself in demand, and Robey packaged her on tours with Otis, Little Esther Phillip, and Junior Parker.

By 1957 Thornton's career was floundering, and she left Houston, Peacock, and Robey to find a place in the San Francisco blues club scene. Although she landed a handful of one-time record deals, none of the albums released during the late fifties and early sixties sold well.

Just as with Lightnin' Hopkins and T-Bone Walker, the sixties blues revival proved a boon to Big Mama's career. She toured Europe and played blues festival circuits both at home and abroad, teaming up with greats like Buddy Guy and Muddy Waters. A whole new audience was discovering and enjoying her, and she released some of her live concert recordings on the Arhoolie label. Her Arhoolie recording with Muddy Waters' band included Thornton's composition "Ball and Chain," which caught the attention of an up-and-coming transplanted Texan named Janis Joplin. Joplin and her band, Big Brother and the Holding Company, included the song on their *Cheap Thrills* album and made "Ball and Chain" the powerful closer of their set at the 1967 Monterey Pop Festival.

That famous performance obviously did wonders for Joplin's career, but it proved a turbo-charge for Thornton as well. She landed a two-album deal with Mercury Records and continued a busy recording and touring career into the seventies. Although years on the road and in nightclubs eventually took their toll on the blues great, she continued performing as late as 1983, when she appeared at the Newport Jazz Festival alongside B.B. King and Eddie "Cleanhead" Vinson, among others. In 1984 she was inducted into the Blues Foundation's Hall of Fame, and she died of a heart attack on July 25 of that same year.

While Thornton provided the first hit for Robey's Peacock label, hers was only the first of many success stories to rise from the Houston recording empire. When Robey heard the single "My Song" by a Memphis-based singer named Johnny Ace, he went to Tennessee and bought the independent label on which Ace had recorded his song. Duke Records was formed early in 1952, but by August of that year Robey had purchased the Memphis outfit and took full control of both labels, operating them from his club headquarters in Houston. He found success with many of the Duke artists he acquired, including Johnny Ace and Roscoe Gordon, and he was able to create formidable package tours by combining artists from both the Peacock and Duke lineup.

In 1955 a young Memphis singer named Bobby "Blue" Bland ended a two-year stint in the Army, only to find that the recording contract he'd signed with Duke Records before enlisting now belonged to Don Robey. Bland, who had started his career at the age of seventeen as a gospel singer, was a member of the Beale Streeters alongside B.B. King, Junior Parker, Johnny Ace, and Roscoe Gordon.

In Bland, Robey found a profitable hit machine, despite the rather unusual fact that Bland didn't play any instruments. Instead, he relied upon a voice that could run the rhythm-and-blues range, from a soulful wail to an earthy growl to an unexpected falsetto. Robey backed him with a horn-driven orchestra and created Bland's signature big-band sound. Joe Scott, a Duke producer, became instrumental in Bland's career, becoming bandleader, arranger, and personal manager for the singer. Bland hit the charts from the beginning, but by the late fifties his singles were going all the way to the top, beginning with "Farther Up the Road" and continuing into the sixties. Despite changes in his band and the eventual departure of Scott, Bland remained loyal to the Duke label until Robey sold it to ABC in 1973.

Robey expanded his Duke Peacock empire through the years, adding a gospel division, a soul music division, and then, in 1963, creating Song Bird, a separate gospel label. Even after selling the lot to ABC, Robey stayed on as a consultant and supervised the release of cataloged material until his death in 1975.

The foundation laid by Texas blues legends in the forties and fifties became apparent in the sixties and took off in a new direction in the seventies. Johnny "Guitar" Watson, Albert Collins, Johnny Copeland, and Freddie King were among the Texans who grew up influenced by such greats as T-Bone Walker, Lightnin' Hopkins, and Clarence "Gatemouth" Brown and then made the music their own.

Watson, who was born in Houston on February 3, 1935, grew up with the blues and later parlayed that into the funk and soul sound of the seventies. He was just fifteen when he left

Houston and headed to Los Angeles, where he cut his first single three years later.

Watson started out playing the piano, and in his hometown he had delved into the urban blues scene, playing gigs with Albert Collins and Johnny Copeland. In Los Angeles he picked up the guitar and at the age of seventeen, poured out the amazing instrumental "Space Guitar," using reverb and echo techniques that were unheard of at the time. It was just a glimpse of what was to come from the string-bending wizard.

His blazing work on the strings, coupled with a cool, laid-back vocal style, could not possibly go unnoticed, and by 1955 he found his first hit with the song "Those Lonely Lonely Nights." He wrote "Gangster of Love" in 1957, which would later be a hit for Steve Miller, and by the sixties was exploring jazz and R&B with moderate success.

The seventies funk scene gave Watson ample room to find a new sound, and he absolutely exploded. Although the blues influence had all but slipped from his sound, he found hits with the R&B records "Superman Lover" and "A Real Mother For Ya" before re-recording "Gangster of Love."

When funk's fleeting fifteen minutes ended, Watson continued recording, once again reinventing himself, this time emerging as a more blues-tinged version of his funk-fortified self. His 1994 album *Bow Wow* picked up a nomination for the Grammy Award in best contemporary blues album, and Watson continued touring until his death from a heart attack in 1996 during a tour of Japan.

Watson's contemporary Albert Collins, another cousin of Lightnin' Hopkins, developed a distinctive sound in the sixties with his sparse, quick-fire guitar approach, which earned him the title the "Master of the Telecaster." Although Collins, who was born in Leona on October 1, 1932, began playing in Houston clubs by the time he was eighteen, it wasn't until the seventies and eighties that he found mainstream success. He scored a hit in 1962 with his instrumental number "Frosty," but even after the million-selling record he had to work day jobs to make ends meet.

A renewed interest in the blues in the mid-eighties put Collins back in the spotlight, and his 1991 release, *Iceman*, propelled him through a successful world tour. But just as his star was finally shining its brightest, Collins was diagnosed with liver cancer, and he died on November 24, 1993—just one month after releasing his final album, *Collins Mix*.

Raised in the same rich Houston blues environment as Collins and Watson was Johnny Copeland, a guitarist and singer who, like Collins, launched his career in the fifties but found success years later. The Louisiana native, who was born in 1937, grew up in Houston and taught himself to play his deceased father's guitar. He found regional success in the late fifties and early sixties, working with greats like Big Mama Thornton and Sonny Boy Williamson II, but he was purely a part-time musician when his flavor of Texas blues struck a chord in the Big Apple in the seventies.

Copeland had headed east when the blues revival of the sixties gave way to the psychedelia of the seventies, and it was in the nightclubs of Greenwich Village and Harlem that his music found a home. He signed with Rounder Records in 1980, enjoyed critical acclaim on two back-to-back albums, and toured extensively throughout the United States, Europe, and Africa.

He teamed up with Collins and a newcomer named Robert Cray in 1985 for the album *Showdown!*, which won the trio a Grammy and secured Copeland's place as a true blues master. Copeland recorded into the nineties, despite being diagnosed with a serious heart condition in 1994. He continued touring and recording while he waited for a heart donor, which he received on New Year's Day of 1997. However, his new heart failed, and he died on July 3, 1997.

Another transplant out of Texas, Freddie King was born in Gilmer in 1934, but his family headed to the Windy City when he was just sixteen. He had picked up some basic acoustic guitar skills from an uncle and his mother, but he could never have guessed what awaited him in Chicago.

In his new town King found a thriving blues scene and fell in love with the sound. (King's birth name was Freddie Christian, but when he fell in love with the blues, he adopted the "King" name—as in B.B. King.) He formed his first band, the Every Hour Blues Boys, by 1952 and began working his way through the club circuit. Eight years later the band had found a tremendous following and he released a recording, "You've Got to Love Her with a Feeling," which made it onto the pop charts. For the next five years, King enjoyed a number of hits, the biggest being his instrumental "Hideaway," which show-cased Freddie's wizardry on the strings and became the song by which future blues players would measure their abilities and agility.

In the early seventies musicians such as Eric Clapton jumped on King's bandwagon, drawing new attention to his music and reviving public interest in his recordings. Albums released in 1974 and '75 were well received, and Freddie was finally enjoying international success when he died of heart failure on December 18, 1976.

The blues revival of the sixties allowed several long-time Texas blues men to assume their rightful position in music history. It also brought to the scene a number of upstarts who would help infuse it with the modern rock influences that would enable it to cross virtually all barriers and fit comfortably with a wider demographic. Of all the singers to emerge during this era, none could claim the powerful impact of Janis Joplin, who was not only recognized as the greatest white female rock singer of the era, but also as quite possibly the best female blues singer of all time.

Her rough start in Port Arthur began on January 19, 1943, where she was born into a comfortably middle class family but grew up ostracized and lonely. Unable to fit into the small and extremely conservative town, she became a loner who found escape in music, poetry, and painting. At the age of seventeen she left home and began singing in clubs in Houston and Austin, working the folk circuit and trying to raise money to finance a move to California. By 1965 she was taking her brand of folk and blues to bars in San Francisco and Venice, California, settling into the Haight Ashbury district before briefly returning to Austin to sing with a country and western band. She was still in Austin in 1966 when she heard that a new San Francisco band, Big Brother and the Holding Company, was looking for a lead singer, so she headed back to the West Coast and landed the job.

The following year Big Brother and the Holding Company performed at the Monterey Pop Festival and dropped a musical bombshell. Her rendition of Big Mama Thornton's "Ball and Chain" closed the set and brought the house down, and with that one single performance Joplin established her musical reputation and changed the course of music history.

Big Brother and the Holding Company released the album *Cheap Thrills* in 1968, scoring a hit with the single "Piece of My Heart" and unleashing a high-voltage combination of blues and psychedelic rock. The album became a million-seller, but Joplin and the band were headed in different directions. The same week *Cheap Thrills* hit the number one spot, Joplin announced that she was leaving the band.

Backed by her new group, the Kozmic Blues Band, Joplin found a commercial success, but her sound lacked the improv feeling that her union with Big Brother had yielded. Her 1969 album *I Got Dem Ol' Kozmic Blues Again Mama* produced the gutsy, gravelly hit "Try (Just a Little Bit Harder)," and Joplin was touring constantly while hitting the TV circuit, appearing on talk and variety shows from Dick Cavett to Ed Sullivan.

Joplin's rendition of blues gems like "Piece of My Heart" resonated with a painful, heart-wrenching honesty that had never been heard in the compositions' original incarnations. Although she didn't write the songs she sang, she certainly adopted their sentiments and made them her own. When she wasn't pouring her pain out in song, she was covering it up with alcohol and drugs. Her heavy alcohol use often covered her heroin addiction from all but those in her inner circle. Despite promises to get clean or stay clean, she was never able to completely walk away from her self-destructive habits.

By 1970, from all outward appearances, Joplin's life was on the mend. She had assembled a new group of musicians, the Full Tilt Boogie Band, to back her on her second solo album, which she named *Pearl*—her nickname among friends. For the first time since leaving Big Brother it seemed she had found a fit, both musically and personally. She was engaged to be married and told friends she would kick her heroin habit for good when she was done recording *Pearl*. Joplin maintained that she was using just enough of the drug to keep from going into withdrawal, and that she'd beat the needle once and for all when the album was finished.

On October 3, 1970, Joplin went to the studio and listened to the instrumentals for "Buried Alive in the Blues," the only track on the album that was missing her vocals. She was to record the vocals the following day but was found dead that morning in her room at the Landmark Hotel in Hollywood. *Pearl* was released posthumously in 1971, earning unprecedented critical acclaim and garnering a number one hit with her version of Kris Kristofferson's song "Me and Bobby McGee."

Where Joplin could have taken the blues and how the music might have changed had she lived, is the subject of futile yet ongoing discussions. Her raw emotional delivery changed the

Alex Moore

The music history books are filled with artists who struggled for many years before finding fame, however fleeting it might have been. For sheer endurance, however, few blues artists can match the story of Alex Moore, a blues legend who toiled in near-obscurity for some forty years before getting his big musical break. As both one of the original and one of the last old-time Texas barrelhouse pianists, the lifelong Dallas resident was a brilliant performer with a penchant for creating poetic lyrics on the spot.

Alexander Herman Moore was born on November 22, 1899, and grew up in Freedman's Town, the black community near Central Tracks and Deep Ellum in Dallas. He grew up listening to the ragtime sound that was becoming so popular in the area's bars, and as a young teenager, he began playing the harmonica. By all accounts Moore's life wasn't an easy one; his father died in 1911 and Moore, then only in the sixth grade, quit school to work odd jobs and help support the family. He was seventeen when he added the piano to his skills, and he soon began experimenting with the barrelhouse sound, creating his own unusual style. He picked up the nickname "Whistlin' Alex" because of the piercing, whistling sounds he made to himself while playing.

Whistlin' Alex joined the Army in 1916 but played at house parties and bars every chance he got. His style poured blues, barrelhouse boogie, and ragtime together, mixing them in a way that had never been heard before and creating an entirely unique musical concoction.

He recorded six songs for Columbia in Chicago in 1929, then he returned to his day job back in Dallas, hauling junk on his mule-drawn cart. At night he played in the nightclubs of Deep Ellum, but he wouldn't record again until 1937, when he teamed up with Andrew "Smokey" Hogg, who had just been discovered by a Decca talent scout.

Moore continued playing live but didn't record again until 1947, followed by his fourth recording session in 1951. All the while, he held a day job—which now saw him working as a hotel porter—and played in clubs at night. But when the blues rebirth began in the 1960s, Moore was rediscovered, this time gaining popularity throughout the United States and Europe. He continued to work his day job, even as he was finding worldwide acclaim, until his retirement in 1965.

By 1969 Moore had found the commercial success that overlooked him in the first blues boom. He toured with the American Folk Blues Festival in Europe, recording the live album *Alex Moore in Europe* in Stuttgart, which found enormous popularity. That led to appearances in other festivals, but Moore never lost his passion for the simple life he led in Dallas. Between festivals, he could be found playing dominoes at the YMCA or playing his piano in local clubs.

In 1987 Moore became the first African American to receive a National Heritage Fellowship from the National Endowment for the Arts. His final album, *Wiggle Tail*, was a live endeavor recorded at a Dallas show and was released in 1988. He died of a heart attack on January 20, 1989.

way women sang the blues as well as the way a whole generation of listeners heard them. By the time of her death, the discovery of blues by an audience that had been raised on rock 'n' roll had begun, and the blues soon became more popular than it ever had been before. New artists worked with revitalized legends, reworking the rich and multifaceted blues tradition into a amalgamation of old-school blues and fresh-faced rock. Elements of jazz and country, poured through a blues filter, happily cohabitates with hard rock in a package that appeals to an impossibly large demographic.

What the future held for the blues as the sixties drew to a close blew open the doors of popular music. The late sixties and early seventies saw Texas blues force Johnny Winter create an international stir with his unrelenting style of blues-flavored rock, and he became the first white artist to be inducted into the Blues Foundation's Hall of Fame.

Austin's blues scene came of age as the so-called "Austin sound" captured national attention and saw the rise of such acts as The Fabulous Thunderbirds, Lou Ann Barton, Angela Strehli, and, most notably, Dallas native Stevie Ray Vaughan. The blues would never be the same once rock entered the scene, and just as it had done since the days of Blind Lemon Jefferson, Texas made certain that the rest of the world heard its influence.

Recommended Listening:

T-Bone Blues – T-Bone Walker (Atlantic)

Blues Masters: The Very Best of T-Bone Walker – (Rhino)

Things I Used To Do – Pee Wee Crayton (Vanguard)

All My Life – Charles Brown (Verve)

Texas Songster – Mance Lipscomb (Arhoolie)

The Complete Aladdin Recordings – Lightnin' Hopkins (EMI)

Alright Again! – Clarence "Gatemouth" Brown (Rounder)

Texas Guitar Killers – Various Artists (Capitol)

The Best of Duke-Peacock Blues – Various Artists (MCA)

Big Mama Thornton—Hound Dog: The Peacock Recordings – Willie Mae Thornton (MCA)

Showdown! – Albert Collins, Johnny Copeland and Robert Cray (Alligator)

Copeland Special – Johnny Copeland (Rounder)

The Best of Freddie King – (Shelter)

Three Hours Past Midnight – Johnny "Guitar" Watson (Virgin)

Cheap Thrills – Big Brother and the Holding Company (Columbia)

Pearl – Janis Joplin (Columbia)

Chapter Eight

Jazz Gets Born Again

A number of cultural changes contributed to a shift in the music scenes of the forties and early fifties, and jazz was visibly affected by the societal changes that came with the end of World War II. The draft had taken both musicians and fans away from the music, and as the war came to a close, the once-swinging jazz scene had become lethargic and disorganized. But the revival that it so badly needed wasn't long in coming.

Swing fans continued listening to the sounds of big bands like those led by Benny Goodman or Duke Ellington, but bebop, which rose out of the predominantly African-American New York jazz scene, brought a different sound to the genre. Characterized by its choppy, staccato style and improvisational nature, bebop put more emphasis on the rhythm section and utilized the cymbals and snare drum in ways that swing had never attempted.

Although bebop emerged as a definite contrast to swing, it clearly borrowed from earlier jazz movements, incorporating sounds of the old territory bands into a new musical framework. The seemingly disorganized format of improv initially drew nothing but criticism from listeners who were accustomed to the more formal, well-rehearsed sound of big band swing. Eventually, though, the emotional mood swings of the up-and-coming bebop sound began attracting both veteran players, who began to see the challenges presented by the style, and mainstream audiences, who discovered it was a fitting soundtrack for the emerging busy urban lifestyle.

Improvisational music, played by smaller groups and combos, opened the door for new instruments to test their limits. Piano-driven trios became popular, and Dallas did its part by providing one of the most outstanding jazz keyboardists of the forties and fifties.

William "Red" Garland, who first found his musical calling on the clarinet, was born in Dallas on May 13, 1923, and started playing both the clarinet and alto at an early age. (He even took lessons from Buster Smith, who at the time still lived in Dallas.)

Red joined the Army when he was eighteen and while in the military, switched from the reed instruments to playing the piano. Following his time in the service, Garland landed a job in a Fort Worth dance hall, and when noted bandleader Hot Lips Page passed through, he claimed the young player as one of his own.

That association led Garland to New York, where the bebop scene was just beginning to bubble to the surface. A quick study, Garland was fascinated by the sounds coming from the city's best bebop pianists, and he began incorporating those new sounds into his own style at the keyboard.

Beginning around 1946, Red began playing with some of the best jazz musicians in New York, and his sound matured into a complex blend of contemporary influences and his own innovative musical experimentation. For the next nine years he would explore new territory with such greats as Coleman Hawkins, Charlie Parker, Lester Young, and Roy Eldridge. But it wasn't until trumpet player Miles Davis heard Garland perform in 1954 that the pianist was able to break out of his obscure sideman role.

Davis assembled a quintet featuring Garland on piano and subsequently produced some of the era's most historic recordings. Garland's block chords created a new foundation for jazz in the fifties. And during his three years with Davis's outfit, he became recognized as one of the greatest pianists of the era, demonstrating an amazing range that could dip into a gutsy blues groove just as easily as it could strike a lighthearted, playful tone.

The musical genius within the Miles Davis quintet provided the music scene with some powerful recordings but also led to a sense of restlessness within the group as players wanted to strike out in their own direction. Garland left the group in 1958 and was replaced by Bill Evans, but not before leaving an indelible mark on music history with his contributions to the landmark *Milestones* album. Although many have argued that Garland's finest work was done while playing in Davis's fold, the piano great's career still had plenty of life left in it.

Garland continued playing, forming his own trios and quartets, cutting a number of solo albums for several different labels. While still playing with Davis, he released three solo albums in 1957 alone and also played on four albums by fellow quintet member John Coltrane. His prolific recording pace continued through 1962. But the following year he returned to Dallas to care for his mother, who was in poor health, and his music wouldn't be heard again until he staged a comeback some fifteen years later. In 1977 he cut the album *Red Alert* and began performing again, albeit at a much slower pace. His final concert was at a jazz festival in Dallas in 1981, and he died at his home on April 23, 1984.

While New York City continued to be a mecca for hot new jazz performers in the forties, cultivating a fresh bounty of bebop artists and drawing talent from the Midwest, Texas was carving its own niche in music history. Building on the master's thesis of a young student in Denton, the state was about to change the way musicians learned to play and for the first time, make it possible to study jazz in a classroom setting.

At the North Texas State Teachers College, now known as the University of North Texas, a student by the name of Morris Eugene ("Gene") Hall was looking for a school where he could learn more about playing big band dance music. Unable to find such a college, he eventually took on the task himself.

Dr. M. E. (Gene) Hall directs an early lab band in an informal concert at the old NTSU Student Union Building, 1950s. *Photo courtesy of Denton Record-Chronicle*

Hall had learned to play the saxophone as a child in his hometown of Whitewright, where he was born in 1913. His father had given him the saxophone to play in church, and with the help of a local violinist and an instructional manual, Hall taught himself basic fingering techniques. He was eighteen when he landed his first professional gig, playing with a five-piece band at a nearby dance hall. Two years later he had joined a nine-piece band in Poplar Bluff, Missouri, where he played for money and meals. But when the hot-tempered bandleader got into a fight with a local patron, the band was fired and Hall returned to Texas, enrolling at Denton's North Texas State Teacher's College in 1934.

At the time, the only available music programs were geared toward teaching inspirational music, although the school's stage band, The Aces of Collegeland, had existed since 1927. The Aces provided weekend entertainment at dances and music programs and later would provide a training ground for such talent as Ann Sheridan and Pat Boone. Hall signed up to study music theory with the hopes of landing a spot in the band. It wasn't until 1936 that he actually earned a chair among the Aces, and he alternated between attending school and playing with other bands until he earned a Bachelor of Arts degree in 1941.

While Hall went after his master's degree, he taught a course in arranging and organized a rehearsal band to play arrangements written by the students. The subject of his master's thesis, "The Development of a Curriculum for the Teaching of Dance Music at a College Level," presented an idea that had never been attempted before. But Dr. Walter Hodgson, dean of the NTSTC music department, recognized Hall's vision and, in 1947, hired him to launch a dance band curriculum.

It was the first program of its kind in the world, and it was met with tremendous opposition both from faculty and parents. Faculty members argued that it would never work; parents objected that such a curriculum would corrupt the morals of their children. Student response, however, was overwhelming.

Initially the public and faculty outcry against the curriculum was so strong that it was listed as a radio writing course, with no reference whatsoever made to jazz, so as not to upset parents. The school attracted a host of talent that went on to play with greats like Stan Kenton and Benny Goodman. In fact, Kenton became so enamored with the talent that his orchestra became a sort of master class for graduates of what later became the Denton university's jazz studies program. Kenton continued a close association with the school until his death in 1979, at which time he bequeathed his entire music library to the University of North Texas College of Music.

Gene Hall continued to head the growing jazz studies program until 1959, when he left to establish and head the jazz program at Michigan State University. Nervous school officials considered dropping the program entirely upon Hall's resignation, afraid that the "wild jazz musicians" would wreak havoc without the tutelage of the program's founder. Instead, they eventually and warily turned to a clarinetist who had played with Arthur Fielder and the Boston Pops Orchestra.

Leon Breeden was carefully scrutinized and questioned by school officials to ensure that the school wasn't bringing a renegade musician on board. Although Breeden was a clean-living family man, his first months at the school were marked by harassing phone calls from parents warning him that he was going to hell for teaching their children that "sinful jazz music." Just two weeks into his tenure, Breeden found the environment so hostile that he penned his resignation, but at the urging of his wife, he decided to stay and fight for the program.

The school continued a struggle in which the jazz studies department blossomed despite the vocal public opposition. Bands were named for the time slot in which they rehearsed, with the premier band kicking things off at one o'clock. Just two years after Breeden took the reins, the One O'Clock Lab Band won top honors at the Notre Dame Jazz Festival, launching an ongoing streak of accolades and performances. In 1967 the band played at the White House by presidential invitation, backing Ella Fitzgerald before a crowd of 7,000. Fitzgerald, impressed with the students' ability, announced to the audience that she wanted to take the band on tour with her. Fitzgerald wasn't alone in her admiration of the talent being cultivated at North Texas. By the early seventies, the One O'Clock Lab Band had solidified its reputation, thanks to appearances at the International Jazz Festival in Montreaux, Switzerland and tours of the Soviet Union and Portugal. Today it has earned no less than four Grammy Award nominations and continues attracting jazz students from around the world.

Breeden led the North Texas jazz studies program until 1981, and upon his retirement, the program was taken over by Neil Slater. Hall went on to serve as the chair of the music departments at College of the Desert in Palm Springs, California, and Stephen F. Austin State University in Texas until his retirement in 1983. He returned to Denton in 1988, occasionally playing in a small Dixieland band until his death in 1993.

The parade of students that passed through the innovative jazz studies program have made significant contributions to the music through the years, but the program also has served as something of a magnet for musicians who didn't participate in the studies but were attracted by the rich creative environment. Denton became something of an incubator for musical talent, encouraging young musicians to test the waters and providing plenty of local bands in which they could play.

Among the people who were attracted to the school was a young man named Bob Dorough, who was born in Arkansas in 1923 but grew up in Texarkana and Plainview. He studied violin, piano, and clarinet before learning harmony and conducting from his high school band director. After a stint in the Army,

Dorough found himself fascinated with jazz and bebop and heard that Denton offered a jazz-friendly environment.

Dorough enrolled in the school in 1946, where he studied composition and piano for three years. His appetite for the music sharpened, Dorough then headed to New York, where he studied bebop and later hosted jam sessions in his flat on the Upper East Side. To make ends meet, he accompanied tap dance classes at a nearby studio. He even played for a time with boxer Sugar Ray Robinson, who at the time was an entertainer as well as a pugilist.

Devil May Care, Dorough's first album, was released in 1956, but it wasn't until 1962 that his career took flight, when he wrote "Comin' Home Baby," which would provide Mel Torme with a hit, and Miles Davis commissioned him to write "Blue Xmas." Dorough enjoys the distinction of being one of the few vocalists ever featured on a Davis recording, but his innovative vocal style has been largely overlooked. His talent for providing lyrics for instrumental jazz solos has won him a place among original American vocalists, and his songwriting easily ranges from love songs to quirky, witty numbers.

It was a "day job," however, that led to Dorough's biggest success. In the late sixties he began doing studio work and composing advertising jingles, which led to his involvement in a project that evolved into a cultural phenomenon: "Schoolhouse Rock." Dorough penned dozens of songs for the catchy, kid-friendly educational program that aired on ABC on Saturday mornings beginning in 1970. The program proved to have more longevity than anyone could have imagined; in 1996 Atlantic Records released *Schoolhouse Rock Rocks!*, a compilation disc featuring contemporary artists performing Dorough's now-famous songs.

Dorough's career has stayed alive through four decades, although he is more of a cult figure than a music icon. He has written music for films and continues performing throughout

Future "Schoolhouse Rock" innovator Bob Dorough plays the piano while Gene Hall leads one of the first lab bands assembled for the innovative Jazz Studies Program at what is now the University of North Texas in Denton. *Photo courtesy University of North Texas School of Music*

North America and Europe, and his most recent release was "Too Much Coffee Man" in 2000.

Four of the North Texas students who are credited with launching the school's jazz reputation predate Hall's prestigious program and were never actually enrolled in the jazz program, although they studied music in some form or fashion at North Texas. Jimmy Giuffre, Herb Ellis, Gene Roland, and Harry Babasin all shared a house in Denton before heading out to California to join the jazz scene there. Ellis, who was born in Farmersville in 1921, fell in love with the guitar while listening to Charlie Christian's pioneering sounds. Christian's recordings with Benny Goodman in the late thirties and early forties inspired Ellis to pick up the guitar, and he taught himself the basics of the instrument before heading to Denton.

The school didn't offer instruction on the guitar, so Ellis majored in bass violin and jammed with his housemates before leaving Denton to go pro. They found an environment rich with opportunity, playing house dances or simply starting up impromptu jam sessions when no audience was available. Ellis landed a gig with The Casa Loma Orchestra in Kansas City then wound up in Jimmy Dorsey's band before forming the Nat King Cole-like group Soft Winds with pianist Lou Carter.

But it wasn't until he was picked up by Oscar Peterson's trio that Ellis found a place to truly make his mark. His hard-swinging guitar lines and Charlie Christian-influenced playing made him something of a standout, and he was included on some Jazz at the Philharmonic tours, which included a veritable who's who of jazz giants. That led to some recordings with Verve, which recorded the Jazz at the Philharmonic events, and after Ellis left Peterson's fold in 1958, he toured with Ella Fitzgerald.

On the West Coast, Ellis earned his reputation as a smooth master of the sound. He became a popular session musician,

Herb Ellis performs at his alma mater—University of North Texas in Denton, 1998. *Photo courtesy University of North Texas*

sitting in with Charlie Byrd, Stuff Smith, and the Dukes of Dixieland. Ellis picked up more speed in the seventies, recording more frequently and spending as much as half his time on the road. Even today he continues a rigorous regimen of recording and touring.

Among the first Denton-schooled musicians to make his mark on the jazz scene was Gene Roland, a Dallas native who joined Stan Kenton's orchestra in 1944, first as a composer and arranger, and later on trumpet and trombone. Roland, whose birth date was September 15, 1921, became the first of many North Texas expatriates to find a home with the renowned band. Having earned a degree in music in Denton, he headed to California in 1944 and was able to contribute a number of arrangements to the bandleader's repertoire, including giving Kenton his first million-selling record with "Tampico." Although Roland stayed with Kenton's orchestra until 1955, he also was a frequent freelancer with other bands, playing with the likes of Count Basie, Dizzy Gillespie, and Lionel Hampton while contributing arrangements to big bands, including working up charts for Artie Shaw and Harry James. Roland worked with Woody Herman from 1956 until 1958 then returned to work with Kenton's orchestra again.

As an arranger, Roland was a prolific, powerful force, but he doubled up his duties in the early sixties to introduce the mellophonium to the jazz world through Kenton's band. The brass instrument required new arrangements, many of which Roland penned, and he also began playing the soprano saxophone for the band. However, that was just the tip of his talent, as Roland also was proficient with the trumpet, piano, and tenor, all of which he played with groups of this own that he formed later in the sixties. He also enjoyed an adventurous approach to the music, attempting arrangements that were far ahead of their time and often were rejected by Kenton.

Roland's dazzling, innovative arrangements were often underrated but ultimately responsible for much of the popularity of Kenton's orchestra during the fifties and sixties. He went on to work with a number of other bands but consistently contributed charts to Kenton's group. He continued writing into the seventies and died in 1982.

Harry Babasin also headed to the West Coast from North Texas State University, where he studied in the early forties, but not before spending time in New York with the big bands of Gene Krupa and Boyd Raeburn. Babasin, a bass player who was born in Dallas on March 19, 1921, landed in California in 1945 and recorded with Woody Herman and Benny Goodman. He later recorded with a number of Kenton's orchestra members, although he never worked with the bandleader himself.

Babasin made jazz history in 1947 when he became the first player to play the pizzicato cello on a jazz record, and by that time he was becoming an active player for the L.A. jazz scene, working with Charlie Parker and a young Chet Baker in the early fifties. Babasin continued recording in the sixties, and in the seventies he created the Los Angeles Theaseum, a jazz history archive that preserves recordings in a digital format. He last toured in 1985 and died of emphysema in 1998.

Jimmy Giuffre followed his housemates to California in 1946, although his initial reason for heading west wasn't a musical one—he had joined the Air Force and found himself stationed there. Giuffre, who was born April 26, 1921, had started playing the clarinet at the age of nine and eventually found fame as a composer, arranger, and master of the clarinet, tenor, sax, and flute.

His time at North Texas had earned him a degree in music education, and although he started working on a master's degree at the University of California at Los Angeles, he never completed the degree, leaving school to begin working with big bands.

Giuffre composed music for Woody Herman's band and found his first taste of success when Herman's outfit recorded his song "Four Brothers of '48." By the end of the decade, he was penning some of the era's most distinctive jazz sounds, breaking away from the conventional compositions and creating a fresh swinging style that defined the new "West Coast sound."

His membership in Howard Rumsey's Lighthouse All-Stars in the early fifties gave Giuffre the vehicle for turning loose his rollicking straight-ahead sound. As both a soloist and a composer, Giuffre was pioneer in the new musical movement, stretching the boundaries and taking musical liberties that hadn't been attempted before. He was among the musicians who had flocked to L.A. and developed a new, mellow sound that drew a razor-thin line between jazz and classical music. This California cool was as mellow as the New York bebop sound was busy. Concise and well choreographed, it gave audiences a new set of tonal combinations to wrap their ears around, and few composers were able to make use of the instruments as well as Giuffre.

His work with trios and quartets yielded a number of new, experimental sounds that established his reputation as one of the most proficient purveyors of West Coast cool. He recorded *The West Coast Sound* with drummer Shelly Manne in 1953, offering a glimpse of the direction the music was heading, and then steadily followed the new path blazed by that album. Two years later Giuffre's *Tangents in Jazz* album introduced the idea of creating jazz without a rhythm section keeping beat, but serving instead as soloists. He scored a hit with his song "The Train and the River," which appeared on his album *The Jimmy Giuffre 3*—another recording that saw him experimenting with instruments. This time around, Giuffre had dropped the traditional piano-bass-drums setup and performed only with a trombone player and guitarist.

The fifties proved to be Giuffre's most visible decade, and his focus changed in the sixties. He stepped out of the high-profile spotlight, choosing to teach music and perform rather than continuing his pace in the studio. Giuffre became a force in the free jazz movement and played throughout the United States and Europe, performing in a relatively obscure trio that included Steve Swallow and Paul Bley. He shifted gears again in the seventies to explore African and Asian influences in a jazz framework, and he began teaching at the New England Conservatory of Music. He continued to perform and compose until recently, when an advancing case of Parkinson's Disease sidelined his live performances.

Denton wasn't the only Texas city to boast a school filled with great jazz talent in the late forties. Some fifty miles and a world away, a Fort Worth high school was quietly grooming a handful of future legends. At I.M. Terrell High School, the band roster in the late forties boasted a membership of one-day jazz giants that included John Carter, Charles Moffett, William Lasha, Dewey Redman, and Ornette Coleman.

Built in the late 1800s, I.M. Terrell was the only school for black students in the area until integration began in the 1950s. That segregation brought together an elite group of musicians who would play together first in Fort Worth and by the mid to late fifties would be reunited on the West Coast.

Cowtown, as Fort Worth is often called, wasn't paying much attention to jazz in the late forties. Blues still ruled the musical roost, and the young musicians mostly were exposed to rhythm and blues or swing music when they weren't blowing their horns for the high school band. Of all the players to come out of Fort Worth, no others enjoyed the prominence achieved by Ornette Coleman, who taught himself to play the sax and by the age of fourteen had bought his own instrument with the money he earned shining shoes.

Coleman's fascination with the sax exploded into a bona fide obsession when, at the age of fifteen, his aunt took him to New York City and he heard Dizzy Gillespie play. Back in the Lone Star State, he began exploring new sounds and even got himself banned from the high school band in 1947 for improvising in the middle of a John Philip Sousa march. It might have been the first time he found himself thrown out of something—or some place—for his unusual musical approach, but it certainly wasn't his last.

His passion for experimentation and improvisation got him fired from bands in 1948 and 1949; he was beat up outside a Baton Rouge dance hall after he unleashed his forward-thinking free jazz solos to a rather unappreciative public. He headed to New Orleans and began experimenting with a sound that would evolve into "harmolodics," a musical system that allows musicians to follow their intuition and invent new melodies and harmonies on the spot. Taking improvisation to a new level and relying on emotions and feelings over structure, the style was widely rejected at first.

After a year in Louisiana, Coleman returned to Cowtown and hooked up with Charles Moffett, a trumpeter who had played alongside Coleman in the high school band. The short-lived reunion ended when Coleman signed on to play with Pee Wee Crayton, something that took him to Los Angeles and initially led to even more rejection of his music once the job with Crayton ended. Jazz musicians were openly hostile toward him, calling him a charlatan and, in some cases, exiting the stage when Coleman showed up to play.

It wasn't until 1958 that Coleman got his break and began finding a glimmer of acceptance. In Los Angeles he had begun playing with James Clay, a Dallas-born tenor player who was open to Coleman's ideas and encouraged him to join Clay's group, the Jazz Messiahs. Messiah composer Don Cherry was impressed enough with Coleman's songs that he bought three tunes and then took him into the studio to record *Something Else! The Music of Ornette Coleman*. The debut album, which combined traditional form with his uninhibited improvisation, in retrospect serves as a signpost for musical change. Music was moving toward a freer form, and Coleman was leading the controversial charge.

He recorded three albums for the Contemporary label, then he was picked up by Atlantic and released the fittingly named record *The Shape of Things to Come*. He continued recording albums that redefined the free jazz sound and reignited tension among jazz musicians. While members of the arts community praised Coleman's artistic approach, many in the jazz community still saw him as a musical interloper.

In 1961 Coleman created a new band that included Charles Moffett, his old high school band mate, and Bobby Bradford, a Dallas-raised trumpeter who had worked with Coleman at a Los Angeles department store. By now Moffett had turned in his trumpet for the drums, and he and Bradford formed part of Coleman's octet. Coleman's early recorded works today have become musical monuments, perhaps accentuated by the fact that Coleman went into a self-imposed exile in 1962, appearing on stage briefly with Bradford and Moffett in January of 1965, then disappearing again for about eight months, resurfacing this time for performances in London and Stockholm.

Coleman re-emerged in the seventies with a fresh free jazz vision and found a warmer reception both from musicians and the public. He not only influenced but recorded with rock and jazz musicians, and by now his style had expanded to embrace funk, R&B, and rock with a nontraditional array of instruments. Forming his legendary Prime Time band, he also traveled through Africa, recording tribal musicians that he incorporated into his recordings back in the states, and in the eighties he recorded with Pat Metheny.

Despite his controversial start, Coleman has gone on to receive widespread critical acclaim, including being named Jazz Musician of the Year both by *Rolling Stone* and *Down Beat* magazines. His hometown of Fort Worth recognized him in 1983, calling him home for the opening of the Caravan of Dreams performance center, a jazz-oriented club in the heart of downtown. In honor of the occasion, the Fort Worth Symphony Orchestra performed Coleman's "Skies of America" and he was given a key to the city. But the greatest evidence of Coleman's impact is found on the numerous albums that bear his work or influence even when they don't bear his name.

While Coleman was obviously the most prominent player to rise from the ranks of I.M. Terrell High School, his schoolmates found their way down jazz-flavored paths that would eventually intersect with their better-known alum.

Charles Moffett gained a certain level of prominence through his association with Coleman but went on to explore other areas of new jazz, performing with Archie Shepp on the classic *Four for Trane* album tribute to John Coltrane. Moffett periodically returned to teaching, which he had pursued after graduating from Terrell, but continued to perform, either with his students, fellow musicians, or his troupe of five musical children, known on stage as The Moffettes. In the 1980s he moved to New York where he taught mentally retarded children and continued to perform and record. He last recorded in 1996, in sessions that yielded albums for Sonny Simmons and Charles Tyler, and he died on Valentine's Day of 1997 at the age of sixty-seven.

Moffett's high school ties with William "Prince" Lasha were among those that endured past school. Lasha, who was born in Cowtown on September 10, 1929, played in a band with Coleman during their days in Fort Worth and had frequently practiced with Moffett and Coleman. Lasha went on to master the alto sax and also proved proficient with the flute and clarinet. By 1962 he was in Los Angeles recording with Sonny Simmons and then invited Moffett to join them on drums for a second recording five years later. *Firebirds* today remains a high-octane piece of work, showcasing both Lasha's emotional and spontaneous style and Moffett's powerful prowess on the drums and cymbals.

Lasha never recorded with Coleman, although traces of the master's hand can be seen in much of Prince's handiwork. Lasha's relatively small library of recorded work belies his role in the free jazz movement; he recorded a few albums for small labels but slipped out of the studio in the eighties and has remained quiet since then.

Yet another Terrell High School alum to venture to California was John Carter, a clarinet player who moved to L.A. in 1961 and began teaching in the public school system—something he continued until his retirement in 1982. He already had put in two years teaching in the Fort Worth school district, where he had provided music instruction to, among others, Ronald Shannon Jackson, a drummer who by the age of fifteen already was playing professionally with Dallas's James Clay.

In 1964 Carter started the New Art Jazz Ensemble with Bobby Bradford, the Dallas-raised trumpeter who had worked with Coleman during his early days in Los Angeles. In fact, it was Coleman who suggested Bradford hook up with Carter, an innovative composer who was also proficient on the flute, sax, and clarinet. Eventually, he focused solely on the clarinet, navigating the music in ways that many didn't even know the instrument was capable of achieving.

Although part of the free jazz movement, Carter placed a great deal of emphasis on the composed elements of the music and, as a composer, managed to convey the loose improvisational style that energized and drove the music. He played and recorded throughout the sixties and seventies then formed the Wind College, a school for improvisation, with a trio of his

John Carter and Bobby Bradford are two Texas jazz legends who teamed up in California. *Photo by Craig Levine.*

fellow musicians. He continued collaborating with Bradford until his death in 1991, by which time Carter had earned a reputation as one of the most melodic improvisers in the world of jazz.

Rounding out the musical powerhouse of jazz greats at I.M. Terrell was Dewey Redman, a man who today is recognized not only as a brilliant tenor sax man but also as the father of renowned jazz artist Joshua Redman. Although his son might currently be seen as the flag-bearer for the contemporary jazz scene, Dewey grew up fascinated with the music from the time he first dazzled the congregation of a Baptist church. He learned the clarinet and alto sax before joining the ranks of the Texas tenor sax legends. Unlike his fellow legends, however, Redman didn't initially set his sights on music.

Dewey Redman performs in Cambridge, MA in 1997. Redman and his high-school bandmate Ornette Coleman reunited in New York and spent seven years playing and touring together before Redman went out on his own again. *Photo by Paul Hilcoff.*

Instead, he earned a master's degree in teaching at what is now the University of North Texas in Denton and spent three years teaching in Fort Worth before heading to California in 1959. Redman spent the next seven years playing in the thriving jazz community of San Francisco, then he moved to New York, where he ran into Ornette Coleman, and the two began a seven-year union that saw them recording albums and touring together before Redman went on to create his own bands.

His innovative playing made him an adept match for Coleman's bands, but audiences found Redman's style more accessible, which generated a lot of work throughout the seventies. He guest performed on Pat Metheny's *80/81* album and then reunited with other veterans of the free jazz scene for the Coleman's reunion band, called Old and New Dreams. Today Redman remains a powerful messenger of jazz, still recording but offering fewer live performances.

The same climate that nurtured Redman, Coleman, Lasha, and Carter also spawned such Dallas-raised jazz giants as James Clay, Bobby Bradford, David "Fathead" Newman, and Cedar Walton, making a generous contribution to the bebop and free jazz movements.

Clay, as noted earlier, made a significant impact on the career of Ornette Coleman by encouraging the sax man to join his group the Jazz Messiahs, where Coleman was able to push the musical boundaries without retribution. Clay, who was born in Dallas on September 8, 1935, grew up playing at area clubs, first on the alto sax and flute, then moving on to become another of Texas's famed tenor players.

Clay cut his first two albums in Los Angeles in 1957, and the second disc saw him teaming up with a young David "Fathead" Newman, a fellow tenor player who had mostly an R&B background at that point. Clay showed a promising start, although he never quite discovered the kind of widespread recognition enjoyed by Newman or Coleman. Not nearly as experimental as Ornette, he was appreciated as a mainstream player. During the sixties his work was found on albums by Billy Higgins and Red Mitchell, and he also performed alongside Newman in Ray Charles's band before slipping into obscurity.

Clay rejuvenated his career in the nineties, recording on ex-Jazz Messiah Don Cherry's album *Art Deco* and then releasing two warmly received albums on the Antilles label, both of which indicated jazz had suffered a considerable loss by his nearly three decades of silence. His comeback was short-lived, however, and Clay died on January 12, 1995.

Newman followed a more brightly lit path than Clay, one that began with his birth on February 24, 1933. He picked up the "Fathead" designation early on, when an obviously frustrated high school band teacher saddled him with the name after Newman botched an arpeggio during practice. Nonetheless, Newman was picking up gigs in high school and, after two years of college, quit school to go on the road with Buster Smith. He played the circuit that included dance halls in Texas, Arkansas, and Oklahoma before heading out to California, where his playing caught the attention of Ray Charles. Charles enlisted Newman as one of his sidemen, starting him off as a baritone sax man and evolving into the outfit's star tenor soloist. Incidentally, Charles was none too fond of the "Fathead" moniker and refused to use it, instead referring to Newman as "Brains."

Newman recorded with Clay and cut his first album as a leader, *Ray Charles Introduces Fathead Newman*, in 1959. His R&B-imbued style of jazz earned him a solid, hard-blowing reputation, and he went on to head his own bands, first in Dallas and then in New York.

Newman led his own combos and gigged with some high-profile artists—including Aretha Franklin, Herbie Mann, and Cornell Dupree—throughout the sixties and seventies, exhibiting a more pop-oriented side. Throughout the 1980s he returned to his more bop-oriented roots and recorded for the Muse label in addition to hitting the road on a regular basis. Newman picked up a Grammy Award nomination in 1990 for his collaboration with Dr. John and Art Blakely on *Bluesiana Triangle*.

Fathead collaborated with his former musical cohort on James Clay's 1990 albums, and today he continues to tour; he even appeared in the Robert Altman film *Kansas City*, playing the role of his mentor and former employer, Buster Smith.

Two of the musicians Newman jammed with in high school also went on to make dramatic musical waves after graduation; both Bobby Bradford and Cedar Wilson performed with the sax star early on. Bradford, who was born in Mississippi on July 19, 1934, but was raised in Dallas, first heard Ornette Coleman play in Fort Worth in 1953 and then went on to play with the stellar sax man in Los Angeles. After working with Coleman and then with John Carter in the New Art Jazz Ensemble, Bradford became a teacher and has continued to teach part-time, heading classes from elementary school to the college level.

His union with Carter continued until the clarinet player's death, and Bradford continues his melodic tradition to this day, leading a quintet known as The Mo'tet and performing as a guest artist with other jazz groups.

Perhaps the most underrated composer of the bop era is Newman and Bradford's high school jam partner Cedar Walton, a funk-flavored pianist who was born on January 17, 1934, in Dallas. His mother was his first piano teacher, and Walton mastered the art and also picked up the clarinet. He enrolled in the University of Denver in 1951 and majored in music then headed to New York to put his degree to work. The Army changed Walton's game plan, and after he was drafted he found himself in Germany, where he played with Leo Wright, a fellow Texan who was proficient on the sax and went on to carve his own place in the jazz world.

Walton moved back to New York after his discharge, playing in a number of small, renowned groups from 1958 until 1961 and then joining Art Blakely's Jazz Messengers, which at that time also included Freddie Hubbard and Wayne Shorter. Walton was a funky soloist who contributed a number of tunes to Blakely's repertoire before leaving the band in 1964 to work with Abbey Lincoln. He then recorded and performed with a number of high-profile artists of the era in addition to forming his own bop quartet, called Eastern Rebellion.

Walton found his most prolific moment in the eighties, when he recorded nearly a dozen albums. He has continued leading his own bands since that time, as well as working with a number of artists and recording for various labels.

The artists who came of age in the forties and fifties ushered in a new era of jazz that included bebop, hard bop, free jazz, and cool jazz. All paths eventually led to a blending of sounds that included rock and funk, which became known as fusion or electric jazz. Acid jazz later combined elements of jazz with soul, funk, and hip-hop, while the contemporary jazz scene saw the explosion of "lite jazz"—music that doesn't swing nearly as hard as its ancestors did, but instead provides a gentle instrumental that is easy on the ears and too delicate for many purists.

Texas has continued making its contributions to the musical mélange, with artists like electric jazz keyboardist Joe Sample and tenor sax man Marchel Ivery, both of whom were involved in the jazz resurgence of the fifties and sixties but found surer footing in the post-seventies era.

Recommended Listening:

Garland of Red – Red Garland (Original Jazz Classics)
The Jimmy Giuffre 3 – Jimmy Giuffre (Atlantic)
Herb Ellis Meets Jimmy Giuffre – (Verve)
Texas Swings – Herb Ellis (Justice)
Right on My Way Home – Bob Dorough (Blue Note)
Firebirds – Prince Lasha Quintet (Contemporary)
Cookin' at the Continental – James Clay (Antilles)
It's Mister Fathead – David Newman (32 Jazz)
One Night Stand – Bobby Bradford (SoulNote)
Among Friends – Cedar Walton (Evidence)

Chapter Nine

Ethnic Accents

The rich cultural diversity of Texas provided the ideal melting pot in which to blend and explore new sounds. The influence of the different cultures that were settling in Texas in the 1800s was evidenced in many ways, from the food they ate to the faiths they practiced. It is, however, in the music that the collision of these diverse cultures formed their most fascinating alliance.

Unlike many other flavors of music, such as blues, jazz, and country, the ethnic sounds cultivated in Texas didn't immediately find the breakout stars who served as musical prophets for a genre. Although the lyrical foundation was laid early on, much of the ethnic music in Texas remained something of a well-kept secret to those outside the individual communities. Ethnic sounds were shared between cultures but didn't reach the popular music front nearly as early as many other genres; local dance halls provided outlets for regionally prominent bands, but few became household names outside of their community.

The door for polka music first opened in the early 1800s, when Czech, Polish, and German immigrants moved to the promised land of central Texas. All three of these cultures were passionate about their music; the early days of this sound of Texas music typically included gatherings in which dancing and singing songs of the homeland were the main event. Eventually these casual gatherings evolved into formal singing societies, which began showing up in Texas as early as 1847 in communities such as San Antonio and New Braunfels.

Many of the Czech and German settlers who came to Texas in the 1800s were drawn there by the opportunities afforded by the trade generated along the railroads from central Texas to Mexico. Scores of Germans headed to the Lone Star State beginning around 1822, creating strong German communities such as Boerne, New Braunfels, and Fredericksburg. Fifty years later, the German presence in Texas was as great as the Spanish influence.

It wasn't surprising, then, that the two cultures would cross musical paths. The European immigrants had brought with them not just the music but the instruments of their homeland—high quality reed instruments, violins, cellos, and pianos, which would go on to help create the state's first symphonies. For the working class Germans, though, the instruments of choice were harmonicas and accordions, played with a brass band backing and churning out the polka party music they had grown up listening to.

The most recognized and most enduring band to develop out of the German presence was the Boerne Village Band, which was formed in Boerne in 1860 by Karl Dienger. Dienger, who had organized a singing club in Boerne, developed the band as an instrumental complement to the choral group.

Dienger headed both the singing and the instrumental groups until 1885, eventually handing the reins over to Ottmar von Behr, whose children played in the group and went on to provide four generations of musicians for the Village Band, including three generations of directors.

Regardless of what societal changes occurred or how much turmoil the country faced, the Boerne Village Band stayed active, playing at events in and around Boerne and keeping its traditional German music alive. Playing slowed during the world wars, but the band always reassembled and resumed playing.

News of the Boerne Village Band has extended far past state lines during its 140 years; in 1988 the Federal Republic of Germany recognized it for the contributions it has made to preserving the German heritage in Texas. In 1990, in honor of the band's 130th anniversary, German composer Peter Fihn dedicated his march "Grusse an Texas" ("Greetings to Texas") to the Village Band.

Today the band continues to be a fixture at German festivals, consistently serving up a reminder of traditional German polkas and culture. It is acclaimed as "the oldest continuously organized German band in the world" that doesn't exist in Germany, and it shows no signs of stopping.

The growth spurt of the Czech population in early Texas came along later than the Germans, with Czechs existing only in small isolated groups until the mid-1800s. But when an immigrant named Arnost Berggman wrote home, speaking of the glories of life in Texas and encouraging other Slavics to join him, they took it to heart. Between 1852 and 1900 the influx of Czech immigrants contributed healthily to Texas's population increase.

As musical as their German counterparts, the Czechs became the first to offer up touring bands who found regional fame. For the most part, the bands played on the weekends and didn't tour. Regardless of their talent, the music was usually just a hobby and did little to generate an income. The popular entertainment of the era came through house dances, where twenty or thirty people might congregate to hear live music and dance away the cares of the day. In many cases bands might play as many as five times a week, loading their instruments into wagons or horse-drawn buggies and going where the crowds were. Still, few saw it as a profession and did little in terms of seeking recognition outside of their own community.

The appeal of the music is obvious; for these hard-working-class immigrants, life offered little in the way of reward beyond the weekend blowout. The polkas and waltzes they smuggled into Texas expressed the common themes of life, love, work, and death and provided an upbeat, universal outlet for expressing their dreams and disappointments. These weren't cry-in-your beer songs but instead provided an exuberant soundtrack to the everyday struggles of life in rural Texas communities.

One of the first Czech bands to rise to regional prominence was the Baca Band, which was formed in 1882 by Frank Baca. Like many bands of the time, the Baca Band was comprised of family members, which wasn't surprising given the close-knit family values of the Czechs. Baca's thirteen children all played in his band at one time or another, and the instrumentation was typical of the time—brass instruments blended with the accordion, with the occasional stringed thing, such as a dulcimer, thrown in.

The Baca Band became the first polka band in Texas to make records, with their first recordings dating back to around 1929 and 1930 on the Brunswick and Vocalion labels. They later recorded for Columbia and O'Keh, but the group split in the thirties to form separate ensembles: Baca's New Deal, the Ray Baca Orchestra, and the John Baca Band.

Many of the traditional bands, the Baca ensemble included, stuck closely to the rigid format of the European music. Sometimes sounding more like a marching band than a dance band, the polka players didn't truly learn how to swing until Joe Patek arrived on the scene.

Patek, who was born September 14, 1907, began heading his Shiner-based orchestra in 1940. A man who would have made an excellent rock 'n' roll sax man in another place and time, Patek breathed new fire into the sound and made the music swing. He had inherited the band from his father, John Patek Sr., who built the band from the ground up in 1920 and

Baca's Orchestra

of Fayetteville, Texas

Will Be On the Air at Houston

STATION KPRC

Wednesday, May 22nd

Playing Old-Time Music---3:~~00~~15 to 3:30 P. M.

TELL - YOUR - FRIENDS!

The Baca Band of Fayetteville became the first polka band in Texas to record albums, with releases dating back to 1929. The original group was formed in 1882 by Frank Baca and later split to form a number of ensembles, including Baca's New Deal and the Ray Baca Orchestra. *Photo courtesy of Julius Tupa/Texas Polka News*

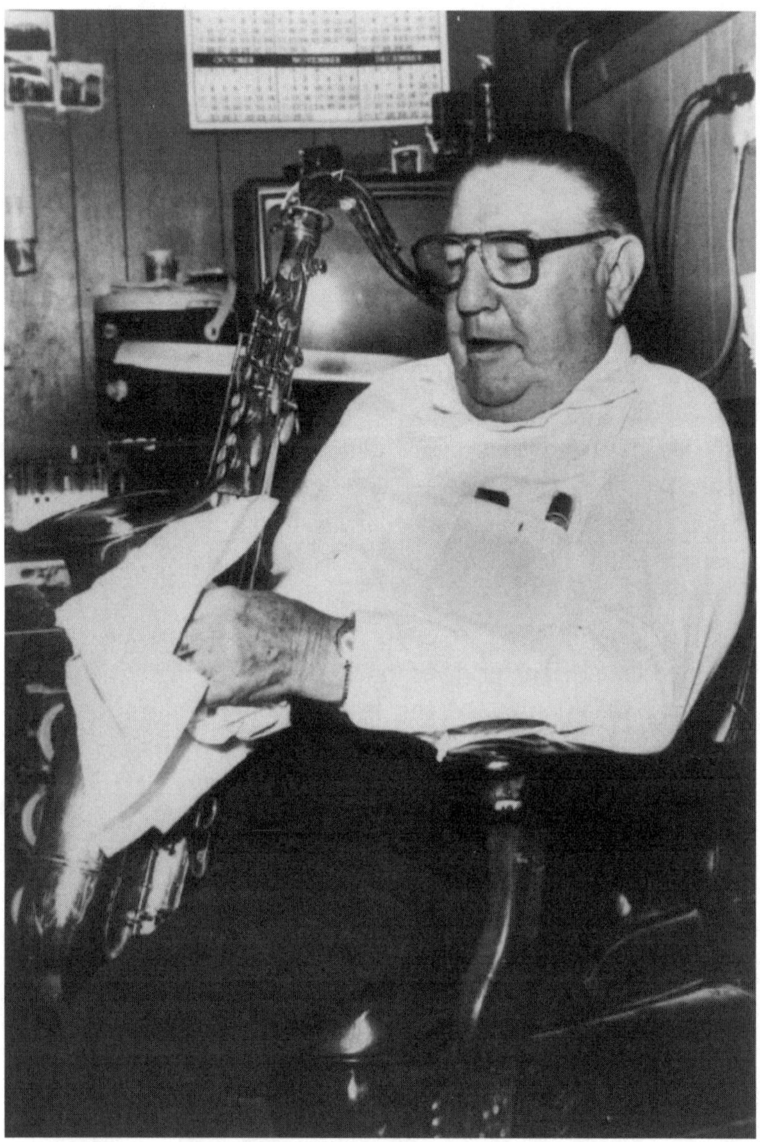

Joe Patek of Shiner, Texas, breathed new life into the polka sound when he took over his father's band in the early forties and subsequently found success with the anthemic "Shiner Song." *Photo courtesy Julius Tupa/Texas Polka News*

ran it for two decades. The band began recording for Decca in 1937, but it was under the younger Patek's direction that the band truly found a following.

Joe Patek's "Shiner Song" became something of an anthem for the outfit and helped propel them to regional success. Like most polka musicians, Patek did his music on the side, as something of a hobby; for his "real" job he ran a meat market and made sausage. However, he recorded a number of songs in the forties, many on the Rosenburg-based FBC label (which stood for Fort Bend County). He continued leading the band until 1986 and died on October 24, 1987.

The Texas environs had a definite effect on Czech polka music; the Texas accent could best be found in the hands of Adolph Hofner, who poured Czech tradition through a filter of western swing and became one of the best-known crossover artists.

Often categorized as a country artist, Hofner successfully combined his obvious pride of his Czech culture with the western swing that dominated the sound during the thirties. He proved to be equally as skilled at ripping out a sizzling swing number as he was at crooning a traditional Czech chestnut, and his innovation helped redirect the sound. From the day of his birth, on June 8, 1916, Hofner grew up listening to the polkas and waltzes of his German and Czech parents. His family moved from rural Moulton to San Antonio in 1928, and by then Hofner already had aspirations of becoming a vocalist. Forming a trio with his younger brother, steel guitar player Emil, Hofner sang and played guitar, eventually landing in Jimmy Revard's Oklahoma Playboys and recording with them. When he recorded the single "Makes No Difference Now" with Tom Dickey's Showboys, his vocals earned enough attention to allow Hofner to strike out on his own, and he never looked back.

Adolph Hofner and His Texans was formed in 1939, but the name later was changed to the San Antonians when the group landed record deals with O'Keh and Columbia. Moving from their native Texas to California, the San Antonians spent three years playing and recording on the West Coast and enjoyed hits with songs like "Maria Elena" and "Alamo Rag" in the early forties. However, it was the "Cotton-Eyed Joe" that was considered Hofner's trademark. It was a song that Hofner once said had been taught to him by a fiddle player during a break. Someone had requested the song, but Hofner wasn't familiar with it, so during the band's break his fiddler gave him a crash course on the song. Hofner might not have known it at the beginning of the night, but he quickly made the old folk tune his own, and his 1941 recording of the song is considered by many historians the definitive version.

He continued playing during World War II but ceased to use his given name when Adolph Hitler came into power. Choosing instead to go by "Dub" or "Dolph," Hofner didn't use his true first name again until after the war had ended.

The band took on yet another name in 1949 when Pearl Beer became the group's sponsor. Adolph Hofner and the Pearl Wranglers became the group's radio handle, while on the record they remained the San Antonians. They continued playing even after the popularity of the western swing movement lapsed, and Hofner went back to playing many of the original Czech songs he had cut his teeth on.

Hofner continued plumbing his rich Czech roots for musical inspiration throughout the fifties and sixties. They changed record labels and personnel through the years, but his devotion to Bohemian and German music was firmly entrenched, and he continued to play regularly in and around the San Antonio area through the 1980s. He was inducted into the Texas Western Swing Hall of Fame in 1990 but was permanently sidelined by a stroke in 1993. He died June 2, 2000, at his home in San Antonio.

The legendary Adolph Hofner and the Pearl Wranglers bridged the gap between western swing and Czech music, becoming a true crossover act and finding fans both in the country-western and the polka community. *Photo courtesy Julius Tupa/Texas Polka News*

Hofner's influence was felt on both sides of the western swing/Czech music coin; he was known both as "The King of South Texas Swing" and "The Prince of Polka." Widely accepted for his western swing tendencies, Hofner lured some country music listeners into enjoying the unfamiliar waters of polka music. Following his lead, many Tex-Czech bands allowed more of their country roots to show. Hofner was the first man ever to play a polka with a steel guitar and piano, and for the music-hungry youth listening to the radio, the impact was huge.

Polka bands began experimenting with the collision between country and Czech or German sounds. Artists like

Jimmy Brosch, whose father, Henry, developed regional fame with his own orchestra, added a fiddle to the mix and created Jimmy Brosch & His Happy Country Boys. The cross-pollination between polka and country music was in full force in the forties and fifties, and it influenced a new generation of performers.

Among them was Alfred Vrazel, a bandleader who was raised near Cameron and bought his first accordion at the age of ten. When his brother, Anton, also picked up the piano accordion, Alfred switched to the tenor and alto saxes and guitar.

The brothers began playing, along with three cousins, in 1953, and Vrazel's Polka Band got its own radio program within two years. They began recording in 1959, putting their own Texas country spin on the traditional Czech sound. Using bass guitar instead of tuba but still maintaining the integrity of the sound, Vrazel's ensemble can share some of the credit (or blame, depending upon how much of a purist you are) for moving Czech music to a more modern fold. The band, now in its forty-eighth year, continues playing.

The Czech and German music influences were largely felt in their own communities, keeping it somewhat quarantined from the rest of the evolving Texas musical landscape. While blues and jazz grew out of ragtime and cowboy songs started spinning off into country and western genres, the polka music of the European immigrants kept to itself, completely able to keep the scene alive within its own demographics. However, it couldn't help but influence Tejano music and deserves much of the credit for the evolution of the conjunto sound.

As the European immigrants made their way to Texas, their accordions caught the attention of working-class Mexican musicians. A number of string bands already populated the border towns, but the accordion brought some new advantages to Mexican musicians: It was inexpensive, versatile, and fairly easy to learn.

The Germans taught the Texas Mexicans not only how to play the accordion, but how to play the polka. Along the border, Mexican string bands already were popular, but the accordion gave the sound an energetic injection. The accordion became the instrument of choice for social events, and by the end of the nineteenth century, these working class musicians had added the *tambora de rancho*, a homemade goatskin drum, and the *bajo sexto*, a twelve-string guitar, to the mix. This musical experimentation created the forerunner of the modern conjunto lineup. After teaching them the accordion, the Germans began hiring Tejano musicians to play for German celebrations, a testament to the musical exchange that was taking place in the 1800s.

Mariachi music already had become firmly entrenched in the Mexican culture, emerging in the late 1700s in small Mexican border towns. Early mariachi groups consisted of the harp, violin, and the vihuela, a small guitar with a rounded back. But by the late 1800s, the instrumentals were complemented by the addition of vocals, and the harp was replaced by the much-more-portable six-string bass. While the Tejano musicians were getting a healthy dose of European music from the Germans and Czechs, their south-of-the-border counterparts were getting a similar education from the ruling of Maximilian and his French army, which occupied Mexico City. There, Mexicans began learning French-European music, including the polka, schottische, and waltz, something they would eventually bring with them when they crossed the border into Texas.

As the Mexicans living in south and central parts of Texas began absorbing the European musical influences, they gave birth to conjunto music. Just south of the border, in northern Mexico, it was being played in much the same way and referred to as nortena music (music of the north). Although rooted in many of the same traditions, the music evolving north and south of the border each had their own distinct sonic characteristics. While norteno music followed a simple, story-based format, conjunto music focused more on the music than the lyrics. More colorful and diverse than its norteno counterpart, conjunto grew to be more flavorful, infused with the pop music of its time and drawing from a broader range of influences.

The music's popularity was well established by the 1920s, but it was the artistry of Narciso Martínez that gave the music a commercial jump-start and made it more accessible.

Martínez, who was born in 1911 to migrant farm laborers in Reynosa, Tamaulipas, arguably has influenced every Tejano musician ever to pick up an accordion. His parents moved to Texas while Martínez still was an infant, and his childhood was spent listening to the musicians playing in the south Texas Valley. He picked up the accordion at the age of seventeen and began playing at dances, where he met local Czech and German musicians. Fascinated by their accordion techniques and musical traditions, he began implementing their sounds into his music.

The same year that Martínez began trying his hand at the accordion, conjunto music took a huge step forward when Bruno "El Azote" Villarreal became the first artist to record an album in the genre. Record labels were already scouring Texas for blues and jazz artists, and some, including Decca and Bluebird, turned their attention to the Mexican American market as well.

Martníez wouldn't get his taste of the recording studio until 1935, but by that time he had refined his sound on the two-row button accordion and had added a *bajo sexto* (Mexican twelve-string bass) to his act, which allowed him to concentrate on the melody and let the bajo sexto worry about the bass line.

With the pair's first recording, a polka called "La Chincharronera," Martínez found a hit. His swift musical attack on the accordion earned him the nickname "El Huracán del

Narciso Martínez (El Huracán del Valle), has influenced virtually every Tejano artist ever to pick up an accordian. Martínez enjoyed success from the forties until his death in 1992. *Photo by Chris Strachwitz. From the film* Chulas Fronteras *by Brazos Films*

Valle" ("The Hurricane of the Valley") and he enjoyed a string of hits, including "Los Coyotes" and "La Parrita." His busy recording career was interrupted by World War II, but in 1946 he began recording with Ideal, the country's first Tejano label. He became one of the most in-demand Tejano artists of the day, providing musical backing for most of the vocalists on Ideal's roster, including the hot singing sister duo Carmen y Laura.

Despite Martínez's escalating popularity, financial hardships remained a reality. His audience consisted of mostly poor Mexican Americans, most of whom couldn't afford to buy his albums, and the record companies of the day paid artists a flat fee for recording, with no royalties from sales.

By the end of the forties, record labels began turning their interest to other styles of music, and Martínez slipped out of the public eye until the mid-fifties, when he became Ideal's in-house accordion player. Appearing on albums by such popular acts as Beto Villa and Lydia Mendoza, his popularity experienced a revival and he recorded again, teaming up with Villa to record a pair of polkas and a couple of waltz numbers.

Another industry slow-down found Martínez looking for work in the sixties, which led him to field work in Florida before he returned to his native state. In Brownsville, he served as caretaker of the zoo but began touring the dancehall circuit, something that took him throughout the Southwest and found him a following beyond Texas, stretching as far north as Chicago. His popularity was furthered in 1976 when he was featured in the documentary *Chulas Fronteras*, a film that rightfully credited Martníez for his pioneering role in the development of Tejano music.

Martínez retired from the zoo in 1977 but continued performing, mostly in Texas dancehalls and at festivals, where he enjoyed an ever-blossoming audience of Tejano music enthusiasts. He became one of the first inductees into the Conjunto Music Hall of Fame in 1982 and the following year received the National Heritage Fellowship Award from the National Endowment for the Arts.

When Arhoolie Records began releasing some of Martínez's old recordings on their label, the accordionist's work found renewed interest and even picked up a Grammy Awared nomination for a compilation of his hits, *Narciso Martinez: El Huracan del Valle*, re-released in 1989.

Martínez died of leukemia on June 5, 1992, in San Benito, Texas. The next year the Tejano Conjunto Hall of Fame renamed the award given to inductees the Narciso Martníez Award.

Narciso Martínez is largely recognized as the father of conjunto music, and if that's true, then Santiago Jiménez is nothing less than its great uncle. Martínez and Jiménez began recording within a year of one another, and both made a dramatic and lasting impact on the music. Where Martínez was recognized for his fast-paced style, Jiménez offered a more fluid style and emphasized the bass chords on his two-row button accordion. He was a simpler player but just as much of a trailblazer as his more flowery contemporary.

Don Santiago Jiménez was born in San Antonio on April 25, 1913, and grew up listening to the accordion played by his father, Patricio, who was fond of German polkas and waltzes. He blended them with the music of his Mexican heritage, and by the time Jiménez was eight years old, his father already had taught him how to play the accordion. The elder Jiménez toted his young son along to the dances where he performed, and when Santiago was twenty he was playing music live on KEDA radio station.

Santiago Jiménez was a musical trailblazer who blended German polkas and waltzes with the music of Mexican heritage. *Photo by Chris Strachwitz. From the film* Chulas Fronteras *by Brazos Films*

In 1936, one year after Martínez recorded his successful debut, Jiménez released his first record on the Decca label, "Dices Pescao" backed with "Dispensa el Arrempujon." The record was warmly received, and his polkas, which were infused with both the spirit of the Mexican rancheras and the German music he grew up listening to, became regional hits. He was a popular radio performer through the late thirties, working as a janitor during the day to support a growing family and playing by night.

With the record industry slowdown that accompanied the Second World War, Jiménez moved to smaller labels and kept his career alive. He had a weekly gig at the Perales Night Club in San Antonio, a twelve-year run that began in 1940. It was also during that time that he recorded his most successful songs, the polkas "La Piedrera" and "Viva Seguin." What was less visible at the time were the contributions he was making to music in a different way; he and his wife, Virginia, had eight children—six sons and two daughters. Of those children, two sons—Flaco and Santiago Jiménez Jr.—would grow up to carry on and extend the conjunto music tradition.

One of the unmistakable contributions Jiménez made to the sound was the addition of a *tololoche*, or upright bass, to the lineup. Following Jiménez's lead, the contrabass became a standard feature of ensembles in the forties and then was replaced by the electric bass in the fifties.

The elder Jiménez quit playing in 1952, and in the late sixties he moved to Dallas, where he worked as a janitor at a seminary. Like Martínez, he was featured in the landmark 1977 documentary film *Chulas Fronteras*, which helped redirect attention to his music. He moved back to San Antonio and began playing music again, sometimes recording with his son Flaco.

Jiménez played steadily after his return to his hometown and was among the first group of inductees into the Tejano

Conjunto Hall of Fame in 1982. He died in December 1984 in San Antonio, but his work continues to live on. In 1986 Flaco won a Grammy Award in the category of Best Mexican American Performance for his recording of Santiago's song, "Ay Te Dejo San Antonio." Four years later the Texas Tornados scored the same award for their cover of "Soy de San Luis."

In the 1940s the paths of conjunto music took some bold new turns. Orchestras, patterned after the popular swing music, created Tejano-flavored big band sounds. Mariachi music, which had become the national popular music of Mexico, began to find popularity in Texas, thanks to the steady stream of immigrants arriving from central Mexico.

Pioneering conjunto players had begun adding lyrics to a previously instrumental form of music, and by the early 1950s, female duets were extremely popular in the Tejano music scene. Although often overlooked, historically, female singers played an important role in the development of Tex-Mex music.

Among the best known of the Tejana singers was Lydia Mendoza, who was born into a musical family in Houston on May 13, 1916. She was just twelve years old when she made her first record, launching a career that spanned four decades and earned her the unofficial title "la alondra de la frontera," or "the lark of the border."

Her earliest work was as a member of El Cuarteto Carta Blanca (the group was named after Carta Blanca beer by her father), a family musical group managed by her mother, Leonora Mendoza. When they learned that O'Keh Records was holding recording sessions in San Antonio, the family quartet signed up and recorded ten songs. It wasn't until 1934, however, that things began to take off for the young songstress, who also played the twelve-string guitar, mandolin, violin, and two-string guitar. She won a radio contest sponsored by Pearl beer and, as the first prize, received a recording contract with Bluebird Records. It was that recording session that spawned her most famous song, "Mal Hombre," which translates to "Cold-hearted Man."

Building on the success of "Mal Hombre," Mendoza went on tour and then enjoyed hits with songs such as "Amore De Madre" and "Celosa." Manuel J. Cortez, owner of KCOR radio in San Antonio, gave her a weekly spot on his station, and when Antonio Montes stepped in to manage Cuarteto Carta Blanca in 1936, the family saw its career begin to accelerate.

For six years the singing Mendoza family enjoyed success as a touring outfit, although their performances were far from the glamorous life. With a vaudeville-style act, they toured the circuit of migrant worker farms, taking entertainment to the dismal lives of immigrant workers. With the beginning of World War II, the touring came to a halt. Tire shortages and gasoline rationing made touring too costly, so the family slid out of the public eye for about five years.

Her younger sisters, Juanita and Maria, began singing together at San Antonio's Club Bohemia during these lean times, accompanied on guitar by their mother, who also served as their manager. The duo became known as Las Hermanas Mendoza and continued performing together after the war, finding more success as a duo than the family had enjoyed as Cuarteto Carta Blanca.

Las Hermanas Mendoza went on to become an important group in the popularization of Tejano music, gaining a faithful following with their beautiful harmonies on traditional Mexican songs. Older sister Lydia sometimes accompanied them on guitar in the recording studio, although she rarely performed on stage with Juanita and Maria. When Maria married in 1951 and then their mother died in 1952, the duo essentially broke up, although they did occasionally record together in years after that.

Lydia Mendoza, meanwhile, continued to play as a solo artist and enjoyed a long and notable career. Her voice carried the

Lydia Mendoza, "the lark of the border," enjoyed a forty-year career that began as part of a family act and led to recordings with Beto Villa and Narciso Martínez. *Photo courtesy of Arhoolie Productions*

emotions of faded dreams and disappointments, while her songs told the stories of the hard lives and hopes of everyman. She recorded for a nearly all the Mexican record labels of the time, including Falcon, Azteca, El Zarape, and Norteno. Over the years her catalog grew to comprise more than fifty albums, including work with such greats as Beto Villa and Narciso Martínez.

Rather than listening to the music of the era and gleaning her musical nuances from it, Mendoza found her inspiration in the music taught to her by her mother, which allowed her to develop her own distinctive, innovative style of playing. In 1971 Mexico asked Mendoza to be their representative in the

Smithsonian Festival of American Folk Life, and the National Endowment for the Arts recognized her with a National Heritage Fellowship Award in 1982. Six years later a stroke left her partially paralyzed and unable to perform. She was inducted into the Tejano Conjunto Hall of Fame in 1991 and still lives in her hometown of Houston.

While the Mendoza family was spreading its musical message, other female sister acts were finding popularity as well. Carmen y Laura became one of the popular acts of the late forties, consisting of Carmen Hernandez Marroquin and her sister, Laura Hernandez Cantu. Carmen's husband, Armando Marroquin, co-founded Ideal Records in 1946 with Paco Betancourt, and the company found an instant hit when Carmen y Laura recorded "Se Me Fue Mi Amor," or "My Love Went Away." The wartime song gave them immediate but lasting success, and the twosome toured well into the fifties and continued to record until the late seventies. Besides their vocal prowess, one of their most significant contributions was their ability to inject Tejano music with other popular sounds, such as blues and swing music.

Another significant Tejana singer was Chelo Silva, a Brownsville-born songstress who got her first singing gigs at school and church but landed a vocal role with the Tito Crixell Orchestra while she was still in high school. She was seventeen when she met Americo Paredes, a folklorist, poet, and composer who hosted a radio program that Silva appeared on. The two later married (and subsequently divorced), but in the meantime Silva met William A. Owens, who in 1941 was conducting a music-collecting project along the Texas-Mexico border and became the first to record her.

Her true recording debut, however, came in 1952. Silva, then thirty, had been singing radio jingles and performing at a Corpus Christi nightclub when she signed a contract with the Falcon label, which was based in McAllen. Almost immediately

Silva became the most popular female singer along the Texas-Mexico border, and her steamy presentation of boleros—a Mexican style of ballad—won her a huge following on both sides.

Silva recorded more than seventy titles for Falcon and by 1955 had a deal with Columbia Records, where she enjoyed a handful of hits and picked up the honorary title "La Reina de los Boleros," or "Queen of the Boleros." During the course of her career she performed with some of the biggest names in Tejano music, and her following was significant in both Texas and Mexico. She remained active most of her life, but the Queen of the Boleros turned in her crown on April 2, 1988, after losing a bout with cancer.

Throughout the forties the music industry as a whole was experiencing significant changes. Just as with blues and jazz, Tejano music slipped out of the spotlight as the country's attention turned to the Second World War. During that time, independent labels popped up, women took center stage, and a new generation of players prepared to take the stage. Leading that charge was Valerio Longoria, an accordion player who became one of the most prominent Tejano musicians during the forties and fifties.

One of the few conjunto players not to come directly out of Texas or Mexico, Longoria was born in Mississippi on March 13, 1924, but grew up in Harlingen. He was seven years old when he saw the legendary Narciso Martínez perform, and Longoria was so affected by the experience that he taught himself to play the accordion. By his teens he was playing weddings and parties, and while serving in Germany during World War II he played an accordion in local nightclubs.

Longoria settled in San Antonio in 1945, where he played in clubs and also began recording for the Corona label. He was among the first to back his vocals with his own accordion playing, but he made a number of other significant contributions as well. Longoria added the bolero to the accordion's repertoire, something that hadn't been attempted on that instrument before. He played standing up—unheard of before that time—and, perhaps his boldest move, Longoria introduced drums to the conjunto sound.

At the same time Longoria was making his alterations to the sound, musicians were being introduced to amplification, something that made a tremendous impact on every genre. By the time modern technology and Longoria had gotten their hands on conjunto, the traditional lineup was reborn to create a band that relied on four instruments: the accordion, *bajo sexto*, electric bass, and drums.

Valerio Longoria y Su Conjunto. Longoria began playing the accordion at the age of seven after witnessing a performance by Narciso Martínez. He was the first to introduce drums to the Tejano music lineup. *Photo by Chris Strachwitz. Photo courtesy of Arhoolie Productions.*

Longoria has remained active for more that sixty years, recording and performing in addition to teaching, repairing, and customizing the accordion. His career has yielded more than two hundred recordings, and he was among the first musicians inducted into the Tejano Conjunto Hall of Fame in 1982. In 1986 he was awarded the National Heritage Fellowship Award.

Like Longoria, Antonoio "Tony" de la Rosa emerged as a formidable accordionist during the forties. Just as Adolph Hofner had integrated western swing into his Czech heritage, de la Rosa fit the spirit of western swing into the framework of conjunto music. From the time of his birth in Sarita in 1931, de la Rosa—one of twelve children born to field workers—was raised on the border music of greats like Narciso Martínez and Santiago Jiménez. His mother taught him to play the harmonica by the time he was six years old, but as he listened to the radio, it was the accordion that caught his attention. De la Rosa managed to get his hands on an old accordion and by the time he was fourteen was picking out chords. When he was sixteen he had saved up enough money—seven dollars—shining shoes to buy an accordion of his own. Playing in the taverns and honky-tonk bars of nearby Kingsville, de la Rosa incorporated the western swing into his Mexican repertoire and even joined a country music band for a time.

A recording session in 1949 saw de la Rosa recording two polka tunes, "Sarita" and "Tres Rios," then launching a string of deals with small independent labels. It was while he was signed to the Ideal label that his music rose to prominence in the Tejano community, and by the mid-fifties de la Rosa's conjunto outfit was one of the most celebrated acts around.

It wasn't just de la Rosa's prowess with an accordion that made him such a lasting musical icon; it was his revolutionary approach to how the music was performed. He borrowed Longoria's innovation of adding drums to the traditional conjunto lineup then took it a step farther when he electrified

Tony de la Rosa was picking out chords of an old accordion by the age of fourteen, then rose to prominence as a major Tejano artist in his twenties. *Photo courtesy of Discos Ideal*

the bajo sexto. Now, with the instrumentation completely wired, de la Rosa was able to move into larger dancehalls, where he gained a powerful reputation for stirring up his own specialized brand of smoking, stomping conjunto music.

In addition to infusing the Tex-Mex music with western swing, de la Rosa also changed the dance movements of the time. His slower tempo polkas created a new style of dancing called tachuachito, one which saw couples moving together around the dance floor in slow, counterclockwise movements. His string of hits included "El Circo," "Los Frijoles Bailan," and "El Sube y Baja," but it is his rendition of the old Mexican polka "Atononilco" that has become something of a signature song for him.

Since he first ventured into the studio in 1949, de la Rosa has gone on to release more than seventy-five albums and numerous singles; he gained his rightful berth in the Tejano Conjunto Hall of Fame in 1982 and was granted a National Heritage Fellowship Award in 1998. Now semiretired, he still performs as his health permits.

As Narciso Martínez and Santiago Jiménez worked to make conjunto music more accessible, another school of Tejano musical thought was taking a different path. Following the big band style of the thirties, conjunto artists developed their own orchestras, catering to the upper class rather than the working class and appearing in ballrooms instead of barrooms. Although the string groups dated back to the early twentieth century, they didn't become a legitimate musical force until the end of the 1930s, when the outfits took a cue from jazz bands and added brass and reed instruments to their lineups.

One of the early orchestras that had found success in Mexico was a band led by Alberto Villa Sr., but it was his son, Beto, who became one of the most readily recognized Tejano bandleaders of the era.

Villa, who was born in Falfurrias, Texas, on October 26, 1915, enjoyed many economic advantages that his fellow musicians didn't. His father was a successful tailor in addition to being a musical leader, and he encouraged his son to take up an instrument as well. By the age of seventeen, the younger Villa had learned to play the sax, and his original band, Sonny Boy, played big band music for area dances and school functions.

Villa continued pursuing music after leaving high school but then decided to give up that career and become a businessman. He opened a meat market and worked as a butcher, but when World War II called him into action, Villa found himself back in a band, this time playing for enlisted men.

The experience changed his musical style, and he experimented with the collision of Mexican and American sounds in a

Beto Villa was an innovative bandleader who put Tejano music into a big band structure.
Photo courtesy of Chris Strachwitz/ Arhoolie Records

big band setting. After his discharge from the Navy, he returned to Falfurrias and opened a couple of dance halls, forsaking the butcher business for the music market.

At the time, the hot-selling music was the European-influenced polka with the Tejano flair. Artists like Narciso Martínez and Santiago Jiménez were dominating the sound, and labels were reticent to gamble on Villa's marriage of big band and Tejano music. He finally got his chance when Ideal records gave him the nod in 1946, and he found success right out of the box with the release of two songs, one a polka and the other a waltz. When he teamed up with Martínez for his next round in the studio, the bandleader found his first hit, "Rosita," and cultivated enough of a following to begin touring throughout Texas and the rest of the country.

Villa paved the way for other Tejano big bands, or orquesta Tejanas, to follow. He remained at the top of the heap for more than a decade, recording with Martínez, Carmen y Laura, and Lydia Mendoza, and cutting in excess of a hundred albums.

The widespread success he enjoyed faltered in 1960, when Villa's health forced him to give up a rigorous touring schedule, but he continued performing and recording periodically. He died on November 1, 1986, in Corpus Christi.

Villa influenced a number of other orquesta Tejanas, and his ability to incorporate other popular sounds and styles into the musical mix raised the bar for other bandleaders. Among those he inspired was Isidro Lopez, who picked up Villa's baton and became one of the most recognizable players in the history of Tejano music orchestras.

Lopez was born on May 17, 1929, in Bishop, and like many of his contemporary musicians, grew up in a family of farm workers. In the fields he listened to Mexican folk music and country music and was fascinated by the sounds. His uncle taught him how to play the guitar by the time he was eleven, and while attending high school in Corpus Christi, he picked up the tenor sax and joined the high school band.

He studied business in college but also began playing with Tejano legends like Narciso Martínez and Tony de la Rosa before joining an orquesta Tejana that played throughout the Rio Grande Valley. He was sitting in with the Juan Colorado Orchestra for a 1954 recording session at Ideal records when the lead singer didn't show, and Lopez found himself behind the microphone, since he had written the song they were recording.

That incident made it abundantly clear that Lopez's many talents were not restricted to the guitar and saxophone. Within two years he had formed his own orchestra and combined the accordion-driven conjunto movement with Villa's big band approach. His innovation effectively changed the sound of Tejano music and opened doors for the contemporary sound that has since emerged. Lopez was a musical experimenter, recording with conjunto and mariachi groups and, as rock music surfaced in the fifties, incorporating some of those rhythms as well. During his three decades as a bandleader, Lopez's band served as a training ground for a number of up-and-coming talents and generated a number of hits. In 1983 Lopez was inducted into the Tejano Music Award's Hall of Fame.

Without the innovations of artists like Narciso Martínez, Santiago Jiménez, Beto Villa, and Isidro Lopez, Tejano music could not have made the leap from its traditional setting to the popular music arena. Changing styles of music were introduced into the Tejano sound, giving it a few runs at the music charts beginning in the fifties, with success stories like Ritchie Valens' "La Bamba." Arists like Flaco Jiménez and Freddy Fender

As members of Texas Tornados, Flaco Jimenez, Augie Meyers, Doug Sahm and Freddy Fender helped bring Tejano music into the mainstream. *Photo courtesy Denton Record-Chronicle.*

began spreading their musical gospel in the sixties, and both gained recognition as world-class musicians—not just as successful solo performers but as members of The Texas Tornados alongside ex-Sir Douglas Quintet co-founders Augie Meyers and Doug Sahm. Jiménez became one of the first musicians to play Tejano music to general audiences throughout the U.S. and Europe and continues enjoying an enthusiastic, diverse following.

Tejano music found mainstream success in the seventies, only to be pushed aside by disco and punk movements, experiencing a revival in the eighties that prepared it for the unprecedented Tejano business boom of the nineties, led by groups like Selena, La Mafia, and Emilio.

Despite its influence in Tejano music, the polka movement in Czech, German, and Polish circles has yet to break out of its homespun cocoon. Many old-time band leaders and observers of the market are concerned by the lack of the music's growth, making note that the exception seems to lie in the Denton band Brave Combo, a rock band that plays traditional polka music in a nontraditional style.

Although the Tex-Mex, Czech, and German influences gave Texas music its strongest ethnic accents, the underlying Cajun influence is small but significant. French and Spanish immigrants came to Texas via Louisiana, bringing with them a rich and spicy heritage that blended well in the working communities of Beaumont, Port Arthur, and Houston.

In Houston the Creole community settled in the city's Fifth Ward in the early twenties, creating a neighborhood called Frenchtown that covered four square blocks. The black French and Spanish immigrants settled there, and while it eventually was absorbed into the rest of the community, the influence of its culture was reflected in its contributions of zydeco music.

Although Louisiana remained the hotbed of zydeco activity, Texas produced its own share of musicians, most notably Harry Choates, a Louisiana-born Cajun who was born the day after Christmas in 1922. His mother moved to Port Arthur during the thirties, and he spent most of his childhood in bars rather than in the schoolroom. He learned to play the fiddle before he was a teen-ager and began playing for tips in area barbershops.

In addition to the fiddle, Choates was proficient on the accordion, guitar, and steel guitar. He reworked the Cajun waltz "Jolie Blone" into the song "Jole Blon" and scored a hit with it in 1946 on the Houston-based Gold Star label. The song became a favorite and was adopted by Aubrey "Moon" Mullican a year later, who found even greater success with it.

The hard-living Cajun never lost his childhood habit of hanging out in bars, something that would ultimately lead to his downfall. Despite the fact that he was a popular artist who recorded some two dozen songs for the Gold Star label, he couldn't replicate the success he had with "Jole Blon." In person, Choates was a charismatic performer who sang both in English and French and incorporated western swing, jazz, blues, and country into his musical Cajun stew.

For all his talent, Choates's lifestyle sometimes overshadowed his music. He often showed up for performances drunk and disheveled, and his habit of ignoring music contracts got him blacklisted from the musicians' union.

The story of Choates's death is as much the formula for a TV movie of the week as his raucous life; jailed for failing to pay child support in 1951, Choates spent three days behind bars in Austin—and not the kind of bars he was accustomed to. Some say that jailers killed him while trying to calm him down as he went through alcohol withdrawal; another story has him beating his head against the bars and slipping into a coma. Regardless of the actual events, he died in jail on July 17 at the age of just twenty-eight. His pauper's grave remained unmarked until

Accordion wizard Clifton Chenier moved to Port Arthur from Louisiana and took zydeco in new directions. *Photo by Edmund Shea Photo courtesy of Arhoolie Productions*

1980, when a Beaumont disc jockey named Gordon Baxter helped raise money to purchase a stone.

One of the greatest zydeco musicians ever to pick up an accordion didn't come from Texas, but he did claim the Lone Star State as his early stomping grounds. Accordion great Clifton Chenier and his brother, Cleveland, moved to Port Arthur in the late forties to form the Hot Sizzling Band and play along the Texas-Louisiana Gulf Coast into the fifties.

By the time he moved to Houston in the sixties, Chenier already had recorded for at least a half dozen labels and had toured nationally. He and Cleveland entered the Gold Star studio in 1965 and recorded "Zydeco Sont pas Sale," the song that would become his signature piece and launch a new era in zydeco music. He began recording for the Arhoolie label and found a large and receptive audience.

Chenier did for zydeco what Narciso Martínez did for conjunto; he preserved an ethnic musical tradition while at the same time taking it in new directions. He won a Grammy Award for his 1983 album *I'm Here,* and accompanied by his aptly named Red Hot Louisiana Band, he continued to perform and tour until his death in 1988.

Recommended Listening:

Texas-Czech, Bohemian & Moravian Bands: Historic Recordings 1929-1959 – Various artists (Arhoolie)

Texas Bohemia – Various artists (Klang)

Play Me a Polka: Tex-Czech Polkas – Various artists (Rounder)

South Texas Swing – Adolph Hofner and His Texans (Arhoolie)

Narciso Martínez – El Huracán del Valle – (Arhoolie)

Santiago Jiménez con Flaco Jiménez y Juan Viesca – Santiago Jiménez, Sr. and Flaco Jiménez (Arhoolie)

Los Primeros Duetos Femininas, 1930-1955 – Various artists (Arhoolie)

First Queen of Tejano Music – Lydia Mendoza (Arhoolie)

Caballo Viejo – Valerio Longoria (Arhoolie)

Es Mi Derecho – Tony de la Rosa (Rounder)

Beto Villa: Father of Orquesta Tejana – (Arhoolie)

Fiddle King of Cajun Swing – Harry Choates (Arhoolie)

Chapter Ten

Rockabilly and the Birth of Rock

Depending on your vantage point, rock music is something that either crept in through the back doors of western swing or burst forth out of the blues; in a sense, both schools of thought are accurate, but neither are entirely true. Western swing in the 1940s cleared the way for rockabilly, a hyperactive hybrid of hillbilly music and rock, which in turn primed the ears of teens for the advent of rock, which came close on the heels of rockabilly.

The blues, on the other hand, had been laying a foundation for rock since the days that Blind Lemon Jefferson performed on the streets of Deep Ellum, playing the rocking boogie rhythms that he sometimes referred to as "booger rooger." The Houston-born Thomas brothers, George and Hersal, certainly did their part for the party by introducing boogie-woogie music to the masses, and blues offered a powerful preview of what rock 'n' roll had to offer when T-Bone Walker wired, reinvented, and thoroughly modernized the sound. His work inspired a number of future rockers, most obviously Chuck Berry and Jimi Hendrix, and the rise of rhythm and blues bands in the fifties and sixties further pushed the music in the direction of rock.

But it was rockabilly, the rhythm that broke through the sound barrier in the early fifties, that forever blurred the lines between genres by throwing together country, rhythm and blues, and hillbilly sounds in one amped-up, high-octane musical package. Doing for music in the fifties what punk rock would two decades later, rockabilly gave longer legs to the careers of several notable Texans, including country boogie pianist Moon Mullican, who found the music a logical and enjoyable extension of the key-pounding barrelhouse style of western swing he'd built his career on during the thirties.

Although the music's roots extend all over the south, the seeds for rockabilly were first planted in Tennessee, not Texas. While shades of rockabilly can be seen in earlier recordings, it is the entrance of Elvis Presley into Sam Phillips' Memphis recording studio that is pinpointed as the birth of rockabilly. His 1954 recording of "That's All Right" jump-started a musical movement that previously only had been hinted at. From the day of that Sun Records release until about 1958, rockabilly became the manic soundtrack for an enthusiastic teen-age nation.

Characterized by twanging lead guitar and slapping string bass, rockabilly fell somewhere in between the music of Hank Williams and Bill Haley. Not surprisingly, many of its innovators moved into country music careers, but others just as easily made the transition into rock. Although rockabilly was dominated by the Sun Records roster of Presley, Jerry Lee Lewis, and Carl Perkins, Texas had no shortage of its own legends, the best and brightest of which came packaged in the short-lived but eternal career of Buddy Holly.

The Lubbock-born Holly made his entrance in this world on September 7, 1936, under the name Charles Hardin Holley. He got his first taste of success at the age of five, when he won five dollars singing in a local talent show. Holly discovered his musical mastery early on, picking up the piano, fiddle, and guitar all before the age of thirteen, and then formed a band with his schoolmate Bob Montgomery.

Their first musical experiments were in bluegrass, and within four years, the duo had picked up both a bass player named Larry Welborn and their own local radio show on Lubbock's KDAV. Although their repertoire was rich with country flavors, Holly was enticed by the new sounds being played on the radio, and the sounds of early rock began to infiltrate his music.

By the time a Nashville talent scout spotted him in 1955, Holly's potential was impossible to miss, and the agent pointed the Decca record label in his direction. His success, however, got off to a slow and shaky start; Holly cut some country singles in Nashville that went unpromoted, and the label refused to release one of his recordings, a number called "That'll Be the Day."

Back in Lubbock, Holly and drummer Jerry Allison performed at the city's youth center, opening for up-and-comers that included a young Elvis Presley. Presley's performance was the inspiration Holly needed to find his rockabilly soul, and he reworked some of his country songs into up-tempo rockabilly numbers. His band, The Crickets, became the first white group to utilize the R&B lineup of lead guitar, rhythm guitar, drums, and bass. When they reworked "That'll Be the Day" from a country tune to a high-spirited rock number, they found the first of a string of hits and carved out a lasting niche in music history.

Holly climbed to number three on the charts in 1957 with "Peggy Sue" and, for the next two years, released several songs that would go on to become rock classics. He left the Crickets in 1958, married, and moved to New York. Although his rockabilly roots still showed in his music, he had added new dimensions to the sound and, it should also be noted, was the first white musician to write the bulk of his own material.

The meteoric rise and bright future crashed to a halt early in 1959, when Holly signed on to perform as part of the Winter Dance Party tour. The tour, which also featured Dion and the Belmonts, Ritchie Valens, and J.P. Richardson, a Beaumont disc jockey who, billed as "The Big Bopper," was enjoying huge success with the song, "Chantilly Lace." An exhausted Holly chartered a plane for him and his band, which included Tommy Allsup on guitar and a relatively unknown bass player named Waylon Jennings, to fly from Clear Lake, Iowa, to the next stop on the tour. Richardson and Valens convinced Allsup and Jennings to surrender their seats and take the bus instead; the ill-fated plane of rising stars went down in a snowstorm shortly after midnight on February 3.

Holly's death seemingly had as much impact on the music as his life had; Don McLean penned the immortalizing tribute, "American Pie" and spoke of Holly's death as "the day the music died." Holly's success continued after his death, as he left behind enough unreleased material to fill a number of albums and collections. He continued scoring posthumous hits into the sixties, and his work continues influencing musicians today.

About the time rockabilly was invading the Memphis studios, it was taking center stage in Dallas as well. At the Big D Jamboree, a stronghold of live honky-tonk and western swing in the forties, rockabilly artists found a welcome audience for their new sounds. The country-based musical brew of rockabilly was frowned upon by many of the Jamboree's contemporaries, such as the Grand Ole Opry, but in Texas, fans were open to the new sounds that accompanied the changing times.

The Jamboree grew out of what originally was called the Texas State Barn Dance at Ed McLemore's Sportatorium in Dallas. The weekend shows began shortly after World War II ended and featured the hot hillbilly acts of the day. When

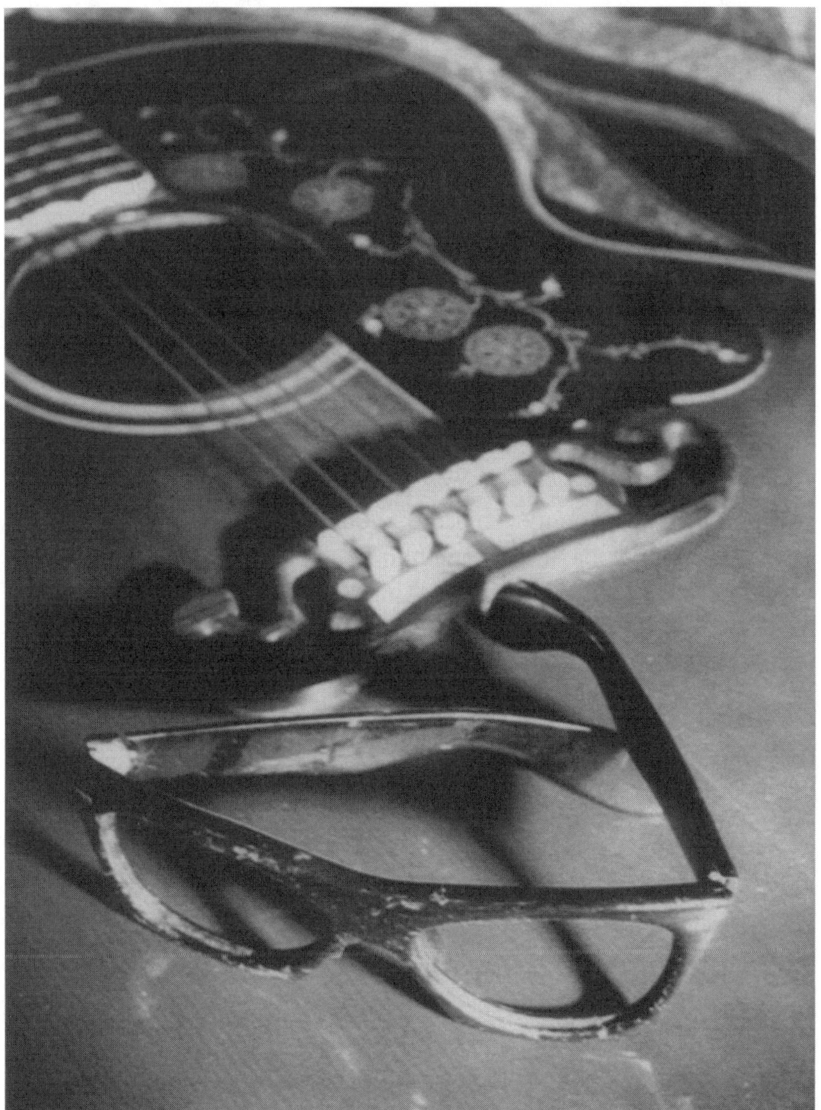

Singer Buddy Holly's black, plastic-framed glasses sit atop his Gibson J-200 acoustic guitar at the Dallas, Texas home of his widow, Maria Eleena Holly. Buddy Holly died in a plane crash in Clear Lake, Iowa on Feb. 3, 1959. *AP photo by Eric Gay/Courtesy of the Denton Record-Chronicle.*

rockabilly began to sneak into the musical consciousness of the masses, the Big D Jamboree was more than willing to give it a listen, even as other live music venues staunchly defended their ground against it.

Rockabilly became one of the first styles of music that was driven more by the radio than by live performances. As Elvis broke out of the traditional musical confines that divided country and R&B, young audiences became hungry for more. The result was packed houses at the Big D Jamboree, with faces in the crowd getting younger seemingly by the week. The Jamboree gained a reputation as a place where rock was welcome and rockabilly could peacefully co-exist with hillbilly music. Elvis played the Jamboree in the spring of 1955, and other stars to parade across the stage, sharing their talents, included Carl Perkins, Johnny Cash, Hank Williams, Gene Vincent, and a string of other legends-in-the-making.

The homegrown talent that performed at those weekly shows often rivaled the imported acts. Ronnie Dawson, Sid King and the Five Strings, and "Groovey" Joe Poovey all provided powerful representation of Lone Star prowess, although none enjoyed the kind of prominence found in their Memphis-based contemporaries.

Poovey wasted no time in starting his career, as if he knew at an early age that the clock was ticking for him. He was just twelve when he began playing the Big D Jamboree, initially with his band, The Hillbilly Boys. Born Arnold Joseph Poovey in Dallas in 1941, he recorded his first songs—a pair of obscure Christmas tunes—at the age of thirteen.

His country roots guided his music until 1955 when, still just fourteen years old, he opened for Elvis at the Jamboree. For a young boy full of talent and hormones, the equation was a no-brainer—the hip-shaking high-octane twang of rockabilly overshadowed any kind of reaction country music ever drew from the crowd—particularly the female portion of it—and

Poovey quickly dropped the western duds and discovered the hair grease.

Two years later Poovey had a small but growing catalog of songs he'd penned with wordsmith Jim Shell, and he began

Joe Poovey got his start performing at the Big D Jamboree at the age of 12. One year later he recorded a pair of Christmas tunes and, as a teen-ager, traded in his cowboy hat for hair grease and found a following with the rockabilly set. Here, he performs at the Cowtown Jamboree in Fort Worth. *Photo courtesy David Dennard*

recording for Dixie records. His first recording, "Move Around," showed the potential of the young performer, and when he followed it up with 1958's "Ten Long Fingers," it seemed fairly certain that he would find the kind of success being enjoyed by Carl Perkins or Gene Vincent. Success side-stepped him, but that didn't keep him off the stage or out of the studio. He worked throughout the Dallas and Fort Worth area both as a songwriter and performer, returning to his country music roots and writing songs that were recorded by artists like George Jones and Johnny Paycheck. By then the packed-house days of the Big D Jamboree were over, but Poovey stayed busy playing places like the Grapevine Opry and working as a disc jockey for country music stations in Dallas and Fort Worth.

In 1980, just when it appeared that Poovey had all but vanished, a small independent label in Sussex discovered and reissued "Ten Long Fingers," and Poovey became an "overnight" rockabilly hero. He toured England where he was treated like rock royalty and began recording overseas, finding a warm reception from small labels in Germany and Sweden.

Back in his hometown, Poovey remained a mostly buried treasure, working as a chauffer on the set of the hit television show *Dallas* and later working on *Walker, Texas Ranger*, where he sometimes appeared as an extra. He finally headed back into the studio in 1990, although it seemed few people noticed. Poovey returned to the studio again in 1997 to lay down some still-rockin' songs, prophetically naming the effort *Final Vinyl*. He celebrated the release of the three-song disc with a performance at the Dallas Bar of Soap club, but no one imagined it was one of the last times Poovey would ever appear behind a microphone.

It seemed, in fact, that all roads were pointing to a comeback for this overlooked legend. Dallas record producer David Dennard, who had almost single-handedly undertaken the task of archiving Dallas's lost music history with his "Legends of the

Big D Jamboree" series, compiled Poovey's first full-length recording, *Greatest Grooves*, for his Dragon Street Records label. Including everything from Poovey's 1954 Christmas recordings to his final nineties sessions, the disc provided two dozen musical snapshots of Poovey's varied career. Two days after its release, Poovey died of a heart attack at the age of fifty-seven.

Like Poovey, many of the stars of the Big D Jamboree enjoyed a brief fling with success, only to slip into obscurity. In the fifties Sid King and the Five Strings became one of the first acts to jump from western swing to rockabilly, and the group enjoyed a rapid rise that snagged a record deal with Columbia. The band was headed by Sid Erwin ("King" was apparently easier to rhyme than "Erwin"), a Denton native who was singing and playing guitar while he was still in high school. Erwin and his buddy Mel Robinson, who was proficient on the sax and steel guitar, played together as a duo before forming a band that included Sid's brother Billy Joe on guitar, David White on the drums, and Ken Massey on bass.

Under the name of the Western Melody Makers, the group played country music and western swing, picking up radio appearances as well as live shows. They signed with the newly formed Beaumont-based Starday label in 1954 and recorded a few songs that went nowhere.

As the more up-tempo rockabilly sound found its way into their music, the Western Melody Makers became Sid King and the Five Strings, and the group got its deal with Columbia early in 1956. One of the first songs they recorded was "Ooby Dooby," a song written by another young Texan named Roy Orbison. Orbison had made his own recording of the song at Jim Beck's Dallas studio, and Beck put it in the hands of a Columbia exec, who was impressed by the song but not the singer and passed Orbison's song onto Sid King's outfit. Orbison would, of course, recover from this slight and go on to record his own version of the song for Sun Records.

Sid King and the Five Strings became one of the first acts to jump from western swing to rockabilly in the fifties. The Denton group was one of the hottest tickets of the time, playing on bills with Johnny Horton and Elvis Presley. *Photo courtesy David Dennard*

With their high-energy rockabilly sound, Sid King and the Five Strings were simply one of the hottest tickets of their time, and they landed on bills with Elvis Presley and Johnny Horton. Popular at places like the Big D Jamboree and the Louisiana Hayride, the band's brand of rockabilly managed to draw crowds without scoring any hits on the charts. Widespread success seemed inevitable in 1956 but instead was short-lived, and the band couldn't quite break out beyond the Texas borders. By the time their contract with Columbia was up in 1957, it was agreed that it was time for them to call it quits.

King surfaced from time to time after that, doing some work in the early sixties with Pat Boone, only to disappear again and take up a career as a barber in Dallas. When the rockabilly resurgence hit in the early eighties, the band found a bit of a revival and even reunited in 1982 to record with the original lineup.

Of all the young performers to grow up on the stage of the Big D Jamboree, perhaps none enjoyed the kind of staying power found by Ronnie Dawson, known onstage as Ronnie Dee or The Blond Bomber. Dawson was born into the music—his father, Pinky, was a western swing bandleader. Born in Dallas's Oak Cliff neighborhood in 1939 and raised in Waxahachie, Dawson may have inherited the talent, but he earned his legendary status the old-fashioned way.

Dawson's father spotted his son's musical interest early on and taught him the basics on the guitar; that was all the younger performer needed. He started his first band, "Ronnie Dee and the D Men," and within two months was performing in a weekly talent contest at the Jamboree. After winning for ten consecutive weeks, Dawson had sufficiently caught the attention of Sportatorium owner Ed McLemore, who also happened to be managing rockabilly wild man Gene Vincent. McLemore liked what he heard and signed Dawson's band.

His first taste of success was practically instantaneous; his 1958 recording of "Action Packed" and "I Make the Love" became a regional hit, and he found himself touring with Gene Vincent and a posse of flash-in-the-pan musical acts. The music even piqued the interest of Dick Clark, who offered him a recording deal and a shot in the national spotlight with a coveted *American Bandstand* television appearance. Just as Dawson's career was poised to take off, though, it was grounded by the music industry's 1960 payola scandal. In the scandal, which resulted in hearings before the U.S. Congress, radio stations and disc jockeys—most notably Alan Freed and

Ronnie Dawson, the King of Texas Rockabilly! *Photo by Rex Fly. Photo courtesy of Crystal Clear Sound*

Ronnie Dawson—performing here at the Big D Jamboree under the moniker Ronnie Dee and the D Men, found regional success in 1958 and even landed on "American Bandstand." England's rockabilly revival in the eighties earned him superstar status across the ocean. *Photo courtesy David Dennard*

Dick Clark—were accused of taking payment for playing songs on the air. With ongoing legal battles at hand, Clark's attention turned away from nurturing artists on his Swan Records label, and Dawson found his career grinding to a halt.

Instead of following a career path to stardom, Dawson found himself as a sideman, playing with the Light Crust Doughboys and sitting in on drums for the hit single "Hey Paula." He kept busy in the sixties, touring with a Dallas-based band, The Levee Singers, and recording R&B music under the name of Commonwealth Jones for the Columbia label.

Dawson turned to his country roots in the seventies, forming the band Steel Rail, writing and performing commercial jingles, and occasionally playing private parties and corporate gigs to pay the bills. He was living the life of a working musician, content to stay outside of the spotlight as long as he could stay in the business. All that changed in 1986, when The Cramps covered Dawson's song, "Rockin' Bones," which he had released on his second recording under McLemore's tutelage.

Almost overnight, but thirty years in the making, Dawson's career enjoyed a superstar status in England. Barney Koumis, a British record collector, made the call that changed Dawson's life, telling Dawson that his songs were getting airplay and selling well in England, and Koumis was interested in any new material that Dawson might have. Dawson began recording and touring again, riding high on the rockabilly revival in England and breathing new life into his career in the Lone Star State as well. Since then, he has recorded no less than ten albums, and he continues maintaining a rigorous touring schedule on both sides of the ocean.

For the most part, the artists who found prominence in Texas during the rockabilly craze were just as quickly forgotten when the movement came to an abrupt halt. Sid King was joined by fellow rockabilly buddies like Ray Campi, Johnny Dollar, and Johnny Carroll as artists who showed incredible promise but never broke out past their rockabilly roots.

Rockabilly enjoyed a brief but brilliant flourish in music history, and despite the Memphis stranglehold on the sound, Texas—and Dallas, in particular—was one of the few areas that gave the music an opportunity to explore new territory in the late fifties. It provided a springboard for future rockers, not the least of whom was Roy Orbison. Despite the fact that he initially was passed over by Columbia Records, the West Texas native had no problem establishing himself as a true legend of the emerging rock scene.

Born in the small town of Vernon on April 23, 1936, and raised in Wink, Orbison found his passion for music as a small child. His father, Orbie Lee, taught him how to play the guitar when he was six years old, and within two years he was performing country music on local stages. He assembled his first band, the Wink Westerners, while he was still in high school.

Orbison's early musical endeavors were all of the country variety, but while still in high school he began exploring everything from hillbilly to big band swing to pop. Once he enrolled in Denton's North Texas State College, however, his musical direction would change dramatically. Orbison began writing and performing in the rockabilly style, drawing on his country roots to provide the proper twang for his rollicking compositions. The Wink Westerners were reborn from a country band into a rock outfit called the Teen Kings, which began playing on local television shows.

Pat Boone, a fellow student and musician at NTSU, provided a major influence for Orbison. Orbison first backed Boone in the recording studio, then recorded his own song "Ooby Dooby" on the tiny independent Je-Wel Records label. By that time Orbison had completed two years at NTSU but dropped out of college to concentrate on his music career full-time.

After "Ooby Dooby" was picked up by Columbia and recorded by Sid King and the Five Strings, Orbison took his own version of the song to a music store in Odessa, which was run by a man named Cecil "Pop" Hollifield. Looking for opinions and advice, Orbison played the disc for him, and Hollifield, who knew his way around the music industry, put in a call to Sun Records owner Sam Phillips and played the single for him over the phone.

Within days Phillips was inviting Orbison and the Teen Kings to his Memphis studios to record, and in March 1956 Orbison recorded his first song to hit the charts.

Roy Orbison, who hadn't yet discovered his trademark dark clothes and sunglasses, gleaned support and advice from Pat Boone at Denton's North Texas State University, then went on to find fame first in rockabilly and then as a rock balladeer. *Photo courtesy David Dennard*

Sun was the powerhouse label of the day, with a rockabilly artist roster that included Elvis Presley, Carl Perkins, and Jerry Lee Lewis. Orbison, however, didn't find the same kind of stardom as his label mates, and the contract with Sun was short-lived.

Although he set out to be a performer, it was his songwriting that found success first. The Everly Brothers recorded and charted with "Claudette," a song Orbison wrote for his wife in 1958. One year later Orbison signed on with Monument, another Nashville record label, and finally found the forum he needed to launch a string of hits, starting with 1960's "Only the Lonely."

By 1960 Orbison, like the rest of the country, had moved away from his rockabilly sound, and his style evolved from country rocker to rock balladeer, with emotional and melodramatic songs that provided a remarkable showcase for his three-octave range. From 1960 until 1964 he enjoyed a run on the charts that included "Blue Bayou," "Dream Baby," and the ever-popular "Pretty Woman." He headlined a tour in England in 1963, appearing on a bill that included a rising quartet called The Beatles.

On stage, his image matched his musical themes of loss and longing; with slicked back black hair, dark glasses, and black clothes, his voice managed to be vulnerable and powerful in the same breath. But while Orbison's career was beginning to soar, his personal life was about to nosedive into tragedy. In 1966 Claudette was killed in a motorcycle accident. Two years later he lost two of his three sons in a fire that destroyed his Nashville home. He ended the decade with a new marriage, which later yielded two more sons, but Orbison's career now had been stymied by the British invasion and the changing musical landscape.

It wasn't until the late seventies that audiences developed a new interest in Orbison's work, something that was led by a new generation of performers, such as Linda Ronstadt, Van Halen, and Emmylou Harris, who recorded his work. By 1987 Orbison was back in the spotlight: He was inducted into the Rock and Roll Hall of Fame and had teamed up with George Harrison, Bob Dylan, Tom Petty, and Electric Light Orchestra's Jeff Lynne to form The Traveling Wilburys.

Roy Orbison in his trademark look. *Courtesy of Denton Record-Chronicle.*

His final year was rich with possibility. A 1988 television documentary paid tribute to his contributions, featuring performances by Orbison as well as some of the many artists who had recorded his work, and the release of the recording *The Traveling Wilburys, Volume One* was both a critical and commercial success. On December 6, however, Orbison, who underwent open heart surgery in 1979, suffered a fatal heart attack at his mother's home in Hendersonville, Tennessee.

The most significant Texas contributions to rock music in its early years obviously were made by Buddy Holly and Roy Orbison, but they were by no means the only architects of the early rock scene. Although the history books tend to overlook his influence, only one artist enjoyed nearly as much time on the charts as Elvis Presley during the calm before the British storm, and that was NTSU student Pat Boone.

Boone, who was born in Florida in 1934, came with a nicely stocked family tree; he was a descendant of frontiersman Daniel Boone and, after high school, married Shirley Foley, whose father, Red, was a country music star. In the early fifties, Boone left David Lipscomb College in Nashville and relocated to Denton, where he began his studies, his family, and his career.

Pat Boone, seen here as a college student, singer, and student preacher during his days in Denton. *Photo courtesy Denton Record-Chronicle*

Studying speech and music, Boone began singing with the Aces of Collegeland, a Saturday night music revue that had been part of the school's tradition since 1927. Getting a spot in the show was "a big deal" at the time, and it gave Boone enough of a spotlight to get work on three different television programs at Fort Worth's WBAP TV. To help make ends meet, he worked as a student preacher at Slidell Church of Christ, working for whatever his youthful congregation tossed in the collection plate.

After winning a local talent show, Boone appeared on *The Ted Mack Amateur Hour* and also snagged a one-year deal to appear on *The Arthur Godfrey Show*. But it was his 1954 recording debut on Dot Records, "Two Hearts, Two Kisses," that shot him out of obscurity. The following year, his cover of "Ain't That A Shame," which Fats Domino had recorded, gave Boone his first number one hit.

Boone began leading a double life, continuing as a student in Denton and crossing the country to record and perform. At the time, R&B was a dominant musical force, and his whiter, politer versions of R&B hits were just the thing for listeners who found themselves uneasy with the rambunctious, rollicking direction the music was headed.

Boone's music was a reassuring, wholesome answer to Elvis' rockabilly, and the performer himself maintained that clean-cut image both on and off stage. Quickly abandoning the R&B cover song repertoire, Boone turned to ballads and found a ready audience of teenagers, but their parents often found his music just as easy to embrace. From 1956 to 1963, the crooning Boone hit the charts no less than fifty-four times, scoring number one hits like "April Love" and "Love Letters in the Sand."

He finished his tenure at North Texas in 1956 and signed a movie deal with 20th Century Fox, which led to starring roles in more than a dozen films. He began hosting *The Pat Boone Chevy Showroom*, a weekly variety show, and continued cranking out the hits.

Like Orbison, Boone found his pop music career all but flattened in the British Invasion, and his run on the Top 40 was over. He redirected his attention, authoring a popular series of self-help books for teenagers and performing with his wife and their four daughters. Boone remained close to his gospel roots from the beginning, releasing religious recordings between his pop hits, and in the seventies he turned his attention almost entirely to the spiritual side of the market.

Boone continued releasing albums throughout the seventies and eighties and in 1983 added a contemporary Christian syndicated radio program to his resume. He found himself back in the headlines in 1997, when a friendship with fellow golfer Alice Cooper led to *No More Mr. Nice Guy*, a big band/lounge style album covering heavy metal hits like "Love Hurts" and "Holy Diver." Most recently, Boone launched Gold Records, a label that supports "vintage" artists like Sha Na Na, The Four Freshmen, and Andy Williams.

Pat Boone retooled his good-guy image with his 1997 album, "In A Metal Mood: No More Mr. Nice Guy." *Photo by Caroline Greyshock. Photo courtesy Hip-O Records*

The late fifties saw a tremendous number of rock bands popping up around the state; Gene Summers, a Dallas-born guitarist began performing in 1955 at high school dances and within two years was making television appearances. He released a few singles that scored regional hits, toured with

Gene Summers in a Jan Records publicity photo, circa 1958. *Photo courtesy Crystal Clear Sound*

Chuck Berry and the Drifters in the late fifties and early sixties, and hit the domestic charts in 1964 with "Big Blue Diamonds" and again in 1977 with "Goodbye Priscilla."

Summers never found the national acclaim he was looking for, though he managed to change with the times and stay afloat in the entertainment industry, including work as a television announcer for Saturday Night Wrestling in the early eighties. His career experienced a huge resurgence in England during the rockabilly revival of the eighties, and in 1997 he released *The Ultimate School of Rock & Roll*, a 32-track career retrospective on Dallas's Crystal Clear label.

The early sixties brought a string of one-hit wonders from Texas, some of whom were able to parlay their moment in the sun into a long-running career and others who slipped out of the spotlight as quickly as they had entered it. Ray Peterson, a Denton-born singer who followed a different career path from most of his contemporaries, created a career that included enough hits to save him from obscurity but never made him a household name.

Afflicted with polio as a child, Peterson's musical career began at the Warm Springs Foundation Hospital, where he sang to amuse himself as much as the other patients. His hobby revealed a four-and-a-half-octave range, and once he left the hospital, he began singing in local clubs.

He moved to Los Angeles in the mid-fifties and by 1957 had a record deal with RCA. His first single was a cover of Little Willie John's "Fever," which failed to heat up the charts. The song would have to wait for Peggy Lee to get her hands on it before it would become a sizzling hit. It took seven singles to score a hit, and that was found with the 1959 release "The Wonder of You," a ballad that cracked the top thirty and even caught the interest of Elvis Presley, who asked Peterson if he could record the song. Presley took "The Wonder of You" to the top ten in 1970.

Peterson's star shone its brightest in 1960, when he hit two musical grand slams, finding hits with two very different songs. His first big success, "Tell Laura I Love Her," unwound a tragic story in the grand tradition of teen angst. In the song, a young boy enters a car race to raise enough money to buy a ring for his girlfriend; he wrecks the car, which goes up in flames with him inside. The song won Peterson a spot at number seven and a permanent place in the hearts of romantic teens in the early sixties.

Peterson recorded two more singles that failed to chart and resulted in him leaving the RCA label, only to begin working with an unknown producer named Phil Spector. His second big song of 1960 was "Corinna, Corinna," an old Scottish folk song once recorded by Bob Wills. Peterson's Spector-produced rendition put something of a Latin feel to the song, and by the end of the year it was riding in the top ten.

He continued cranking out singles until 1971, none of which matched the success of his 1960 hits. Peterson's last appearance on the charts was a brief showing at number seventy with the 1964 re-release of "The Wonder of You." He has, however, continued performing through the years.

A handful of flash-in-the-pan acts popped up about the same time as Peterson, such as Johnny Preston, the Port Arthur-born singer who skyrocketed to the top of the charts with "Running Bear" in 1960. Preston was attending Lamar University in Beaumont in the late fifties when his band, The Shades, caught the attention of local D.J. J.P. Richardson (the Big Bopper).

Richardson took Preston to Mercury Records, where Preston recorded the song Richardson had written about Indian love gone wrong. The Big Bopper himself produced the song, which took some four months to find its way onto the charts but then went to number one both in the U.S. and England. By the time the single became a smash, Richardson already had been killed in the same plane crash that killed Buddy Holly and Richie Valens.

Preston continued to record, but he didn't see the top of the charts again. Bruce Channel, who lived in Grapevine, shared a similar fate. While making a demo recording in his home studio in 1962, he threw in a new song he'd just written, called "Hey! Baby." Six months later the song hit number one and stayed there for three weeks, launching the young singer's career, but he never repeated his initial success. He continued touring and recording for about a decade, settled in Fort Worth for a few years, and then moved to Nashville in 1978, where he has enjoyed success as a songwriter. "Hey! Baby" was among the songs featured in the hit movie *Dirty Dancing*.

A duo by the name of Ray Hildebrand and Jill Jackson, working under the name Paul and Paula, found one-time success with the song "Hey, Paula" in 1963. And, around the same time, Ray Sharpe surfaced out of Fort Worth to gain his fifteen minutes of fame with the rock classic "Linda Lu."

Out in the Texas Panhandle, where one might surmise they had little else to do but play music, the state contributed a couple more players to the big leagues. Buddy Knox, who was born in the small town of Happy, near Amarillo, in 1933, formed his first band in 1954 when he went to West Texas State University. The Rhythm Orchids put Jimmy Bowen on bass, Don Lanier on guitar, and Dave Allred on drums, while Knox provided vocals and lead guitar.

Knox and Bowen teamed up to write their material and found two big hits, the first one in 1957 with "Party Doll" and shortly afterwards with "I'm Stickin' With You." The group also produced the highly (and understandably) controversial teen angst song, "I Think I'm Going to Kill Myself," which was banned at many radio stations and probably didn't get picked for many homecoming dance themes, either.

Both Knox and Bowen enjoyed long careers behind the scenes. Bowen went on to top positions with a number of record labels, including MCA and Warner Brothers/Reprise, and Knox worked behind the scenes as well as continuing to perform. He opened a nightclub in the Pacific Northwest in the seventies and died of a heart attack on February 14, 1999.

Rock music changed dramatically in the first half of the sixties, drawing fire from critics and raising the ire of parents. Outsiders saw the new sounds as uninspired and lacking originality, and the fact that television was bringing live musical performances into American homes each week only emphasized the ways in which music was becoming a pale imitation of its ancestors. The music was ripe for change, and like many musical movements that followed, this one began on college campuses. By the end of the fifties, a renewed interest in folk music was being poured through a filter of rock 'n' roll, laying the foundation for the music to move into the political and social unrest of the sixties.

The folk boom occurred mostly in larger cities and was concentrated in California and New York, where many Texas performers headed. A few artists managed to score a hit or two despite the isolation from the social movement; in 1963 Dallas's Trini Lopez found a smash hit and instant success with his recording of "If I Had a Hammer." Lopez, who found a successful career by blending Latin rhythms with a rock recipe, enjoyed a handful of lesser hits after that initial success. He also went on to host his own television program, appeared as one of the Dirty Dozen in the famous 1967 movie, and had a number of guest appearances on television programs including *Adam 12*. Lopez, who was born in a poor neighborhood in Dallas in 1937, remains active today, touring internationally and recently inking a deal with Sony International.

Carolyn Hester came out of Waco via the Austin club scene to become a driving folk force in California and New York. Her

Trini Lopez found a smash hit with "If I Had A Hammer" and has remained active as a performer.

1962 debut album for Columbia featured a newcomer named Bob Dylan on harmonica, and Hester's vibrant vocals kept her a favorite on the folk circuit for many years. She was largely responsible for bringing another Texas folkie, Nanci Griffith, into the national spotlight and appeared on Bob Dylan's thirtieth anniversary album, which was recorded in 1992 at Madison Square Garden. Today she rarely performs in public, although she serves on the board of directors for the annual Kerrville Folk Festival.

In the wake of the Beatles and the British Invasion, the nation's youth became more obsessed with music than ever before and new bands, it seemed, were popping up everywhere. America's answer to the Beatles came in the form of The Monkees, which featured Dallas-born Michael Nesmith. Nesmith had become a mainstay on the folk circuit while attending college in San Antonio and was a starving musician in 1966 when he landed a berth on the Monkees. He enjoyed overnight success as one of the prefabricated four, and when the show ended in 1969 Nesmith picked up his solo career again. His work has gone largely unrecognized but has included a few minor hits, major contributions to the development of video discs, and penning the Linda Ronstadt hit "Different Drum."

The Tex-Mex answer to the Moptops hailed from San Antonio, where producer Huey Meaux assembled the Sir Douglas Quintet, featuring Doug Sahm, Augie Meyers, Jack Barber, John Perez, and Frank Morin. The band found a hit in 1965 with "She's a Mover," sort of a Texas version of the Beatles' song "She's a Woman." Sahm went on to enjoy a long and diverse career, and his musical union with Augie Meyers remained intact. They both recorded for a number of labels throughout the seventies and eighties, finding their greatest success when they decided to create a Texican version of the Traveling Wilburys and formed the Texas Tornados. Joining with fellow musical legends Flaco Jiménez and Freddy Fender, the Tornados have released six CDs, winning the Best Mexican American Performance Grammy in 1990 with a cover of Santiago Jiménez's "Soy de San Luis." Sahm died of a heart attack in 1999.

Sam the Sham and the Pharoahs grew out of Dallas, where front man Domingo Samudio combined Tex-Mex with rock and ended up with a record deal for MGM. The band's biggest hit was the eternal "Woolly Bully," and they followed that up with the successful "Li'l Red Riding Hood," but other efforts fell flat, and the band, frustrated by being perceived as nothing more than a novelty act, broke up. Samudio released a solo album in 1970, which featured Duane Allman on guitar, and won a Grammy for his liner notes, then became a street evangelist.

Texas musicians continued making contributions to the national scene in the early to mid-sixties, with Dallas's Sylvester Stewart going on to lead Sly and the Family Stone, B.J. Thomas emerging as a folk-flavored singer before meandering into country music territory, Shawn Phillips putting his own lasting spin on the folk-rock sound, and El Paso's Fuller Four making it big with the single "I Fought the Law." A young Dallas man named Stephen Stills headed for California in 1966, resurfacing as part of Buffalo Springfield before becoming part of the super group Crosby, Stills, Nash and Young.

As the winds of change reached gale force in the mid and late sixties, the music reflected the turmoil of the era, and Port Arthur-born Janis Joplin became the most visible troubadour of tragic times. The list of coming attractions from the Lone Star State was seemingly endless as the sixties headed toward the seventies: Edgar and Johnny Winter, Mother Earth, Thirteenth Floor Elevators, ZZ Top, Boz Skaggs, Steve Miller. The state provided the Eagles with Don Henley and gave the world the seventies acts Meat Loaf, Johnny Nash, J.D. Souther, and Christopher Cross.

Music, in Texas or anywhere else, was never the same after the trials and tribulations of the sixties. It splintered and expanded in ways that couldn't be imagined when Elvis kick-started the rockabilly movement back in 1954. By the early seventies, Austin became the focal point of the Texas music scene, driven largely by the social consciousness and idealism that tended to incubate in college environments. The University of Texas provided a hungry audience for a bar scene that began to evolve in the mid-sixties, with honky-tonks and coffeehouses co-existing with rock clubs and frat hangouts. By the seventies Austin had become a visible, viable musical hotspot, and the "Austin sound" encompassed country and rock with a sort of wise narrative that was lacking in much of the music produced elsewhere.

Television in the fifties and sixties played a major role in changing the face of music and its place in pop culture. Just as music videos would send the sound in new directions in the eighties, television in the sixties gave teens and young adults a new perspective on the world in which they lived and exposed them to new sounds, sights, and insights. That inevitably sent them exploring new paths, both socially and musically, with the two often being intertwined. As the sixties ended, it was clear that Texas, a state that already enjoyed a rich and varied past, had really only just begun to write its musical history.

Recommended Listening:

The Buddy Holly Collection – (MCA)
The Big D Jamboree Live Volumes 1 & 2 – Various artists (Dragon Street Records)
Greatest Grooves – "Groovey" Joe Poovey (Dragon Street Records)
Rockin' Bones: The Legendary Masters – Ronnie Dawson (Crystal Clear)
For the Lonely: 18 Greatest Hits – Roy Orbison (Rhino)
At Town Hall – Carolyn Hester (Bear Family)
Texas Music, Vol. 3: Garage Bands & Psychedelia – Various artists (Rhino)

Appendix

Texas Music Timeline

1847 – German singing societies are formed in New Braunfels and San Antonio

1860 – The Boerne Village Band is formed

1868 – Scott Joplin is born in Texarkana

1882 – Frank Baca forms the Baca Band

1887 – Alexander "Eck" Robertson is born in Arkansas

1888 – Huddie "Leadbelly" Ledbetter is born in Louisiana

1890 – Gates Thomas transcribes the blues song "Nobody There"

1895 – Kentucky's Ben Harney publishes the first ragtime tune

– Mance Lipscomb is born in Narvasota

1897 – Blind Lemon Jefferson is born in Coutchman

– Jimmie Rodgers is born in Mississippi

1898 – Beulah "Sippie" Wallace is born in Houston

1899 – Scott Joplin publishes "The Maple Leaf Rag"

– "Whistlin' Alex" Moore is born in Dallas

1902 – Al Dexter is born in Jacksonville

1903 – Milton Brown is born in Stephenville

1904 – Henry "Buster" Smith is born in Alsdorf

1905 – Leo "Jack" Teagarden is born in Vernon
– Woodward Maurice "Tex" Ritter is born in Murvaul
– James Robert "Bob" Wills is born in Kosse

1906 – Eddie Durham is born in San Marcos
– Victoria Spivey is born in Houston

1907 – Lammar Wright is born in Texarkana
– Orvon Gene Autry is born in Tioga

1908 – Oran "Hot Lips" Page is born in Dallas

1909 – Copyright laws are enacted in America
– Moon Mullican is born in Corrigan
– "Dallas Blues" becomes the first copyrighted "blues" song

1910 – Aaron "T-Bone" Walker is born in Linden

1911 – George Thomas writes "New Orleans Hop Scop Blues," the first boogie-woogie piece; it is published five years later
– Narciso Martínez is born in Reynosa

1912 – Sam "Lightnin'" Hopkins is born in Centerville
– Dale Evans is born in Uvalde

1913 – Santiago Jiménez Sr. is born in San Antonio

1914 – Floyd Tillman is born in Oklahoma
– Ernest Tubb is born on a cotton farm near Crisp

1915 – Beto Villa is born in Falfurrias

1916 – Adolph Hofner is born in Moulton
– Charlie Christian is born in Bonham
– Lydia Mendoza is born in Houston

1917 – Eddie Vinson is born in Houston

1919 – Brothers George and Hersal Thomas compose the quintessential boogie-woogie number "The Fives"

1920 – A young T-Bone Walker signs on as Blind Lemon Jefferson's guide

– Charles Brown is born in Texas City

1921 – Herb Ellis is born in Farmersville

– Gene Roland is born in Dallas

– Jimmy Giuffre is born in Dallas

1922 – Eck Robertson and Henry Gililand become the first performers to make a country music record

1923 – Sippie Wallace scores her first hit with "Up the Country Blues"

– William "Red" Garland is born in Dallas

1924 – Vernon Dalhart becomes the first country artist to have a million-selling single ("The Wreck of the Old '97")

– Clarence "Gatemouth" Brown is born in Louisiana

1925 – Dallas's Alphonse Trent Orchestra becomes the first black band to have its own radio program

– Hank Thompson is born in Waco

1926 – Blind Lemon Jefferson is "discovered" on the streets of Deep Ellum and releases his first recording

– Ray Price is born near Perryville

– Willie Mae Thornton is born in Alabama

– Johnny Gimble is born in Tyler

1928 – Gene Autry gets his first singing job as "Oklahoma's Singing Cowboy" for KVOO radio in Tulsa

– Bruno "El Azote" Villareal makes the first Tejano music record

– Lydia Mendoza makes her first recording

– Lefty Frizzell is born in Corsicana

1929 – T-Bone Walker records his first songs for Columbia under the name "Oak Cliff T-Bone"

– Blind Lemon Jefferson is found dead in a Chicago snow bank

– "Whistlin' Alex" Moore records his first tracks

– William "Prince" Lasha is born in Fort Worth

1930 – Bob Wills and Milton Brown team up as the Aladdin Laddies

– George Jones is born in Saratoga

– J.P. Richardson ("the Big Bopper") is born in Sabine Pass

– Ornette Coleman is born in Fort Worth

1931 – Jimmie Rodgers is named an honorary Texas Ranger

– The Light Crust Doughboys are formed

– Tony de la Rosa is born in Sarita

1932 – Milton Brown forms the Musical Brownies

– Albert Collins is born in Leona

1933 – John and Alan Lomax discover Huddie Ledbetter in a Louisiana prison and successfully petition the governor for his release

– Jimmie Rodgers dies in a New York hotel room

– Willie Nelson is born in Fort Worth

– David "Fathead" Newman is born in Dallas

1934 – Freddie King is born in Gilmer

– Cedar Walton is born in Dallas

– Bobby Bradford is born in Mississippi

1935 – Jazzman Eddie Durham introduces the electric guitar solo

– T-Bone Walker and Pee Wee Crayton move to California

– Narciso Martínez makes his first recording

– Johnny "Guitar" Watson is born in Houston

– James Clay is born in Dallas

1936 – Milton Brown dies of pneumonia five days after a car accident

– Al Dexter records "Honky-Tonk Blues," the first song to coin the phrase, "honky-tonk"

– Santiago Jiménez releases his first record

– Buddy Holly is born in Lubbock

– Roy Orbison is born in Wink

– Roger Miller is born in Fort Worth

– Kris Kristofferson is born in Brownsville

1937 – Cliff Bruner forms the Texas Wanderers

– Freddie Fender is born in San Benito

– Waylon Jennings is born in Littlefield

– Trini Lopez is born in Dallas

1939 – Leadbelly serves time at Riker's Island on an assault charge

– Ted Daffan writers "Truck Drivers Blues," the first of many songs dedicated to the trucking profession

– Ronnie Dawson is born in Oak Cliff

– T-Bone Walker plugs in to the electric guitar

– Flaco Jiménez is born in San Antonio

1941 – Ernest Tubb earns his first hit with "Walkin' the Floor Over You"

– Adolph Hofner records what many call the definitive version of "Cotton-Eyed Joe"

– Five-year-old Buddy Holly wins his first talent contest

– Joe Poovey is born in Dallas

1942 – Charlie Christian dies in a sanitarium at the age of 26

1943 – Janis Joplin is born in Port Arthur

1944 – Sly Stone is born in Dallas

– Gene Roland joins Stan Kenton's orchestra

1945 – Eddie "Cleanhead" Vinson signs with Mercury and immediately records a two-sided hit

1946 – Beto Villa takes the Tejano big band concept into the recording studio for the first time

– Armando Marroquin and Paco Betancourt launch Ideal Records, the first Tejano label

– Bob Dorough enrolls in North Texas State Teachers College to study composition and piano

1947 – North Texas State Teachers College in Denton launches the world's first jazz studies program

– Harry Babasin makes the first jazz record featuring a pizzicato cello

– Ornette Coleman is kicked out of his high school band for improvising on a John Philip Sousa march

1948 – Vernon Dalhart dies of a heart attack

– Woody Herman becomes the first band to record a Jimmy Giuffre song

1949 – Don Robey launches Peacock Records to record Clarence "Gatemouth" Brown, a guitarist he discovered in his Peacock nightclub

– Gene Autry records "Rudolph the Red-Nosed Reindeer"

– Leadbelly dies six months after his last performance

1950 – Lefty Frizzell has his first two number one hits

1951 – Willie Mae "Big Mama" Thornton signs with Peacock Records

1952 – Ray Price joins the roster of artists at the Grand Ole Opry

– Don Robey's Peacock Records buys the Memphis-based Duke label, inheriting Bobby "Blue" Bland

1953 – Willie Mae "Big Mama" Thornton scores a number one hit with "Hound Dog," which would bring Elvis Presley success three years later

– Oran "Hot Lips" Page dies

– Pat Boone enrolls at North Texas State University

– Pappy Dailey and Jack Starnes found Starday Records in Beaumont

1954 – Red Garland teams up with Miles Davis

1955 – George Jones takes his song "Why Baby Why" to number four on the charts

– Joe Poovey opens for Elvis at the Big D Jamboree

– Roy Orbison backs Pat Boone in the recording studio, which leads to making his own recording

1956 – Buddy Holly makes his first recordings on the Decca label

– Columbia Records passes on Roy Orbison, giving his song "Ooby Dooby" to a hot Texas rockabilly act named Sid King and the Five Strings

– Roy Orbison scores his first hit with "Ooby Dooby" on Sun Records

– Ray Price gets his first number one song with "Crazy Arms"

– Pat Boone leaves Denton and, for the next seven years, shows up on the charts 54 times

1957 – Buddy Holly makes his television debut on *The Ed Sullivan Show*, singing his hit, "That'll Be the Day"

– Johnny "Guitar" Watson writes "Gangster of Love"

- James Clay records his first two albums in Los Angeles
- Buddy Knox and the Rhythm Orchids have two hit singles: "Stickin' With You" and "Party Doll"

1958 – Beaumont songwriter and disc jockey-turned-singer J.P. Richardson finds a number one hit with "Chantilly Lace"

1959 – Buddy Holly, Ritchie Valens, and J.R. Richardson (The Big Bopper) are killed in a plane crash near Clear Lake, Iowa

- Ornette Coleman releases his landmark album, *The Shape of Things to Come*, and launches the free jazz movement
- The album *Ray Charles introduces Fathead Newman* is released
- Ronnie Dawson makes his national television debut on *American Bandstand*
- "Running Bear," a song written by The Big Bopper and recorded by Johnny Preston, becomes a number one hit
- Johnny Horton wins the Grammy Award for Best Country Western Performance

1960 – Charles Brown records the seasonal smash "Please Come Home For Christmas"

- Roy Orbison records "Only the Lonely," launching a string a hits
- Denton's Ray Peterson gets two top ten hits, "Tell Laura I Love Her" and "Corinna, Corinna"
- Mance Lipscomb makes his recording debut on Arhoolie Records

1961 – Jimmie Rodgers becomes the first person inducted into the Country Music Hall of Fame

– Cedar Walton joins Art Blakely's Jazz Messengers

1962 – Bruce Channel of Grapevine spends three weeks at number one with "Hey! Baby"

1963 – Paul and Paula (Texas college students Ray Hildebrand and Jill Jackson) get a number one hit with "Hey, Paula," which features Ronnie Dawson on drums

– Fort Worth's Ray Sharpe enjoys success with "Linda Lu," his only hit

– Trini Lopez of Dallas records "If I Had a Hammer"

1964 – Jim Reeves dies in a plane crash

– Roger Miller wins five Grammy Awards

– John Carter creates the New Art Jazz Ensemble with Bobby Bradford in Los Angeles

1965 – The Sir Douglas Quintet gets a hit with "She's a Mover"

– Roger Miller wins six Grammy Awards

1966 – Janis Joplin joins Big Brother and the Holding Company

– Stephen Stills leaves Dallas for California

– Dewey Redman teams up with his former high school band mate Ornette Coleman

– Dallas's Michael Nesmith joins the cast of *The Monkees*

1968 – Bob Wills is inducted into the Country Music Hall of Fame

1969 – "Whistlin' Alex" Moore records the album *Alex Moore in Europe*

1970 – Janis Joplin dies of a heroin overdose in Hollywood, California

– Bob Dorough composes the songs for "Schoolhouse Rock"

– Ray Price wins a Grammy Award for "For the Good Times"; T-Bone Walker wins in the category of Best Ethnic Recording

1971 – Al Dexter is inducted into the Nashville Songwriters Hall of Fame

– Janis Joplin's final album, *Pearl*, is released and finds both critical and commercial success

1974 – T-Bone Walker dies in a nursing home

1975 – Bob Wills dies of a heart attack in Fort Worth

– Lefty Frizzell dies after suffering a stroke

– Willie Nelson wins his first Grammy Award

1976 – Freddie King dies of heart failure

1980 – Lightnin' Hopkins is inducted into the Blues Foundation Hall of Fame

– A rockabilly revival in England makes an international star of "Groovey" Joe Poovey

1982 – Lightnin' Hopkins dies of throat cancer

– Clarence "Gatemouth" Brown wins the Grammy Award for Best Blues Album

1984 – Al Dexter dies at his home on Lake Lewisville

– Ernest Tubb dies of emphysema

– "Big Mama" Thornton is inducted into the Blues Foundation Hall of Fame; she dies later that year

– William "Red" Garland dies at his home in Dallas

1985 – Gene Autry wins the Hall of Fame Award at the Grammy Awards

1986 – Buddy Holly is inducted into the Rock and Roll Hall of Fame

– England "discovers" Ronnie Dawson and the rockabilly performer becomes a huge star overseas

1987 – Roy Orbison is inducted into the Rock and Roll Hall of Fame

– T-Bone Walker is inducted into the Rock and Roll Hall of Fame

1988 – Roy Orbison dies of a heart attack at his mother's Tennessee home

– Eddie "Cleanhead" Vinson dies of a heart attack

1989 – "Whistlin' Alex" Moore dies in Dallas

1990 – Adolph Hofner is inducted into the Western Swing Hall of Fame

– Herb Ellis wins a Grammy Award for Best Jazz Instrumental

1991 – T-Bone Walker is given the Grammy Hall of Fame Award

1992 – Narciso Martínez dies in San Antonio

1993 – Johnny Gimble wins a Grammy Award for Best Country Instrumental Performance

1996 – Johnny "Guitar" Watson dies of a heart attack while touring Japan

1997 – Buddy Holly is given the Lifetime Achievement Grammy award

1998 – Gene Autry dies in California

– Harry Babasin dies of emphysema

– Bob Wills and the Texas Playboys earn the Grammy Award's Hall of Fame award

1999 – Charles Brown dies

2000 – Valeria Longorio dies in San Antonio

– Adolph Hofner dies at his home in San Antonio

Index

R

S

T